Victor Hugo in Exile

Victor Hugo in Exile

From Historical Representations
to Utopian Vistas

William VanderWolk

Lewisburg
Bucknell University Press

Associated University Presses
2010 Eastpark Boulevard
Cranbury, NJ 08512

The paper used in this publication meets the requirements of the American National Standard for Permanence of Paper for Printed Library Materials Z39.48-1984.

Library of Congress Cataloging-in-Publication Data

VanderWolk, William, 1949–
    Victor Hugo in exile : from historical representations to utopian vistas / William VanderWolk.
        p.   cm.
    Includes bibliographical references and index.
    ISBN 0-8387-5628-X (alk. paper)
    1. Hugo, Victor, 1802–1885—Exile.   I. Title.
PQ2297.V36   2006
848'.709—dc22   2005024413

PRINTED IN THE UNITED STATES OF AMERICA

Contents

Acknowledgments

I AM GRATEFUL TO THE BOWDOIN COLLEGE FACULTY RESOURCES COMMITtee for awarding me a Kenan Fellowship, which gave me the time to complete the research and writing of this book.

Many thanks to Natalie Handel and Alex Harris for their excellent translations.

Many colleagues who work on French literature and history were involved in this project in one way or another, but I would like to acknowledge especially Allan Pasco for sharing sage advice; Kathryn Grossman for giving me encouragement and a glimpse of her vast knowledge of Victor Hugo; and Charlotte Daniels for her flawless critical eye.

Thanks to the University of Chicago Press for permission to reprint sections of Paul Ricœur, *Memory, History, Forgetting*. Translated by Kathleen Blamey and David Pellauer. Chicago: University of Chicago Press, 2004.

Introduction

IN LATE 1851, AS HIS FOUR-YEAR TERM AS PRESIDENT OF FRANCE WAS COMing to an end, Louis-Napoléon Bonaparte launched a bloody coup d'état that would pave the way for his establishment of the Second Empire (1852–1870). Playing on the nation's reverence for his uncle, he crowned himself Napoléon III and set up an authoritarian regime. Republican politicians, including Victor Hugo, fled. While many returned after a short period, Hugo remained abroad for eighteen years, returning to Paris triumphantly in 1870 after Louis's defeat by the Prussians. From the island of Guernsey off the Normandy coast, Hugo wrote and clandestinely published a series of scathing critiques of the new regime. Each portrayed the Second Empire as the antithesis of the republican values the French had come to hold dear since the revolution of 1789. Each represented an alternative to the empire's official propaganda machine, exemplified by state-run newspapers as well as public attempts to create and control the emperor's image, including museums, ceremonies, and even the remaking of the city of Paris. Today, Hugo's works such as *Les Châtiments* and *Les Misérables* remain cherished texts and over time have helped form the French collective memory of the era. This study, examining these two works and the non-fictional *Napoléon le petit*, argues that through such texts Hugo can be seen as an important historian of his time, a polemicist and prophet whose version of past events and vision of the future proved to be more lasting than those accepted during the empire. His words were woven into individual citizen's memories of the times and as such became part of France's collective memory.

No comprehensive study of Hugo as a historian has yet been written. While commentators have closely studied every aspect of Hugo's life and literary work, they have not taken Hugo the political historian terribly seriously. He is often portrayed as politically naive and a latecomer to liberal, prorevolutionary politics. The following pages build on previous scholarship by emphasizing the power of literature to act as a historical text. Examining the role of literature

9

in the writing of history poses a certain number of questions: What role can literature play in the formation of collective memory? What time lapse is necessary for texts to have their full impact on a society? To what extent does the reputation and background of the author affect the reception of the works? What is the difference between an author of literary texts dealing with historical events and a historian? These questions are central to my analysis, and the answers to them present the thesis that Hugo was a historian of his time and that, as such, he influenced the way in which future generations remembered Louis-Napoléon and the Second Empire. Viewing Hugo as a historian redefines the historical process, as literature is highlighted as a powerful creator of collective memory. The literary creates a shared sense of past, a more personal interpretation of events that have been lived through, archived and analyzed. Theorists such as Paul Ricœur and Maurice Halbwachs have been thinking about these relations in ways that allow us to better understand Hugo. Hugo's work, in turn, allows us to better understand the process of creating history.

During his eighteen-year struggle against Louis-Napoléon, Hugo found three sources of power that eventually tipped the scales of history in his favor: message, voice, and genre. His was a message about freedom and justice, incorporating all the revolutionary ideals of the late eighteenth century. Louis-Napoléon had the family name evoking France's imperial past, but Hugo had ideas on his side. He also had the prestige of his position as the best-known writer of his century. Throughout this study, we will never lose sight of the fact that Hugo was far more than an author in the eyes of the French public; he was a philosopher, politician, and father figure as well. In addition, he was a poet in exile, a position that gave him a romantic air, the lone voice in the wilderness speaking out against injustice. These roles all contributed to the legitimacy of his arguments against a powerful government and its repressive policies. Lastly, Hugo was a master of every literary genre, and the three texts to be studied here are representative of his range. The political essay, *Napoléon le petit* (1852), delivered as a two-hundred-page diatribe against the emperor and his coup d'état, releases every emotion in Hugo's arsenal and directly impacts the reader's emotional core. The poems of *Les Châtiments* (1853) reconfigure the events of 1851 to 1852 in metaphorical terms that recall to the reader the great flights of Hugo's romantic verse. The novel, especially one on the scale of *Les Misérables* (1862), delivers the knockout blow, in which the literary master at his grandest and most bombastic appeals to the great masses of the French populace, including many new readers ironically created by educational advances under the Second Empire. Message, voice, and genre combine to give overarching force to Hugo's cause.

The three texts to be examined here show that Hugo was both an influential historian and a keeper of the national memory, a concept that lies at the heart of Hugo's view of the world. By emphasizing the universality of themes such as freedom and social justice, Hugo worked on his readers' emotions as well as on their memories of the history they had been living in recent years. The power of this combination can be seen in the stunning success of a novel written from exile by an outlawed author. While at first metaphorization might seem a move *away* from the historical, it is actually, as Paul Ricœur has seen, an essential part of historiography. Through these three works, moving from testimonies to poetry to a romantic fresco of a novel, Hugo not only establishes his vision of the revolution and the empire, but he ensures that, through various forms of sentimental engagement on the part of the readers, it will become part of who they are, part of their sense of being French. While Hugo was revered throughout the world for the ideals he espoused in works such as these, we will view them specifically in the context of the contest between Hugo and Louis-Napoléon for the hearts and minds of the French public.

This study finds its theoretical underpinnings in a number of sources, but Paul Ricœur will be a constant companion throughout. Two of his texts in particular, *Time and Narrative* (1983) and *Memory, History, Forgetting* (2000), will provide a framework for looking at the relationship between historical events and their representation in both fictional and non-fictional texts.[1] Ricœur sees the writing of history as a three-part process: eyewitness accounts and their inclusion in archives; a process of explanation and comprehension of the eyewitness accounts; and a transformation of memory into literary form. I will follow these ideas through analyses of *Napoléon le petit, Les Châtiments*, and *Les Misérables*. These texts represent different literary genres and different ways of writing history, but they all express Hugo's distaste for the empire and his vision of how France's glorious past could impact her future as a republic.

An analysis of Hugo's written work of this period is no more objective or subjective than a biography. Its originality lies in its approach to the works Hugo wrote as a reaction to the "official" history of his era. I will look at these works through the lens of collective memory in an attempt to see what effect they had on the thinking of the French people about Louis-Napoléon, all the while conscious of the existence of competing collective memories within any society. When we talk about how a society remembers, we try to determine how that society came to its set of contemporary values, who defined them and whether or not they were rooted in a particular time period. At the same time we must look at who controlled the perception of those values and their historical context. In most cases, those in power have the privilege of communicating their values to the public with more efficacy than the opposition. That was certainly the set of assumptions motivating Louis-Napoléon's control of his opponents and the press. Yet Victor Hugo engaged the emperor in a long-distance debate on all of these questions, and it is Hugo's voice that we hear more clearly today.

This book has five chapters. The first two explore the relationship between memory, history, and literature while laying the theoretical groundwork for my view of Hugo as a historian. The final chapters correspond to the three works being studied: *Napoléon le petit, Les Châtiments,* and *Les Misérables.* In the conclusion, I look briefly at Hugo as a prophet of a republican future, a vision of twentieth-century Europe that has largely come true. Hugo's keen ability to see past, present, and future, and weave them into his literary and political project, made him a powerful historian whose words have long outlived those of his hated rival, Louis-Napoléon Bonaparte.

Abbreviations

C:	*Correspondance entre Victor Hugo et Pierre-Jules Hetzel,* Sheila Gaudon.
CS:	*Les Cadres sociaux de la mémoire,* Halbwachs.
FT:	*Figuring Transcendence in "Les Misérables": Hugo's Romantic Sublime,* Grossman.
HR:	*L'Homme révolté,* Camus.
HSR:	*How Societies Remember,* Connerton.
LM:	*Les Misérables,* Hugo.
LMF:	*La Mémoire des Français,* Crubellier.
MM:	*Matière et mémoire,* Bergson.
MHF:	*Memory, History, Forgetting,* Ricœur.
"P:"	" 'Problematization' as a Mode of Reading History", Castel.
R:	*Revolution and Repetition,* Mehlman.
R&H:	*Histories: French Constructions of the Past,* Revel and Hunt.
T&N:	*Time and Narrative,* Ricœur.

Chronology
1848–70

1848	Revolution in Paris (February 22–24), abdication of Louis-Philippe
	Proclamation of the Second Republic (February 25)
	Louis-Napoléon Bonaparte elected President (December 10)
1850	Elimination of universal suffrage (May 31)
1851	Coup d'état (December 2–4), Victor Hugo and other republican politicians flee the country
1852	Proclamation of the Second Empire, Louis-Napoléon crowned Napoléon III (December 2)
1852–60	Repression of all opposition, restrictions on public and private freedoms, loyalty oath required of all public employees, tightly controlled press and educational system
1854–56	Franco-British victory over Russia in the Crimean War
1857	Official candidates win 90 percent of the seats in the legislative elections
1858	Felice Orsini attempts to assassinate Napoléon III (January 14)
	National security law allowing conviction without trial of any recidivists or simple "suspects" (February 19)
1860–70	Beginning of liberalization of social laws in France, including the right to strike (1864) and more freedom of the press (1868)
	Opposition gains seats in legislative body, whose powers increase
1870	France declares war on Prussia (July 19)
	French capitulation at Sedan (September 2)
	Proclamation of the Third Republic (September 4)

Victor Hugo in Exile

1

Memory as Historiographical Process

MEMORY IS A FORCE OF NATURE THAT SEEKS TO MERGE CONFLICTING strands of personality and experience. The various aspects of memory are no more unified: recall is not reminiscence, voluntary is not involuntary. Similarly, memory is not history, the recounting of a memory is not historiography.[1] And yet our desire for union remains. We want a single strand of events to represent chronology; we want the person we were to be the one we are. The process of maturing is partly the realization of the impossibility of such unity, and yet we persist in the desire, however subconscious. It is part of the battle against aging, against death, for death is the final separation, the end of the dream of uniting past and present. Perhaps that is the force of religion: it keeps alive the dream of unity (soul and body, past and present) beyond the grave.

We are not alone in this enterprise of desire; our fellow humans are going through the same process. And so we share our memories, compare them to other people's, combine them (unity again) into a coherent common story. This we call collective memory. It can never be wholly one because it is a collection of such different stories, but it has a life, a force of its own that is separate from the individual. It is a public manifestation of a private dream.

One day one member of the collective ownership of these memories decides to write it down, to tell it to a wider audience, for reasons of pride, competition or a simple sense of sharing. This historian, with the historiography he creates, becomes a privileged yet feared member of the community that has donated its memories. For some he seems too brash or merely incorrect. The way he remembers their common story is different from others. He seems to be writing it for some personal gain or retribution. He has lost his objectivity in a web of human desire. And so a second historian takes up his pen and rewrites the text, blending his mixture of fact and interpretation into a tale that suits his own personal memory, his

19

own need for unity of experience. This counter-discourse accounts for some of the things the first historian left out or distorted.[2] It takes into account the political and social forces that drive the individual world of the second writer. This counter-memory fulfills a need not only of the writer but also of the people who agree with him, whose memories correspond most closely to his.[3]

The impossibility of reconciling the two versions presented is not a new story; it is the history of politics, sociology, and history itself. We as a society have the same desire for unity as the individual; we want a society that resembles our model of it. Any deviance from the ideal represents a dangerous sedition that can only take us further from our goal of a utopia in which everyone speaks the same language, everyone has the same dream, and everyone has the same memories. The seditious one must be driven into exile where his words will no longer have any impact. His individual memories will not threaten the new order, which he deems the new tyranny. Only when the hope of that new unity fades will his voice drift back into our consciousness. What if he had been right all along?

As the community reabsorbs the exiled member and his voice becomes heard, the old communal voices must readjust to the new voices within it. Thus begins the creation of a new history, a new voice, and a new collective memory. The mature society, made up of diverse voices that recognize the inevitability of, and even the need for, difference will thrive. The community that rejects either the returning exile or the new voices born during the exile's absence will flounder. Yet in order to thrive, the diverse community must again rewrite its history, must again look for a common ground, a common experience that allows it to understand the new world in which it exists. Hopefully, the new history will draw upon the lessons of the old and add its own knowledge to it.

Victor Hugo was a historian who dared to tell a different story. His counter-discourse left him open to charges of sedition and the possibility of exile, both physical and communal. His voice was unwanted at the time of expression because his community was not ready to reevaluate its common past. He was an uncommon crusader because he was a teller of tales, a writer of autobiography, poetry, and fiction, who dared to enter the realm of politics and historical struggle, who dared to take on the establishment in order to right a wrong ingrained in the collective memory.

Hugo's desire to be heard resulted in a number of influential texts whose words were eventually heard and whose message resonates today. The collective memory of Western twenty-first-century societies, and specifically of France, is imbued with the ideals Hugo professed. France has accepted, at least in part, the telling of memories that its ancestors did not want to hear. The country has been willing to adapt, at least in the majority, to accommodate the point of view espoused in Hugo's texts. A powerful voice produced significant texts whose basis lay in a feeling of righteousness and in a desire to unify the community.

I do not seek to justify Hugo's opinions, although the fact that I have chosen him reflects my sympathy with his views. My aim is to explain why these texts were important, to analyze their relevance to the topics and events of the time, and to show how their views correspond to those of the succeeding generation. This will not be a sociological study with figures and charts showing how these texts changed public opinion or how they led to political or social change. It will be a literary analysis, one that examines a few texts closely in order to show the motivations that spurred their creation and the corresponding forces that came after them that justify their views, however unpopular they may have been at the time of the writing. Hugo's counter-discourse attempted to change the way a society remembered, to unify the competing forces in the collective memory. The degree to which Hugo succeeded is in the eye of other historians who have analyzed the era, and there can never be a full consensus among them. What we can agree on is the course of history after the writing of these works, and it is in this aftermath that the traces left by these texts can be seen and appreciated.

INDIVIDUAL AND COLLECTIVE MEMORY

Saint Augustine represents the first modern view of memory and autobiography. For Augustine, memory provides the basis on which rests the individual's conception of time, and as such it is a very personal experience. "In remembering something, one remembers oneself " (*MHF*, 96). My memories are not yours. For each of us, our sense of time has a double orientation, from the past toward the future, through a "push from behind" (*MHF*, 97), but also from the future toward the past, from expectation to remembrance, passing through the living present. What Augustine called "the tradition of inwardness" (*MHF*, 96) was constructed through a common perception of the passage of time. For Augustine, memory represents "the present of the past" (*MHF*, 101).

Paul Ricœur gives a detailed analysis in *Memory, History, Forgetting* of how Husserl's thinking moved "inwardness" closer to collective memory (97). For Husserl, "the difficulty [is in] passing from the solitary *ego* to the other, capable of becoming, in turn, an us" (*MHF*, 115). Another person is constituted as a stranger, but it is in me that he is constituted (*MHF*, 118). This process results in what Husserl calls "communalization" (*MHF*, 119). The inner unity of the individual depends upon his ability to recognize himself as a member of a number of diverse groups (*MHF*, 123). Husserl's view of the relationship between individual and collective memory will resemble closely that of Maurice Halbwachs. It is in relation to the individual's consciousness and memory that we take collective memory to be a collection of *traces* left by events, which have affected the course of history. This relation also allows us to recognize the power of these common memories in the mise en scène of occasions such as holidays, rituals, and public celebrations.[4]

Halbwachs's seminal works on collective memory elucidate the theoretical underpinnings of the effects over time of historiography on the collective psyche of a nation.[5] During the 1920s, Halbwachs wrote a number of texts on the subject, the most useful of which for us is *Les Cadres sociaux de la mémoire* (1925). Here Halbwachs outlines the relationship between individual memory and the dominant discourse of the time, a rapport critical to the understanding of how a society remembers and then writes its own history.

Halbwachs begins by recognizing that individual memories do not exist in a vacuum; they are not just a spontaneous expression of an interior experience. There is always an exterior stimulus, a catalyst that may come from nature but more often is the result of interaction with another person: "More often than not, if I remember, the reason is that others incite me to remember, that their memory comes to the rescue of my own, that mine depends on theirs." (*CS*, vi). Most memories are triggered not by an involuntary sensory experience like Proust's narrator's but by a conscious remembrance of some human interaction: a request, an expectation, an expressed sentiment, a glimpsed acquaintance, an overheard narrative, etc. Our memories live thus in a community inhabited by other people. Each individual memory is a point of view on the collective memory, and this point of view changes according to the place that I occupy, and this place changes according to relationships that I maintain with another's milieu (*MHF*, 124).

When an individual memory is spoken, it enters into the domain of language, where each memory can be said to be already "spoken," in a kind of discourse that the individual has had with himself. The enunciation takes the form of the common language of the individual's social group, most commonly the mother tongue (*MHF*, 129). The memory enters the collective conscience through narration and becomes part of the public repository of memories. Such narratives form the building blocks of collective memory, as members of the group are conscious of sharing memories (*MHF*, 130).

It would be erroneous, however, to extrapolate from this that collective memory is just an agglomeration of individual memories. The collective memory of a society is always already present, in the form of the dominant discourse, and it is into that particular construct that individual memories must be added in order for them to be part of the collective experience. Halbwachs puts it this way: "It had to be shown, moreover, that the collective frames of memory are not made up after the fact by a combination of individual memories, that they are not simple, empty shapes into which foreign memories come to insert themselves, and that they are, on the contrary, precisely the instruments used by collective memory to build an image of the past that agrees with the dominant thoughts of society at every period of history" (*CS*, viii). Each individual defines himself by his place in the collective conscience (*MHF*, 121). Louis-Napoléon's rise to the throne, for example, would never have been possible without the collective remembrance of his uncle, a collective memory fueled principally by the individual memories of those who had lived through the first empire. The discourse, as Michel Foucault would appreciate, determines the historical viewpoint.

In general, individuals are only aware of the influence of their milieu when rival influences confront one another (*MHF*, 122). In order for the dominant discourse to stay that way, it must appeal to the commonly accepted view of the past to maintain a certain coherence of thought among the people: "The memory of society had to be called upon in order to obtain an obedience that later would be demanded based on the usefulness of services rendered and on the competence of the magistrate or clerk" (*CS*, 224). The example of Louis-Napoléon is pertinent here as well. In order to maintain the calm in the streets necessary to establish the empire, Louis had to convince the people that he was the legitimate heir to that throne.

To do that he had to convince them that they needed more stability, more order in their lives and in the conduct of national politics. The best way to bring about such obedience of action was to appeal to their memories of Napoléon I. The strategy worked masterfully, as Louis convinced the public that he was the legitimate emperor, and an elected one at that. Thus, Hugo had a daunting task ahead as he set out to change that way of thinking and remembering.

Hugo's task was to persuade the French people that Louis-Napoléon was more "clerk" than "nobleman." The distinction is critical since the clerk is judged on his present performance while the nobleman must be evaluated in the context of his and his family's history.[6] Louis-Napoléon would have had the French people believe that his was a noble tradition, based principally on the historic contributions of his uncle. He was the legitimate heir to such heroism and would lead France back to the heights that the French people remembered so vividly, even if they had not lived through that period. Hugo, on the other hand, wanted people to know that Louis was nothing more than a functionary with no credit to his own past, a meaningless figure in French history who had used the only trump card he had: his family name. Yet Louis did not possess the name as a true nobleman; if he had, he would have treated his uncle's accomplishments with more respect by letting them stand. He would not have attempted to re-create history in his own, inferior image.

Continuing the theme of social class, Halbwachs points out the crucial role class has in determining the dominant discourse. The nobility used historical titles to determine the value of a person's worth and word, while the "capitalist bourgeoisie" relied on a person's aptitude and his connections (CS, 256). Such value markers were important in the formation of a discourse for a society still rooted in an identifiable class system. Such human qualities are traits that a class can reinforce and transmit to its members through a kind of social discipline (CS, 256). Louis-Napoléon and Victor Hugo each tried to impose discipline in his own way—Louis by force and propaganda, Hugo by persuasion—yet each in the end was subjected to the greater flux of time, as the people, represented by their social classes, determined which discourse would prevail.

One factor in Hugo's favor is that memory, whether individual or collective, is not static. Because of such fluidity, he could hope that he would be able to work a revision among his readers powerful enough to effect a shift in the popular view of Louis-Napoléon. Halbwachs sees such changeability as critical to the very existence of collective memory: "[The] memory of recent and current events cannot stay fixed. Its purpose is to adapt its frame of reference to new memories: its very frame of reference is itself made of such memories" (*CS*, 241). If Louis-Napoléon had been allowed to appropriate recent collective memory without being challenged, then all would have been lost for Hugo. His work from exile was the result of his taking up this challenge. In the end, however, he had to wait almost twenty years for the dominant discourse to change with events.

Collective memory, while influenced by time and by social class, begins always with the individual, and it was to each individual reader that Hugo aimed his polemics. "We maintain that it is beyond work, in the part of society where men do not exercise their profession, that the most important collective memories are born and conserved" (*CS*, 244). Each group in a society is constantly revising its collective memory through the input of new individual memories. The two cannot work independently because no individual lives in a vacuum and every society is composed of individuals. "The individual evokes his memories aided by the framework of social memory. In other words, the different groups that make up society are capable at any moment of reconstructing their past" (*CS*, 289). At the same time, evolution of collective memory comes at a price. Halbwachs calls it the deformation of collective memory. While reconstructing a new collective memory, society is deforming it at the same time, according to the current ways in which the social classes are interacting at the time.

Such deformation comes about as a complex set of interactions between the individual and his social group, each of which tries to maintain its equilibrium and strength by distancing itself from anything or anyone who is different. Ricœur calls the social group one's "close relations" (*MHF*, 131), a group that resides somewhere between the self and the others. This intermediary group is the one with whom we are contemporary and with whom we share memories. "It is, therefore, not with a single hypothesis of the polarity between individual memory and collective memory that we enter into the field of history, but with the hypothesis of the threefold attribution of memory: to oneself, to one's close relations, and to others" (*MHF*, 132). But society does not easily accept the separation into groups: "Society tends to separate from its memory anything that could alienate individuals or distance groups from one another, and in each era it modifies itself in order to harmonize with the variable

conditions of its equilibrium" (*CS*, 290). Thus we can see the importance of instruments of persuasion such as propaganda and polemical writing. The goal of each is to bring the wayward back to the
flock, to transform the dialogue between the individual and the
group, to strengthen the group by purifying its way of thinking. And
the thought process of a group is nothing more than its collective
memory (*CS*, 296).

Memory's power lies both in the emotions of the narrator and in
the combination of his story with those of millions of others who
lived through the era. The collective memory of a group, whether it
be a family, a town, a tribe, a religious sect or a nation, is composed
of individuals' memories and forms a whole through the affinities
that bind the group, whether they be familial, religious, national or
experiential. This idea is the crux of Halbwachs's explanation of collective memory. The personal sphere gives life to the collective.

Social thought is thus conceived of as the memory of individuals
who re-create their society at each instant. In the conclusion to his
study of Halbwachs, Gérard Namer likens this aspect of society to a
Janus-like figure: "Halbwachs will base progress on an ontology
linked to collective thought; progress will be like Janus (the two-
faced god): one side a memory faithful to the tradition it witnesses,
and the other a reasoned attitude as attentive to the values of the
present world as it is to the intentions of the present. . . . Memory is
almost the hope of progress in this book, which seems to be written
for our postmodernity" (*CS*, 367). Collective memory turns toward
the past for the raw materials of its existence and re-creates a present
which is always facing forward toward the future.

Such sensitivity to contemporary mores renders Halbwachs's vision of collective memory more complex. It does not look strictly to
the past, as one would expect any memory to do. Instead, it faces the
past and the present, an interaction that ultimately forces a society
to contemplate its future. The word progress immediately brings us
back to Hugo because that was his watchword. His association with
the concept of progress is particularly appropriate here because he
also is a Janus-like figure, facing both the past and the future. He
calls for the French people to remember their tradition of *liberté, égalité, fraternité*, while at the same time moving into a new world, one in
which a new republic, based on past ideals, will be able to realize the
dreams of the past.

Historical evidence shows that practice does not always follow Halbwachs' Janus-like scenario because, in order for a new regime to

flourish, it feels that it must eliminate all memory of the preceding one. Paul Connerton has studied these phenomena in a book entitled *How Societies Remember*. Even though "all beginnings contain an element of recollection" (*HSR*, 6) that solidify the principles on which the new regime is founded, there is no place in the collective memory for the powers who have been overthrown. "Those who adhere most resolutely to the principles of the new regime and those who have suffered most severely at the hands of the old regime want not only revenge for particular wrongs and a rectification of particular iniquities. The settlement they seek is one in which the continuing struggle between the new order and the old will be definitively terminated, because the legitimacy of the victors will be validated once and for all. A barrier is to be erected against future transgression" (*HSR*, 7). By executing Louis XVI in public, the revolutionaries eliminated the physical as well as symbolic obstacle to their newfound power. By basing his legitimacy on his uncle's, Louis-Napoléon effectively eradicated all memory of everything that had happened in between the two empires. Hugo's project was to fill in the gaps.

One complication in this elimination of collective memory is how far back you must go in order to cleanse the collective spirit of the elements you find undesirable (*HSR*, 9). For the Revolution, the public execution of the king was sufficient notice of the changing of the guard; for Louis-Napoléon, the evocation of his uncle provided the necessary shroud over the intervening years; for Hugo, however, the task was not so simple. Turning back the clock to 1850, for example, would not be enough to provide his reader with an image of a stable government that kept Hugo's individual and group interests in the forefront. Hugo had to return instead to the same place as his adversary, the first empire. How ironic it was that two bitter enemies were vying for the same legacy as descendants of the great emperor. Louis would have the people forget 1815, 1830, and 1848 in order to remember the glory of his ancestor. Hugo would have them recall 1789, 1830, and 1848 in order to remember the glory of the ideals Napoléon I represented as a symbol of the Revolution.

Connerton reminds us that social memory is not the same thing as historical reconstruction (*HSR*, 13), yet they are interdependent: "The practice of historical reconstruction can in important ways receive a guiding impetus from, and in turn can give significant shape to, the memory of social groups. A particularly extreme case of such interaction occurs when a state apparatus is used in a systematic way

to deprive its citizens of its memory . . ." (*HSR,* 14). The most obvious examples of such phenomena are found in totalitarian states in
which all sources of information are controlled by the forces in
power. Hugo would argue that such was the case under the Second
Empire. The difference between Louis-Napoléon and Hitler, however, is that the former did not try to eliminate all the people who
opposed his regime. The ultimate danger in a society such as the
Third Reich is that there will be no one left to remember what it was
like before (*HSR,* 14).

   For Hugo, the Second Empire represented a totalitarian state that
attempted to control all aspects of life and to eliminate dissent, and
he saw it as his task to provide an opposing voice. Every totalitarian
society that has tried to control the collective memory has had what
Connerton calls "relentless recorders" (*HSR,* 15). Alexander Sol-
zhenitsyn and Elie Wiesel are two examples of writers who give voice
to those who would be otherwise silenced (*HSR,* 15). Hugo was the
relentless recorder of the Second Empire. He was an eyewitness to
the events of December 2, 1851, and he spent the following nine-
teen years reminding the French people not to forget where they
came from. By rejecting Louis-Napoléon's historical reconstruction
and accepting his, the people would have a more accurate memory
of the events they had lived through. Without such relentless recorders, society would undergo what Ricœur has called "historical sui-
cide."[7] While it is not always easy to say what collective memory is,
its absence would be catastrophic.

   Another element in this type of historical reconstruction and its
relationship to collective memory is desire. No historical remembrance is done in a vacuum, and, as we can see through Foucault,
the writing of the history of the present is determined by the relationship between past and present.[8] This relationship is fostered by
what people believe to be true and what they believe to have remembered. The role of propagandists and relentless recorders is to convince people that their desires are represented in the particular
memory being proposed as true. In cases like this, historical accuracy is sometimes discounted in favor of political expediency: "It is
necessary that the people and events retained in memory be *believed
true* [emphasis Crubellier's]; it is not necessary that they have actually been so. Have we not seen many times over at the most serious
junctures of a nation's destiny, historians silence their critical tendencies? Legend is then recognized as being useful. . . . The overly
thorough investigation exhausts the contagious virtue of the model"

(*LMF*, 8–9). Just hearing the name Napoléon triggered memories that made people believe that the nephew was the equal of the uncle. They did not need empirical evidence that such was the case. Hugo, on the other hand, developed a legend of Napoléon I that engendered memories of the positive aspects of the Revolution. By substituting one myth for another, each tried to win over the belief system of the public at large.

This notion of desire is always associated with the imagination because in order for a legend to be believed, it must be based on what the public imagines to be the truth. "Resemblance to reality is more esteemed than truth. The essential factor is conformity to a type or stereotype. . . . This presents a great opportunity for imagination, which is more effective than reality at fortifying confidence in a world order or in human nature" (*LMF*, 9). As time goes on, the role of imagination becomes that much stronger because the empirical evidence becomes less and less relevant. What the people believe becomes more important than what actually happened. The reconstructed version of history becomes the history remembered in the collective consciousness. Such belief based on a mixture of fact and imagination helps a society remember certain events such as the Holocaust or Hiroshima that cannot be fully grasped by the objective historian. And of course adroit manipulators of the collective imagination, such as Louis-Napoléon and Hugo, can play to the beliefs of the people in order to have them accept their particular version of the myth of historical reconstruction.

A brilliant example of how the image replaces the event is related by the historian of the cinema, Marc Ferro, when he describes how Eisenstein's film *Potemkin* has come to embody the historical event in the imagination of the spectator: "In the case of Potemkin, the legend ended up overtaking history. Today it is Eisenstein's film that remains the most powerful account of the revolution [of 1905]; the masterpiece stays alive while analyses contradict each other, neutralize each other, and the event distances itself, loses its relevance, and slowly dissolves."[9] While Louis-Napoléon and Hugo may have represented "contradictory analyses," Hugo's interpretation, digested in 1870 after the fall of the Second Empire, appealed to a wider audience through their imagination. Napoléon I was once again the only great member of his family, and the process of forgetting had begun apace. Hugo's reconstruction was the one that remained the dominant version of historical events, even if it was not wholly true. One myth had replaced another because the collective memory had accepted it into its imaginary space.

Myth can seem more real than history because the readers or viewers want it to. History is a mixture of authenticity and invention, while myth exists in a realm of imagination and belief that has fewer constraints. A powerful myth recounted by a skillful narrator such as Eisenstein can have more effect on the public: "We understand, then, how memory can satisfy itself with romanticized history and historical fiction. Balzac and Zola testified for their century with exceptional force. Their works composed, for fictional actions, an irrefutable background that could potentially disqualify the laborious reconstructions of historians" (*LMF*, 10). Hugo's initial writings from exile were a hybrid of history and fiction but were written in the same powerful style as a novel such as *Les Misérables*. The force of conviction coming through the prose would overwhelm any historian's attempt to render the same images. The weight of the mythology presented would drown any metaphor a historian could conjure up.

The reason that authors and film directors can have such an effect on collective memory is that society is made up of representations that in themselves are partially fictitious. Memory plays the role of frame for the tableau of these representations and as such lends them their meaning.[10] In the vast fresco that is society, memory has the task of keeping disparate traditions together in a collective tradition. While the stories differ somewhat from group to group, a common thread of collective memory gives the whole its cohesion. Within the confines of the tableau, different representations, such as Louis' and Hugo's, can vie for supremacy by appropriating the collective memory of the society.

Crubellier establishes a parallel between the way a society is constructed and the way memory functions within that society. Every culture, according to the Russian-American sociologist P. A. Sorokin, supposes the conjunction of these three terms: a constituted group; the content of representations of value; and the means of communication, which we have come to call the media. So it is with memories since they are those of a group; they are memories that are chosen, always alive, and values, new rules of action; and they have established themselves in a large variety of guises: narratives, celebrations, a moral code, etc. (*LMF*, 19). While it is easier to identify the group and its ideals, the variety of ways in which the group reinforces those beliefs can cause confusion, contradiction and strife. A totalitarian government tries to limit such conflict by controlling the means of communication, while a free state attempts to avoid chaos by creating a legitimate dialogue among different interpretations in order to form a collective story, based on collective memory, that can satisfy the needs of the whole culture. In the case of Louis-Napoléon versus Hugo, a dialogue of the deaf (*dialogue de sourds*) developed as the man in power tried to ignore the writer in exile, while the totalitarian state attempted to silence any dialogue about its interpretation of cultural myths and memories.

The elite tends to dominate the representation of cultural memories because of their control of the media, but the diversity of both the group being targeted and the beliefs that they hold to be true go a long way in undermining any attempt on the part of the elite to monopolize the message. A certain lack of focus reigns in the domain of the group, and even more so in the content of the message. Borders between groups are often uncertain and fluctuating; some groups overlap. One can, from a cultural standpoint, be at the same time Breton, Occitan, and French, peasant or city dweller. In the end, however, the influence of the elite on the masses tends to prevail because it is the most focused (*LMF*, 19).

As Robert Gildea has so succinctly put it, "there is no single French collective memory but parallel and competing collective memories elaborated by communities which have experienced and handle the past in different ways" (*French History*, 10). Louis-Napoléon and Victor Hugo represented different parts of the elite: the government and its dominant discourse on the one hand, the intelligentsia and its power over the collective imagination on the other. Both were able to transcend the differences in class and ethnicity that their society possessed, and both had powerful means of affecting the collective consciousness by promising things such as order and stability on the one hand, and liberty and justice on the other, that directly touched popular sensibilities. While Louis initially had the upper hand because he controlled the media, history evened out the odds and presented Hugo with the final victory.

Hugo's victory came both as a direct result of historical events and of the way those events were represented. The power of historical representation depends essentially on the distancing of the actual event from the observation of the event through the lens of time and representation: "What is striking is the retreat of the political, social, or religious event, in the face of the rising tide of news items, passages of narrative, that is to say the linking of cause and effect to the refraction of current events, *a flattening of memory*" [emphasis Crubellier's] (*LMF*, 33). This flattening of memory, far from weakening the historical import of the event, renders it both mythical and historical and thus enters it into the collective memory. The way in which the media allow such entry is the stuff of the battle over the control of the message.

Crubellier sees history as a crossroads of memories (*LMF*, 58), an amalgam of all the different representations of certain historical events. Yet not all of the narratives will ultimately carry equal weight in the collective memory, and it is only time that determines which will be the preponderant version of events. As various types of media have flourished in our modern society, the competition for the domination of the collective memory has intensified. This has given added weight to the whole notion of collective memory as a repository of the history of a culture. We can no longer rely on the dominant discourse alone to provide us with information about our past. As Jacques Le Goff has written: "History writes itself, much more so than before, under the pressure of collective memory" (*Histoire et mémoire*, 170. Cited in *LMF*, 58).

MAKING HISTORY: TRACES, DOCUMENTS, QUESTIONS

As I noted earlier, Paul's Ricœur's conception of "historical knowledge" (*la connaissance historique*) is divided into three sections: documentation, explanation/comprehension, and representation. As Hugo's role changes from eyewitness to archivist to analyst to novelist, we can see Ricœur's model at work. During the coup d'état of December 2, 1851, Victor Hugo was actively involved in resisting the course of events planned by the government. *Napoléon le petit* is the documentary account of his experience, based on Hugo's experience and the testimony of over two hundred people whom he interviewed immediately after the events took place. In Ricœur's scheme, this corresponds to the first phase of the making of history. An individual's memories are combined with those of other individuals to form an archive that becomes the repository of the collective memory of an event. These archives help answer two key questions: "Of *what* are there memories? *Whose* memory is it?" (emphasis Ricœur's. *MHF*, 3). No pretense is made of complete objectivity in these accounts because the reporter is clearly biased against the government. This absence can been seen as a potential for the abuse of memory or, on the other hand, an opportunity to create a counter-memory to the version of events being propagated by the government.

At this stage in the making of history, there can be no confusion between memory and imagination. In order for the witnesses' accounts to be believed, they must be separated from any association with the imaginary, which is always linked to what is possible or even fantastic (*MHF*, 6). Memory, on the other hand, represents what actually happened, what was real in the past. Hugo, in his account of the events of December 2, will present elaborate documentation in order to persuade his reader of the validity of the memories of the witnesses he cites. Memory is the best tool available to ensure that an historical account is based on fact.

Since the eyewitness account is the fundamental structure of transition between memory and history, each reporting must have the goal of being true to the past that it is recounting. Problems arise when one of two things occurs: the witness lies or a competing version of the memory is shown to be more truthful. In Hugo's case, his version of the events of December 2 will stand in stark contrast to the government's. These contrasting narratives will do battle throughout the course of the Second Empire, and only the passage of time will allow Hugo's to emerge as the more truthful of the two.

Marc Bloch's notion of the historical trace (*la trace*) is essential to Ricœur's thinking about historical knowledge.[11] Memory is the equivalent of a written historical document that we have created in our head through sensory perception (images, sounds, etc.). Like the written text, memories are composed of traces of our past experience, traces of that which has happened and no longer exists. The key ingredient in memory is a human's ability to be aware of time and its passage. Hugo will eventually be successful in his attempt to influence the collective memory thanks to what Ricœur calls secondary memory (*MHF*, 39). Primary memory is what we recall in the immediate present or what we retain from memorization; secondary memory (recollection or *ressouvenir*) is what we reproduce in our memory over time (*MHF*, 32). Since memories are formed over time, their development corresponds to the development of an archive concerning a certain historical event. When enough documentation is stored in the archive, we can say that we have a history of the event. When enough time has elapsed, we can say that we have a memory of something. This time lapse may be long or short, but the longer the lapse, the more comprehensive the memory. This facet of the memory process will come into play in my discussion of the role of long duration (*la longue durée*) of Fernand Braudel. Because Hugo's works were read and appreciated after as well as during the Second Empire, they were able to affect the collective memory of the time.

The things that we remember tend to be dominated by events (*MHF*, 23). While Proust has shown us the power of sensation in the formation of memory, particularly involuntary memory, the fact remains that we tend to remember what happened before we relive how it felt. This is a crucial point in the making of an historical account because history is made up of a series of events. In *Napoléon le petit*, Hugo describes events in great detail. He was either present at the unfolding of the events described or he allows his witnesses to give their own detailed testimony. These types of memory can be classified under Bergson's "memory as distinct recollection" (*mémoire-souvenir*) rather than his "memory as habit" (*mémoire-habitude*), which describes memories that are part of our everyday life.[12] Memory as habit is experienced as something lived rather than something represented (*MM*, 227).[13] Memory as distinct recollection takes on a more unique quality stemming from its relation to specific events.

Memory as distinct recollection takes us closer to the world of imagination, while still retaining its pretense of being the truth of what happened. The further the event recedes into the past, the greater the tendency for memory to embellish and change it (*MHF*, 25). This is the paradox of the memory as distinct recollection, as we have seen that time allows memory to act as an archive, deepening our understanding of the events being remembered. So while we may have a better grasp of what happened, an occurrence may not be the same event in our memory as it was in real life. Hugo will see it as his duty to interpret for his reader what he and others saw on December 2, 1851. The analytical side of this paradox will be the subject of the section on explanation/comprehension in the second chapter.

When societal influences are added to an individual's memories, we move closer to commemoration and away from remembrance (*MHF*, 26). The formation of collective memory depends on the stockpiling of individual memories and the habits and rituals of society that form the direction the collective memory will take. It is thus essential that those who want to influence collective memory claim the high ground and formulate a strong enough argument to fight

back challenges to its hegemony. Governments do this by controlling the flow of information to the people in order to make individuals believe that they themselves experienced what the government is
telling them. Myths are created using traditions and beliefs that reaffirm traditional values in the collective consciousness. The force of
these myths makes it extremely difficult for a counter-memory to
take hold, even when it is being proposed by a widely respected
voice such as Hugo's. Hugo had, in fact, to create his own, very personal myth as a weapon.

This relationship between the individual's memories and societal
pressures will be central to this study because it helps us understand
how individual memories become part of the collective consciousness. Ricœur writes about the difference between reflexivity (*réflexi-
vité*) and worldliness (*mondanéité*), where the former represents the
interiority of memory while the latter designates the spatial context
surrounding the remembered scene (*MHF*, 36). In the first instance,
the individual says to himself in his heart that what he has seen, experienced and learned is true.[14] In the second, the individual remembers the space in which the event took place, including the
people, the decor, and so on. These two polarities combine to create
a full memory, but they also create a paradigm for the relationship
between an individual and collective memory. One does not exist in
a vacuum, and therefore one's memories always already belong to a
collective greater than the individual's store of memories. This notion will come into play in the discussion of Camus' version of the
man who revolts by saying "no." Each individual act of revolt impacts those around him in an ever-widening circle, resulting in a climate of revolt that may effect change. Hugo is obviously a man who
said "no" to the regime of Louis-Napoléon and who took it upon
himself to make sure that his refusal was heard by the greatest number of people.

The enemy of memory is always forgetting, a topic I will discuss in
the conclusion. It is important to mention it here, however, because
it is one of the primary motivating factors for the formation of the
archives of a society. We remember in order not to forget (*MHF*, 27).
This is true for the individual as well as the society in which he lives.
Hugo wrote his texts in order to stimulate the memories of the
French people, in order to create documents that would form the
archives of the collective memory of the Second Empire. His
competing version of the official record ensured that the collective
memory did not fall into the void of the government's self-serving

account. Hugo's goal was to create what Ricœur calls "happy" memory (*la mémoire heureuse*) (*MHF*, 28), which, simply put, is a successful culmination of our effort to remember something. We are far from Proust's involuntary memory, as Hugo exhorted his countrymen to make a conscious effort to remember not only the truth of December 2 but also the traditions of France and the ideals of the French Revolution.

The effort to remember involves the development of a structure that will form the eventual representation of that which is being remembered (*MHF*, 29). Opposing forces are at work in the formation of this scaffolding: habit and imagination, intellect and emotion (*MHF*, 29–30). Hugo had to take all of these factors into account as he appealed to the various facets of the French collective memory. His fight was as much against a collective forgetting as against Louis-Napoléon's version of history. He had to convince his reader not only that he was telling the truth of what happened December 2 but that his interpretation of those events was the right one, while at the same time reminding the reader of the glorious French past that the empire had eliminated from view.

If memory is the enemy of forgetting, then so is history. The function of the historical record, whether in the form of archives or narratives, is to create a basis on which the memory of the events at hand can be conserved in the collective memory. An important aspect of this type of remembering is what Pierre Nora has called the realms of memory (*lieux de mémoire*): monuments, commemorative ceremonies, plaques, dates, and places that help us remember what took place there, when, and why. These function as reminders, a weapon against forgetting (*MHF*, 41). Hugo took up these issues in all his texts written from exile, as he showed how a government could manipulate the collective memory by its appropriation of these realms of memory.

In every society, and particularly among those who could be classified as victims of a certain regime, there exists a "duty of memory" (*MHF*, 86) that is essential if the group is going to retain its identity. The more difficult the memories, the more important it is that they not be forgotten. In order for the process of mourning to take place, memory must precede forgetting. Only time and a sense of justice, "that gives the form of the future and of the imperative to the duty of memory" (*MHF*, 88), will allow the mourning process to be successful. "The duty of memory is the duty to do justice, through memories, to an other than the self" (*MHF*, 89). Ricœur sums up Hugo's project succinctly.

Another aspect of the duty of memory is the debt that each of us and each society has toward the memory of those who have come before. Yet even the means by which a society remembers its victims can be abused by those who have the power to control those means. A "frenzy of commemoration" (*MHF*, 90) can take the place of a thoughtful and comprehensive system of remembrance by replacing a national, historical remembrance understood by all with a fragmented, local and cultural system of commemoration. "Thus the very dynamics of commemoration have been turned around; the memorial model has triumphed over the historical model and ushered in a new, unpredictable, and capricious use of the past."[15] While Louis' use of commemoration was less local than national, he significantly altered the way France remembered its past in order to put himself in the best light. Hugo continually compared him to his uncle in order to counteract such revisionism.

The fight against forgetting results eventually in a document that permits the collective memory to outlive the individuals who originally compiled it. Ricœur sees the process as perception, memory, and fiction (*MHF*, 49). These elements correspond roughly to documentation, explanation/comprehension and representation. His use of the word fiction is interesting because we have come full circle from the need for truth found in the first stage, where an eyewitness must establish his credibility in order for his testimony to be made part of the record. The final version can be seen as fiction not because it is not true, but because it relies on a metaphoric image for its formation. When a memory is transformed from the original sensory experience into an historical document, it inevitably will rely on its ability to translate sensation into image for the benefit of the reader. This process replicates the way fiction is created. Thus we see how Ricœur arrived at this concept through his reading of Bergson's view of how a "pure memory" becomes a memory-image (*MHF*, 52). I will look closely at the relationship between history, memory, and fiction throughout this study and will rely on Ricœur's *Time and Narrative* as a guide.

One consequence of a memory like Hugo's is its obsessive nature. Hugo felt personally attacked by the coup d'état, and his campaign to rectify the situation takes on the nature of a religious crusade. Ricœur, through Bergson, sees obsession as having a fundamental role in the creation of both individual and collective memory be-

cause a memory refuses to take its place in the repository of past
events that is collective memory (*MHF*, 54). This "pathological mod-
ality" (*MHF*, 54) is a kind of torment that corresponds to hallucina-
tions in the individual. Hugo, for his part, never allowed his
obsession to become hallucinatory because his eye was always on the
future. The only way to eliminate the obsession is to eliminate its
cause, and that, according to both Hugo and Ricœur, requires the
individual and the society to take action.

The Use and Abuse of Memory

Memory consists of two distinct operations: reception and recall.
We can either receive an image from the past, triggered by sensation
or association with another memory, or actively search what we have
"forgotten" in order to retrieve a memory that has been temporarily
put aside. Bergson calls this active recall "effort of memory," and
Freud calls it "the work of remembering" (*MHF*, 56). These operations, one cognitive, the other pragmatic, provide the core of the
interaction between memory and history, with the more pragmatic
recall function corresponding to the active making of history (*MHF*,
57). Within this framework lies, however, the potential for the mal-
functioning of memory or the abuse of history. Ricœur places these
potential problems in three categories: on a pathological-therapeu-
tic level, troubles can arise from memory that is restricted for one
reason or another (blocked memory, *mémoire empêchée*); on a practical level, memory can be manipulated (manipulated memory), by
another individual or by a group; and on an ethical-political level,
collective memory can be abused when commemoration equals recall (*mémoire obligée*) (*MHF*, 57).

The abuse of collective memory is most interesting for this study,
because it is precisely the thing of which Hugo accuses Louis-
Napoléon. Each generation has the task of passing traditions on to
their descendants, but they must do it in good faith. Collective memory becomes, in this way, the root of a society's history (*MHF*, 69).
As each generation passes the torch to the next, a transitional process of mourning takes place, as the previous generation's memories
are archived and the next generation makes its own history. Without
this period of mourning and remembrance, both generations would
be subject to melancholy and inaction (*MHF*, 72). One of Hugo's
principal arguments against Louis-Napoléon was that the emperor

represented a past generation that could not let go, could not liberate itself in order to see the future. Ricœur puts the relationship between mourning and memory most succinctly: "The work of mourning is the cost of the work of remembering, but the work of remembering is the benefit of the work of mourning" (*MHF*, 72). The abuse of collective memory comes, therefore, from the refusal of the first generation to allow the second to move through its period of mourning into a new phase of action that looks toward the future.

Along with the mourning process, violence is one of the motors of history because it is through violence that historical change takes place. Such violence engenders different memories for the groups involved and opens up a whole new realm of potential abuse of collective memory. One group's glory is another's shame. A cause for celebration on one side is a reason for execration on the other (*MHF*, 79). Wounds that are stored in the collective memory take a long time to heal, and the healing process is even more complex than the passing of the torch from one generation to the next. Hugo could not forgive the violence of the coup d'état, and his graphic descriptions of the killing in the streets of Paris were calculated to work on the collective memory of his readers. For Louis, on the other hand, the coup d'état was the beginning of his glorious reign as emperor, and December 2, 1851 lived as a day to be celebrated. In Hugo's eyes, the celebration of violence was the worst possible abuse of collective memory.

The collective memory of a society is the temporal component of its identity, and any abuse of it will upset the fragile balance of forces that allows that identity to exist (*MHF*, 81). Every society asks both who and what it is, and the tradition stored in its depository of memories helps answer both questions. When that identity is destabilized through contact with a competing version of history, the very existence of the society is jeopardized. Competing ideologies create a climate of violence, as one camp denounces the beliefs of the other. Ideology and power go hand in hand, as efforts to gain and maintain power revolve around each group's attempt to achieve semiotic dominance. Each group needs a belief system, a basis on which to explain why they should obey the dictates of the powers that be. The paradox of authority comes from the need for a legitimate power structure coupled with the potential for abuse inherent in any governmental system.

Attempts to control the language of communication of a given society are often a distortion of reality and lead to the manipulation and abuse of collective memory. If representatives of competing ideologies are allowed to air their views in free public discussion, then a power structure legitimized by the people will emerge. If not, civil war will result (*MHF*, 84). Hugo's texts from exile can be seen as an attempt to reestablish the free flow of discussion and eliminate the futile *dialogue de sourds* between his pamphlets on one side and Louis' propaganda on the other. Narrative thus plays a crucial role in incorporating memory into a society's identity. By constantly reminding his readers of the positive nature of their past, Hugo hoped to strengthen their identity as a free and just nation.

The battle lines between Hugo and Louis were thus drawn on a battlefield of narration. Every tyrant needs a spokesman, an orator to intimidate and seduce. He needs speeches and proclamations about his nation's foundation and its glory to nourish his discourse of flattery and fear (*MHF*, 85). The "official history" is learned and celebrated. Forced memory is followed by commemoration of events chosen by those in power. "A formidable pact is concluded in this way between remembrance, memorization, and commemoration" (*MHF*, 85). Hugo had a formidable task ahead of him when he set out to write the counter-memory to the one being created in Paris. Louis had the newspapers as his mouthpiece and had the means to limit distribution of opposing voices. Hugo had to overcome such resistance to convince his readers that his cause was just, not simply that his version of the facts was true. His most powerful tool became his view of the future, because that is where lay hope of a return to a system of freedom and justice.

CONCLUSION

Memory becomes an integral part of the historiographical process as each individual creates a personal history that takes its place as part of the greater collective memory. In the following chapter, I will examine how this movement from memory to history takes various narrative forms. In the hands of a master writer such as Hugo, personal stories are woven into a highly metaphorical representational process. A specific historical event, such as the coup d'état of December 2, 1851, becomes the linchpin of a number of literary works that culminate in the timeless novel, *Les Misérables*. Throughout the

1850s and 1860s, Hugo's narrative grows in scope and power, as the French people come to see the wisdom of his words.

Narrative, specifically that written by a revered national figure, develops a form of collective unity that people find so elusive in their own lives by reminding them that the ideals of the past need not die. We cannot relive the past, but we can return to what the past stood for. For a time during the Second Empire, Louis-Napoléon provided the dominant narrative by appealing to time-tested values such as order and unity. Hugo's goal was to write a competing narrative that would expose Louis's values as simple buzz words concealing a perfidious agenda of enriching himself and his colleagues. The emotions triggered by Hugo's writings of this period are the base on which trust built between him and his readership, a trust he had to rekindle from exile. Only by appealing through emotion and memory could Hugo's metaphorical case be made for acceptance of his history of the period as the legitimate one.

2

Memory as Narrative

I HAVE MADE THE CLAIM THAT MEMORY AND HISTORY, OR MORE PRECISELY, memory and recorded history, are distinct. Memory plays a role in the narration of historical events because even the most clear chronology narrated by the most reliable observer depends at its core on the memory of that narrator. When a monumental historical event such as Louis-Napoléon's coup d'état takes place, observers may often agree on the basic chain of events. Memory's role comes later, as the individuals who were there or others who heard about it remember where they were, what they were doing, whom they were with, and how they felt at the first moment of recognition that an important event had taken place. Each individual recounts that memory to someone else, and the process of retelling and of interpretation is launched.

The interlocutor asks questions about what the narrator saw, heard, and felt. The narrator tries to recall the exact moment of realization that his world has changed and finds that there are things missing. What exactly had he heard just before the dull thud of the first shot hitting the wall next to him? What were the exact words used by the soldiers as they attempted to clear the streets? Even the most experienced journalist could not replace every sight and sound, could not put every small event into its exact place in the chronology. The writing of history thus begins as an immediate distortion of the facts, and memory's hold on historiography increases as the distance between the event and the narration of it grows.

To use a more recent example, the Vietnam War was the first war to be televised, some of it live, back to the United States. As such, it was supposed to be the first time that people not on the scene could see war for themselves. And yet, even these images, as stark as they were, came filtered through a camera with a limited scope of vision, run by a human being who was responding quickly to events and making quick decisions about the choice of shot. There could be only a pretense of objectivity here since we were seeing the action from one point of view in a limited visual range. The spectator was deprived of all senses except (limited) sight and sound. No smell, taste, or touch came through the television screen. We were unable to ascertain what the North Vietnamese were thinking or feeling or even seeing since the camera was not turned on the Americans and South Vietnamese. The result of this limited scope was a narration so restricted the spectator had to rely on imagination to complete the scene. Our imagination was fueled by our own memories of war or war as seen through books and films. A second-hand memory thus came into play and threatened to destroy the "objectivity" of the television's story. Only the memories of the soldiers, journalists and other first-hand observers could keep events in their historical perspective. But their stories came much later, long after they had been removed from the action being described.

History most often has at least the intention of respecting chronology. A recounting of the Second World War makes more sense if told from the beginning to the end. The uninformed reader would not understand the ramifications of the Battle of the Bulge without knowing anything about the German attack on and occupation of France. This kind of history must, however, be limited because it can only narrate the broadest picture. It can include events that have preceded its story, the motivations of the people who put the events into motion, and the aftermath of the action being described. It cannot write the story of the individual soldier who lay terrified in a ditch while German tanks drove by or of the French farmer who watched helplessly as his land was destroyed by battle. Only these individuals can complete the picture, and they do not do so in any chronological way. Memory does not work that way. It is based, as Proust has shown us, on sensations hidden in our psyches.

Memory is more than a complement to the official writing of history; it is a fundamental part of the writing or telling of any historical event. Memory is a web of collected material that becomes the framework of history. Paul Ricœur, in *Time and Narrative III*, makes the distinction between representation (history) and self-representation (memory), "representation in the sense of 'standing for' something and representing something to oneself in the sense of giving oneself a mental image of some absent external thing" (*T&N*, 143).[1] Memory and history could not exist without one another; they enrich each other and enable their society to better comprehend the past in order to work toward progress in the future. The next question that interests us here is *how* history is represented and the role that memory plays in that representation.

Are history and memory synonymous or do they provide different ways of recording the past? Is collective memory sufficient for telling a nation's, or any other group's, story? Marc Ferro is of the opinion that memory alone is not sufficient. In a 2002 interview for the French television program, *Histoire,* Ferro stated that if you tried to string together a series of personal testimonies, the result would be a disjointed, incomplete, nonanalytical version of events. The professional historian, as separate from the eyewitness, is vital to the process because he is the one who can weave the memories together into a coherent whole. He can do so because he has the requisite distance—physical, temporal, affective—from the events to decipher the meanings of the eyewitness testimonies. Films such as *The Sorrow and the Pity* and *Shoah* needed to come out well after World War II, and they needed the critical eye of their creators, Marcel Ophuls and Claude Lanzmann, to formulate the footage into a coherent story. While the narrative techniques of film create the director's own and oftentimes highly emotional truth rather than a substantive or statistical truth, the use of eyewitness testimony is a powerful force. Only after the film has been viewed, distanced from the event, could the audience be expected to make sense of these hundreds of different witnesses, each representing a unique point of view. Paul Ricœur would seem to agree with Ferro when he writes: "History has always been a critique of social narratives and, in this sense, a rectification of our common memory" (*T&N,* 119).

MEMORY AND LITERATURE

Historians write historiography, writers write novels, poetry, theater, and essays. Some of Hugo's literary texts are historical in nature, and these are the ones that interest us here. When an author sets out to write a historical novel or play or poem or essay, he does so with the knowledge of the historical events he is narrating. His goal may be to rewrite the accepted version of events in a way he finds more exact or more politically accurate, it may be to add an imaginary element to the known events, or it may be to protest the official version of what happened.

When a government writes its own version of events, it adds a level of distortion to that of the historian's account. Individual governments have an agenda, whether it be political, social, economic, humanitarian, etc. They also have the power to determine how and when historical representations will be presented. Whether they control the dissemination of information or not, governments have the power to monopolize at least part of the information system. This may come in the form of a newspaper sympathetic to the party in power or a state-controlled television system. Governments use the promise of monetary advantage to buy favorable coverage in the media, or they might fund costly research projects at universities in exchange for a friendly reception in the academic community. The problem, of course, is that such a system leads to abuse of the power held by the government. Opposing views do not receive the same amount of coverage and are not as favorably portrayed. The government mouthpiece can be used for slander and exaggerated critiques of those that oppose it. Only historical perspective can correct the corrupted message.

In this context, we can begin to see what a literary work can add to a reexamination of history that another historical account cannot: imagination, a different point of view, and the animation of the personalities involved. In addition, the author of fiction, particularly if he is well known, has a certain stature in society, especially in France, that a politician does not. He also has distance from the halls of power, even if he is a politician such as Hugo. This distance gives him legitimacy in the eyes of his readers that a politician does not generally have. If he is as celebrated an author as Hugo, his readers will hear his voice even from abroad, where Hugo's opposition to the government of Louis-Napoléon necessitated his exile. The reading of literature, again particularly in France, is a privileged pastime, and the populace takes its authors seriously. (The popularity of televised literary talk shows such as *Apostrophe* and *Bouillon de Culture* is an obvious example.) While one might never see an American on a beach reading the most recent work by the latest hot contemporary philosopher, in France, this would be common. Many French writers have held elected office; conversely, almost all high-ranking French politicians of note have dabbled in literary enterprises. The symbiosis between government and literature is as old as the French state itself.

When a government abuses its power of representation, the literary world is often the first to raise its voice in protest. Yet its effect is often delayed. Rare is the example such as "J'accuse," where the text sparks immediate comment and action. More commonly, a writer's attempt to refashion the prevailing view is not immediately accepted, whether because of government suppression, as in the case of Hugo, or because the public was not ready to accept the view of someone from outside official channels. The text may come later, as a reaction to the historical portrayal of events. Such was the case for Hugo's *Histoire d'un crime* (1877), which was intended to set the record straight, not to change history that had taken place years before. In Hugo's situation, he had to work on influencing the individual memory of the reader and the collective memory of the reading populace. His goal was to revise historical impression and to rewrite official versions of historical events in order to prevent similar happenings in the future, in order to work for progress.

In *Time and Narrative III*, Paul Ricœur gives fiction a privileged role in the recounting of history: "It is precisely one of the functions of fiction to detect and to explore some of these temporal significations that everyday experience levels off or obliterates" (*T&N*, 190). The pact established between author and reader allows for the reader's belief that he is reading events that belong to the author's past. "Fiction is quasi-historical, just as much as history is quasi-fictive. . . . Fictional narrative is quasi-historical to the extent that the unreal events that it relates are past facts for the narrative voice that addresses itself to the reader. It is in this that they resemble past events and that fiction resembles history." (*T&N*, 190). The different functions of the historian are clearly distinct: "History takes care of the actual past, poetry takes charge of the possible" (*T&N*, 190). That which is possible is persuasive because it is not restricted by time. It acts as a secondary memory, one that comes after the initial recall of the event, much as Proust's Marcel uses involuntary memory to recapture lost time. This critical distance that both memory and fiction have is what gives them their power to effect change through their influence on the reader. Equal yet different, memory and history find a critical link in fiction.

Just as fiction is quasi-historical, history is quasi-fictive. We have seen above possible reasons for distortion in the writing of history. Ricœur goes further by equating the reading of history with the reading of a novel (*T&N*, 186). While historians no longer invent dialogues between protagonists, they are conscious of giving the reader the impression of being present at the time of the events being described. Quasi-fictionalization serves the historian in the evocation of emotion as he tries to communicate what Ricœur calls the "uniqueness" (*l'unicité*) of the event.[2] While fiction has the power to provoke the impression of presence, it is still controlled by critical distance.

History and memory have thus a number of common characteristics: they use eyewitness accounts to construct a narrative; the story that is told can never be wholly objective since it is constructed from individual memories and since each historian has a personal point of view; collective memory and historiography are specific to a community, each group within it having its own history, mythology, and system of beliefs. The fundamental difference between memory and history lies in the distance identified by Ferro. Without the distance possessed by the historian, there is only personal memory.

Both the historian and the writer of historical fiction become critics of history through distance. More than just a damper on emotion or a change of temporal perspective, distance endows the writer with the critical powers that enable him to make more sense of events in the past. Whereas the historian's distance is physical, temporal, and affective, the writer of fiction has the added dimension of fictionality. Even as he is writing a historical fiction, his characters and their thoughts and feelings are not remembered but invented. While the historian has a certain liberty of invention, it is nowhere near as great as the fiction writer's. Consequently, the work of history critiques events more directly than does fiction, which has in its arsenal invention, exaggeration, allegory, and metaphor. The original memory of the historical events is enhanced and eventually replaced by historical and fictive versions that impose their own critical stance on the narrative. The power of these narratives comes from such critical distance because they have as ammunition all that has happened—and been remembered—between the occurrence of the events and this historical or fictive narration of them. A large dose of the propaganda Hugo was attempting to combat was based on historical myth. The government had carefully constructed its own mythology, based on past glory, in order to protect its interests. Louis-Napoléon based his legitimacy as emperor on his uncle's legendary exploits, using the people's memory of them to create his own contemporary mythology.

Professional historians, most notably Michelet, developed their own more literary tools, including memory, to recount historical events and trends. By the twentieth century, memory was a powerful technique in the writing of history. What began with Freud, Bergson, and Proust, has continued up to the New History.[3] No longer content with "objective" renderings of events, historians began looking at the same eras with a new perspective, whether through individual reminiscences or the collective memory of a certain group.[4] Memory informs virtually every event of historical note, whether it is a war, a political scandal or changes in the way a society goes about its business. The problem for historians is how to put memory to work in order to create a coherent whole.

One of the most striking contemporary examples of how personal memory becomes history is the Second World War. As the twenty-first century begins, we are faced with the death of the generation that lived through the war. Once they are gone, only their testimony will remain: diaries, photographs, recorded narration of events, and memories retained by their successors of stories told to them by those who lived through the horror. Yet these are not the only ways in which memories can be preserved. Art, and particularly modern art aided by new technology, provides a record that, while not as "objective" as the traditional historical account, is a powerful tool in the recording of events. Documentary films such as Resnais' *Night and Fog* or Marcel Ophuls's *The Sorrow and the Pity*, will forever conserve images of the camps and the angst of occupied France. Literature in all its forms commemorates the ideals and the realities of all aspects of war. Whether it be Céline's *Voyage au bout de la nuit*, Sartre's *Les Mains sales*, Camus' *La Peste*, or Modiano's *La Place de l'Etoile*, the specifically French view of war has been examined and, in part, shaped by a vast variety of writers.

Despite the presence of materials that would seem to move memories from the personal to the collective and historical, memory is never fixed. Bergson effectively destroyed the notion of a fixed and lasting memory by identifying our individual desire to step outside the time line and view our own history from afar. In so doing, we become historians of our own life, subjective ones at that. In "writing" our own history, we bring into play certain prejudices, as does the historian who is writing a more dispassionate account of an era. Since individual memories are never objective and never fixed, collective memory is also constantly evolving, and the recording of history reflects these changing perceptions of historical events. Hugo puts his personal stamp on memories of historical events in the three texts to be studied here, and his refusal to accept the "official" memory proposed by the government sets the tone for the revision of the nation's memory of the times.

In what has become one of the most influential essays of the twentieth century, "L'Homme révolté," Albert Camus presents the scenario of a slave who, after a lifetime of servitude, finally stands up to his master and says: "No." Camus' point is that each of us can and does reach the same point of frustration at some point during our life. It is this "no," this refusal to accept further oppression that represents our revolt and gives us life: "Je me révolte, donc nous sommes"(38). [I revolt, therefore we are.][5] The use of the subject pronouns in this sentence is ingenious because it succinctly explains the relationship between the individual and his fellow human beings. On a grander scale, we can see the relationship between an individual and his surroundings. For my purposes, the sentence presents a synopsis of how Hugo uses individual memories to appeal to the collective conscious concerning certain historical events. Hugo had the courage to say "no" to the myths being promulgated by Louis-Napoléon, who had control over the dissemination of information and therefore over the collective memory of past events. Hugo reaffirmed the power of the written word to influence how a society remembers.

In the same television interview cited above, Marc Ferro says that it is through these moments of revolt that history is written. These privileged moments provide us with the grist that the historian can mill. The import of each refusal to acquiesce to the unjust use of power varies from the beginnings of the French Revolution to the voice of an individual slave. As Camus points out, each of these declarations has an effect on the world surrounding the speaker. "The revolutionary acts in the name of a value, still inarticulate, but through which he at least senses that he is united with all people. We see that the affirmation implied in every revolutionary act stretches to something that surpasses the individual in the sense that it pulls him out of his supposed solitude and gives him a reason to act" (*HR*, 30). If no revolt ever took place, history would grind to a halt under the weight of routine and the status quo. In fact, following Camus' argument, revolt is inevitable because it is what gives us life. In a personal sense any interaction between human beings involves relationships of power, and the person without power will eventually rise up against the one who has it. In a political sense revolt is inevitable because any established system of government is inherently unjust. Tyranny cannot last forever because the oppressed will eventually demand to be free, and the consequences of individual revolt are felt throughout the surrounding community.

If no one but the slave owner hears the slave say "no," then the slave owner can simply put down this small protest by using his physi-

cal power, the same power that established the slave/owner relationship in the first place, but the memory of the event will linger with
the slave owner. He will become more vigilant, in order to prevent
future outbreaks. In so doing, he will increase the tyranny built into
the relationship. The original slave and eventually his fellow slaves
will feel the added weight of this new oppression, thus beginning a
cycle that will inevitably end in a collective revolt powerful enough
to overthrow the slave owner and subsequently the system he represents. The process may take many years, even centuries, but eventually the voice of the original slave will be heard throughout his
community. At that point, the historian will have his material and
will be able to interpret the effect of the original "no" on the subsequent years.

The courage of writers to say "no" helps prevent future atrocities.
We must never forget the horror of certain events such as the Holocaust. Such remembrance constitutes the ultimate tribute to the victims and the ethos of their story. Victimization is the obverse of
history in the sense that no reason can legitimate the horror. The
role of fiction is a corollary of the power of this horror in its ability
to portray these events in their uniqueness (*T&N*, 187). As the historian—or writer of fiction—delves deeper into the problem, the horror grows: "The more we explain in historical terms, the more
indignant we become; the more we are struck by the horror of
events, the more we seek to understand them" (*T&N*, 188). The
"no" of the historian/writer of fiction evolves from this desire to
understand and the desire to prevent similar horrors from happening again.

PRIMARY AND SECONDARY MEMORY

Ricœur picks up on Husserl's conception of primary memory (*réten-
tion*) versus secondary memory (*protention*). He describes Husserl's
use of a simple sound to demonstrate the difference between them.
The length of the sound itself enters the realm of duration, but as
soon as the sound has ended, it falls into "the ever more distant
past."[6] The sound takes its place among others, just as any present
moment takes its place on the chronological time line. The concept
of duration is inherently linked to this line, and while time continues incessantly, the movement that is created by associations between points on the line can cease momentarily through the act of

remembrance. In other words, we are consistently moving forward in time and changing as we do so, but as each "retained" moment becomes part of our past (the secondary memory), it can only be recalled through voluntary or involuntary memory. This moment of using memory marks the succession of "nows" that Husserl calls "phases" or "points" on the time line. The emphasis is on the continuity of the whole or, looked at another way, the totality of continuity, as implied in the term duration. To last means that something remains, even while changing. What remains is not a logical unity but a temporal totality (*T&N*, 30).[7] This notion of endurance is closely linked with Braudel's long duration because they both insist on the importance of secondary memory. The continuous progress and change we undergo as we pass along the time line would have no meaning if we did not stop the movement and look back. We would be plunging headlong into the blackness that is the unknown future, without assigning any significance to the experiences we have lived through.

Ricœur calls primary memory "an enlarged present" that assures the continuity of time (*T&N*, 30). At the same time, the original impression experienced at the present moment enters into retention only in a form that is progressively "shaded off" (*dégradé*) (*T&N*, 30). This is because it now takes its place on the time line with every other experience from our past. As each new experience joins the line, the previous one is pushed farther into the past and becomes part of secondary memory. Each act of recall is colored by all the experiences that have occurred between the original occurrence of the time being remembered and the present of the person doing the remembering.[8] When one sound is heard and continues to resonate in our mind, it joins others to form a melody. As the melody passes by, it becomes part of the repository that is our memory.

The conscious act of recalling the melody, even long after it has been heard, constitutes a central question of this study because it brings into play the notion of how to represent the past through memory. In order to remember the melody, we repeat it back to ourselves until we are confident that we have re-created it in our mind. Yet this re-creation is only that; it is what Ricœur calls a "quasi-hearing" (*T&N*, 32) because it is different from the original. Herein lies the fundamental difference between primary and secondary memory, and the problem of representing memory is "the basis of historical consciousness, for which every past that is retained can be set up as a quasi-present endowed with its own retrospections and anticipations, some of which belong to the retained past of the actual present" (*T&N*, 32). By creating a representation of the melody through memory of it, we have brought into play the complicated relationship between past and present. No memory is untainted by our present state, and therefore no representation of a remembered event can be wholly free of interpretation based on experiences that have come between its origin and the time of remembrance. This process of re-creating the past through memory is what Ricœur calls "recollection" (*ressouvenir*).

The fundamental difference between remembering a recent event (retention) and remembering something further in the past (recollection) is the freedom accorded the latter by its distance from the event being recalled. "Recollection, with its free mobility and its power of recapitulation, provides the stepping back of free reflection" (*T&N*, 34). As we remember and re-create original events or sensations, we are conscious of the reconstruction taking place. In this most voluntary of memory processes, we contemplate the images that remain in our consciousness and analyze their effect on us. Our present self who is doing the remembering is not the same one who experienced the original sensation. We have compiled a whole series of other experiences in between. Our present self is, however, the one doing the representation of the past, and it is necessarily colored as a result.

We must be careful not to confuse "recollection" with imagination. Ricœur emphasizes here the similarities between retention and recollection rather than their differences in order to contrast them with the notion of imagination. The primary difference between any memory and imagination, as Ricœur sees it, is their "positional value," that is to say their relationship to the present on the continuous time line. There is a conscious association between the reproduction/ representation of an event and the event itself. This "intentionality" is what gives memory its uniqueness and distinguishes it from imagination.[9]

Let us return now to the relationship between memory and the present, for it is here that the key to historical representation lies. Ricœur points out that the present is not only that which we are experiencing at the moment, but the realized or unrealized expectations that we had in the past. We look back on what we had been expecting this moment to look like and take stock of whether we have achieved our goals or not. The present becomes therefore a dual experience: living the present moment and remembering past expectations. This is a crucial point in the study of historical representation because historical expectations are what drive government policy or help individuals decide on a course of action. Historiography is the recording in the present of the outcome of those expectations.

In this study, we will see a fine example of the importance of this notion of the present as remembrance of past expectations. Victor Hugo wrote the poems of *Les Châtiments* between 1851 and 1853. These pieces look toward a future in which the emperor, Louis-Napoléon will have been deposed, and France will have returned to a republican form of government. In 1853, the time for the realization of Hugo's expectations was not right, and the collection had little popular success. In 1870, however, after the fall of the empire, Hugo reissued the poems, with a few new pieces included, to great acclaim. The poems served as a written memory of the events of 1851 to 1852 and also of the realization of Hugo's expectations. The success of Hugo's hopes was not essential for his poems to serve as a memory of a certain time, but it did color the way in which the poems were received.[10] While Hugo did not write all of the poems in 1870, they serve the same purpose as if he had. They are written markers of personal and cultural memory of the outcome of expectations.

History naturally outlasts individual memory, and so the distinction between primary and secondary memory becomes that much more important when talking about the writing of history. As the actual memory of an event fades, the written record describing the event takes the place of memory. It has its own present (the moment of writing) that will recede into memory, but the written record will remain. The point of view of the historian, who wrote the account during his present moment, will be a matter of discussion, disagreement, and revision, as future generations read the written account, but the record will still exist. It will be up to future historians, who may or may not have any memory of the events at hand, to revise and rewrite the historical record. This constant rewriting of history acts in much the same way as our replacement of one memory by another more recent one.

Hugo rewrote history in order to obliterate Louis-Napoléon from the collective memory of the French people. He wrote the texts I will study while the empire was still in place, and they represent both the historical present of the author and the remembrance of the expectations that he had while the events were taking place. Hugo is re-creating history, through the writing of either his own memories or the projection of himself into the memories of others, a process made possible by the existence of eyewitness accounts of the times. One of the keys to studying these re-creations of history is the order in which they are presented. By structuring the historical re-creation in one way or another, the author can "remember," and make his reader "remember" in any way he wants. In *Les Misérables*, for example, Hugo's narration covers the years 1815 to 1834, but we are always conscious of the fact that the novel was published in 1862. Once we have it in our mind that Hugo's own memory is in play here, it is a simple step to project the narrator into the years of the coup d'état and the Second Empire and to see the narrative as a commentary on his whole century as he has lived it. Even as Hugo appropriates the memory of the historical record and the memories of people who have lived through the period, he forces us to project our own imagination and memories along with him. By ordering his narrative in a certain way, Hugo manipulates the imagination of the reader. He thus creates a kind of tertiary memory, one based on a combination of history and imagination, and one in which the reader is fully engaged. This ordering of memory, whether personal or historical, is what Ricœur calls the indirect way the representation of time manifests itself" (*T&N*, 49).[11] The allegorical aspects of *Les Misérables* are a good example of this phenomenon.

The three kinds of memory I have identified in this section— primary, secondary, and tertiary—correspond more or less to Ricœur's summary of Kant's view of the order of time: simultaneity, succession and duration. The simultaneity of the present gives way to a secondary ordering of memories that in turn gives way to a more permanent historical record. Hugo uses these three ways of "remembering" in different ways, yet he finishes with three texts that are his own reordering of events.[12] *Napoléon le petit*, *Les Châtiments*, and *Les Misérables* become Hugo's historical record, arranged in such a way as to make his arguments more forceful.

"PROBLEMATIZATION" AND MEMORY

One of Michel Foucault's lasting contributions to the philosophy of history is his call for "a history of the present."[13] In delineating this project, he coined the phrase "problematization" as "a means of utilizing history to account for the present."[14] Foucault defined problematization as "the totality of discursive and non-discursive practices that brings something into the play of truth and falsehood and sets it up as an object for the mind."[15] It is neither a representation of a preexisting object nor the creation through discourse of an object that does not exist. These "discursive and non-discursive practices" refer to institutions, regulations, and scientific, philosophical, and moral propositions. These things are neither true nor false but at a given moment become "part of a debate on truth and falsehood that has incontestably theoretical claims and repercussions" ("P," 238). Problematization is also a way of governing and of shaping the conduct of others. Foucault's goal was to understand how we govern each other by "means of the production of the truth." He places "the register of the production of truth and falsehood at the heart of historical analysis and political debate."[16] These definitions are crucial to this study. Hugo tries, in his own way, to turn a falsehood into truth, to modify the institutions that allowed that falsehood to flourish, and to do so using the power of the written word.

Victor Hugo is a historian of the present. He becomes such a historian by relocating events of the past in the present context. His role is to update history, allowing the present to play itself out without ever forgetting the legacy of the past ("P," 238). The uses of memory in the process are evident and abundant, whether we speak of personal or historical memories. Each of the three texts written by Hugo is an updating of the past, an attempt to reorder the present by learning the lessons memory and history bring us. He "problematizes" his particular era in order to better understand it in terms of the present, and even to effect change in the present based on past experience.

Robert Castel immediately recognizes some of the potential pitfalls of Foucault's formulation of problematization: historiography can always be influenced by the present preconceptions of the author; it is sometimes impossible to pinpoint the beginning of the historical era at hand (although, fortuitously, this is not the case for Hugo); the choice of which historical evidence to choose is always subjective; problematization is generally undertaken by nonhistorians, who may base their conclusions on historical documents, but who are not trained in the painstaking methods of the historian; because of the previous problem, there is always the danger that the problematization will slip into fiction ("P," 239). It is my contention that most, if not all, of these objections can be overcome through the lens of memory. When memory is added to the equation, it introduces a subjective element that renders moot some of the problems, such as that of fiction versus reality. By substituting memory for history where appropriate, we can see the rapport between past and present in a new light, one that allows us to choose data in a way similar to that of the human consciousness, as it sifts through remembered information to form a coherent whole that will allow it to function most efficiently in the present.

The relationship between problematization and historical representation is obvious but problematic. The first of Castel's worries is how the writer of the history of the present can keep his own preconceptions out of his account. Obviously he cannot, and the historian is no more immune from this problem than is the "amateur." Castel writes that this "presentism" is a type of ethnocentrism since we attach to the past a concern that is principally rooted in the present (239). This phenomenon leads to historical distortion. Yet we could argue that all historiography contains a certain distortion because it is written in the present of the historian. He cannot be oblivious to how the past is affecting his present, particularly those aspects of present life that affect him personally.

Hugo is an extreme example of the amateur historian who projects his own present on events of the past, but his situation was complicated by two factors: he was a participant in the events being discussed, and the events took place not long before Hugo wrote about them. This lack of physical and temporal distance would seem to be a problem, for we have seen that distance creates the conditions necessary for a certain objectivity in historiography. On the other hand, Hugo's proximity to the coup d'état of 1851 had its advantages. First, he had no need for secondary or even primary sources since he himself was a primary source; second, he did not need to rely on competing views of what happened since he was convinced that his version was correct; and third, with the moral conviction that his version was the authentic one, he used the power of the pulpit to harangue and cajole his reader until they came around to his point of view. Hugo had no pretense of objectivity in the texts written from exile; his only goal was to persuade. Seen from Hugo's vantage point, the writing of the present was a straightforward matter of putting the facts on paper in a dramatic and persuasive style.

One could ask whether Hugo's type of writing the history of the present, based on memory instead of documentation, represents a distortion of history. The answer is of course that Hugo did not pretend to write anything other than a one-sided account. On the other hand, such distortion does not render this type of historical account invalid because if it were, we would have to disqualify all historiography, since every text contains its biases. Hugo's texts have great value in their immediacy. What better way to write the history of the present than by first having been present and then immediately writing about it?

Castel's second issue with problematization is the difficulty in identifying a beginning to the period under discussion. "A problematization emerges at a given moment. How can that appearance be dated? What gives one the right to interrupt the move toward an undefined past with the assertion that this current question can be formulated at such and such a moment in the past?" ("P," 239) For Hugo, these questions presented little problem at all. The immediate problem, the repression of freedom by the Second Empire, can be identified as having begun on December 2, 1851. The larger question of restoring the ideals of the Revolution finds its roots in the late eighteenth century, specifically on July 14, 1789. The modern world began on that day, and Hugo saw his role as the restorer of the ideals represented by the acts of 1789. He had no need to return to the Greeks for notions of freedom; he had living examples in his own life of what freedom meant to him. He had especially his memories, of accounts of the events of the last decade of the eighteenth century and of his own life. These accounts and memories were all the documentation he needed, and they provided him with the beginning—and end—of critical time periods.

The third problem Castel sees is the difficulty of identifying "historical periods." While a problematization does not repeat itself, significant changes have taken place within the context of historical continuity, and thus we could speak of the same problematization being possible at different times ("P," 239). We have just seen, however, that for Hugo, defining the historical parameters of the events at hand presented no difficulty. The Revolution gave rise to the empire on which the Second Empire based its claims of legitimacy. The only time that was unknown was the date of the fall of the Second Empire. As for the relationship between past and present, this would not seem to have been a problem at all because the ideals on which Hugo based his pleas never changed. The immediate problems addressed by Hugo, what to do about the empire and how to restore revolutionary ideals, could only hope to be resolved by resorting to the past through memory. He did not worry about what history would eventually call this time period; for him, time could be neatly divided into before 1851 and after 1851, or on a larger scale, before 1789 and after 1789. Hugo wrote the history of the present through the immediate past.

The next problem for the historian, amateur or professional, is the choice of events he will treat, since he cannot study every aspect of his society. Hugo decided on a limited subject, just as Foucault chose relatively minor topics such as confinement in the seventeenth century. Hugo went right to the heart of the matter and chose the Second Empire, its sources, its vices, and the possible means of overthrowing it. This choice of material had advantages and disadvantages. For someone like Foucault, who relied on intimate knowledge of a great deal of minutiae, Hugo's choice would have seemed impossible, but Hugo would have responded that his memory provided him with precisely the kind of intimate knowledge of his subject that Foucault's research afforded him. Hugo, the individual, the poet, and the amateur historian, had the same ability to analyze large events as the historian had of looking at small segments of a certain society at a certain point in its history.

Castel's final problem is one that may prove more difficult for the analyst of Hugo to overcome. "Generally a problematization covers a long span of time. It cannot be completely constructed from primary sources, unpublished discoveries, or historical 'scoops.' It is largely the outgrowth of the work of historians, which, however, it reads in a different way" ("P," 240). Clearly, Hugo was not dealing with phenomena that lasted over a long period of time, but does this really matter if he was still writing the history of the present? He was certainly writing the history of his time in a different way than the dominant discourse of his time. If the Second Empire's propaganda machine represented the "historians'" view, then Hugo's counterdiscourse would seem to fulfill the requirement of writing history in a new way. Hugo relied on their version not for information but for material to attack.

The rules of the game are a problem because Hugo is not a traditional historian, even one as original as Michelet. Hugo would not have disagreed that his methods were different from Michelet's, and he would not worry about whether his works were fiction or not because his fiction, he would argue, holds as much truth as the historian's history. The methodology is certainly different but can we question the power and accuracy of Hugo's accounts? His claim for legitimacy was based on memory, a historical source as strong and as true as historical documentation. And who determines what the "rules" of documentation are? Hugo would have maintained that there is no more accurate account than that of an eyewitness.

Foucault is careful to distinguish the historian, who must do an exhaustive treatment of the material in order to present all aspects of the events being studied, from the person who chooses to study only one problem of a certain era. In his case, he "must follow other rules: the choice of material as a function of the givens of a problem; the focus of the analysis on those elements likely to resolve it; the establishment of relationships that permit the solution. Hence the indifference to the obligation to say everything, even to satisfy the assembled jury of specialists."[17] Hugo's texts that react directly against the continuation of the empire satisfy each criterion set forth by Foucault. His choice of material clearly arose out of the givens of the problem; he always had his sights set on ways to resolve the problem; and he was uniquely qualified, through his experience and memory, to know what relationships had to be developed in order to bring about the desired result. Even Castel's warning that those writing Foucault's type of history must be careful in choosing what material to keep does not apply to Hugo. Since his material was supplied by his own memory, the limits of his material were self-selecting.

A problematization, no matter how limited its subject, must fit into a larger historical context. Hugo, whose main goal may have been the overthrow of the empire, also set the era into the greater context of the late-eighteenth and early-nineteenth centuries. The presence of two emperors from the same family made this a task that Hugo undertook with great vigor. To focus only on Louis-Napoléon would minimize the greater questions of freedom, justice, and truth that are more easily associated with the revolutionary period.

One major question concerning Hugo's treatment of the Second Empire is whether a history of the present based on individual and ultimately collective memory can say something about empire in general or whether it is limited to the specific empire in question. Does Hugo's history take what Castel calls "a double look back, [shedding] light on how contemporary practices function, showing that they continue to be structured by the effects of their heritage, [while also shedding] light on the entire development [of empires] by showing that the history of this development began before its official birth"? ("P," 244) Again, Hugo would seem to have satisfied this requirement, as he related the Second Empire to the first as well as to others, particularly the Roman Empire, that had come before. By making such comparisons, Hugo could show specifically how Louis-Napoléon and his henchmen fell short of their historical models. The lessons of the present always have their roots in the past, whether it is the immediate past that provides a specific model or a long lost past that provides the ideals.

One of the fundamental problems of Foucault's methodology, as Castel sees it, is that Foucault did not always recognize how much he depended on historical documentation. Foucault "discerned a powerful interpretive grid—even if it is not the only one—that is valid for the history of these institutions as well as for their contemporary structure" ("P," 248). If Foucault had appreciated the power of historical documentation to an even greater extent, he would have seen that it is necessary to look at other ways of interpreting the material at hand. Hugo can certainly be faulted along the same lines. For him, historical documentation meant primarily personal experience, but he also had at his disposal the propaganda coming out of Paris during the period of his exile. In order to correct the false documentation, he had to provide his own. The result is clearly the limited view that Castel accuses Foucault of having, but no one can argue that these men did not make significant contributions to writing the history of their present.

Castel does not mean to imply that history is only a matter of documentation done by professionals. Memory does play a significant role in the collection and analysis of data: "If the present is indeed a conjunction of the effects of the past and the effects of innovation, one ought to be able to discern the basis of the 'discursive and non-discursive practices' that have formed it. In this instance, it is an attempt to recover the memory that structures today's formulation of the social question" ("P," 250–51). Beyond documentation, which is itself a kind of memory, individuals and societies remember in their particular ways. Only by looking at the way these memories coincide and conflict can we hope to discover how the past communicates itself to the present. Hugo does this masterfully, by comparing his own memories with those of the official historian, the government of France.

There is one area of problematization where Hugo's direct approach to a very recent event fell short. Castel rightly points out that Foucault's manner of writing the history of the present relies on categories, "in this case, social categories such as instability, vulnerability, protection, exclusion, insertion, and so forth that are not utilized by historians to organize their own corpus. In other words, a problematization constructs *another* account from historical data" ("P," 251). Hugo certainly creates his own categories: political and military power, the emperor, the poet, exile, the people "asleep," ways to revive them, the ideal. He studies each one with the thoroughness of a professional historian or philosopher or sociologist. The problem comes when, as Castel says, a problematization "must be compatible with the accounts of historians" ("P," 251). In 1853, when Hugo wrote *Les Châtiments*, it was clearly too early for the historians to have spoken about the Second Empire, even about its turbulent beginnings. Only in 1870, when the poems reappeared, could Hugo and the nation look back over the past seventeen years and try to determine whose version of events was true at the time and whether Hugo's version of seventeen years later now coincided with that of the historians of the new era.

A problematization contributes to the writing of the present by adding something to the professional's historical account. In order to increase our knowledge of a certain subject that touches on our present, a problematization "must be tested using other approaches" ("P," 251). For Foucault, such approaches could include "empirical sociology, the ethnography of psychiatric practices, or the administrative or professional literature of psychiatry" ("P," 251). For Hugo, we could mention political philosophy, the sociology of mass behavior, or the psychology of power. In his own idiosyncratic way, Hugo added something to the knowledge of all of these areas by taking his appeal for the restoration of fundamental liberties straight to the people.

Nor does Hugo's historical view violate the final requirement that a problematization not contradict historical knowledge. From the privileged viewpoint of 1870, Hugo's writings of 1853 proved to be remarkably accurate about the future, without violating any critical interpretations of the past. His faithfulness to the first emperor colored but did not fundamentally distort his vision of the second. The only historical accounts that Hugo intended to rewrite were the histories written by Louis-Napoléon's propagandists. Their version of history turned out to be partially fabrication. Hugo did, however, propose to help revise and rewrite the nation's collective memory of Louis-Napoléon and the Second Empire. By 1870, it was clearer that his project would have some success.

LONG DURATION

It is not enough to simply state that a nation's view of history changes over time. We must examine how these changes take place and how a writer such as Hugo was able to take advantage of them. Fernand Braudel's conception of long duration (*la longue durée*) helps explain Hugo's contribution to the revision of the collective memory of the events of the Second Empire.

In his writings, particularly in *Les Annales* in the late 1950s, Braudel outlined his definition of long duration as a series of structures: "Good or bad, [the word *structure*] dominates the problems of long duration. By *structure*, the social observers mean organization, coherence and fixed relations between realities and social masses."[18] Long duration, through the edifice of these structures, reveals itself to be more faithful and less capricious than short duration (*R*, 153). While we may see an event clearly in the present, its true historical significance cannot be ascertained until much later, until all the structures of the passage of time have been put into place.

Ideas built up over time can be cumbersome and can seem outdated, yet they are more legitimate than new, undeveloped, untested formulations. "Within the different historical times, long duration thus shows itself to be a cumbersome figure, complicated, often undiscovered." (*R*, 158). This difficulty is complicated by the fact that the true meaning of the ideas developed over time can be hidden in the heavy structures that have been created at the same time: "The difficulty is to detect long duration within the [dominant or surviving domains]—that is, old ways of thinking and acting, stubborn frames of mind, slow to die, occasionally against all logic" (*R*, 157). In order for the historian to interpret and understand the importance of the developed ideas, he must be able to separate the significant from the encrusted tradition. Hugo's role was to facilitate the historian's task by bringing the notion of long duration to the forefront. His ideas, whether written immediately after the fact or several years later, were to stand history on its head and provide a new way of looking at the accepted versions of historical facts.

We saw earlier how Braudel uses the development of myths as a way of explaining what he means by long duration. Myths develop over long periods of time and come to correspond to structures of comparable longevity. "We may, without worrying about choosing the oldest, assemble the different versions of the myth of Oedipus, the problem being to arrange the diverse versions and to bring to light beneath them a profound statement that orders them" (*R*, 171). In other words, the historian must tease out the significance of that which has developed over the years. In so doing, he will alter the way in which his present society reads the myths so as to more accurately reflect the present era. Braudel thus gives us another way of writing the history of the present.

When applied specifically to politics, the notion of long duration takes on a particular significance. For Braudel, "political history is not necessarily factual, nor is it condemned to be" (*R*, 153). The model he uses here is Karl Marx since Marx knew the importance of developing, fostering, and implementing an ideology over the long term: "The genius of Marx, the secret of his prolonged power, has to do with the fact that he was the first to create real social models based on the historical long term" (*R*, 177). No social program and no historical project could function effectively in a short period because the missing perspective that the long term affords would doom it to oblivion in the minds of the very people it was supposed to be influencing. Revel and Hunt sum up Braudel's ideas on Marx as follows: "[Marx's] models have been frozen in all their simplicity by being given the status of laws, of a preordained and automatic explanation, valid in all places and to any society; whereas if they were put back within the ever changing stream of time, they would constantly reappear, but with changes of emphasis. . . . In this way, the creative potential of the most powerful social analysis of the last century has been stymied. It cannot regain its youth and vigor except in the *longue durée*" (*R&H*, 141–42). Hugo may not have been as astute a political strategist as Marx, but he proposed a set of ideals that act in similar fashion to Marx's models. Freedom of the press, liberty of movement and thought, respect for the rule of democratic law are "laws" that would not disappear simply because a usurper of legitimate power declared them defunct.

Hugo, while obsessed with short-term goals, knew that he would ultimately have to be patient. The political structure that he was attacking was doubly difficult to overthrow because it was both a recent phenomenon and an echo of past glory that the nation seemed to need to cling to during the turbulent middle years of the century. The complex nature of the needs of the French people—order and stability on the one hand, memories of grandeur on the other—made Hugo's calls for republican ideals fall on deaf ears, at least at the outset. The multiplicity of temporal aspects in this situation is precisely what Braudel refers to in his conception of long duration. "From the recent experiments and efforts of history an increasingly clear idea has emerged . . . of the multiplicity of time, and of the exceptional value of the long time span. . . . We find a history capable of traversing even greater distances, a history to be measured in centuries this time" (Braudel, cited in *R&H*, 118). Hugo was more than happy to produce a new headlong, breathless rush of historical narrative, complete with polemical overtones, but the actual political ramifications of his writings from exile would only develop over time.

One thing that Hugo had in his favor was the geographical distance exile afforded him. This, coupled with the length of his absence, gave added force to his writing. Braudel recognized the power of distance, both temporal and spatial in the formulation of political and social attitudes: "Live in London for a year and you will not know much about England. But by contrast, in light of what has surprised you, you will suddenly have come to understand some of the most deep seated and characteristic aspects of France, things you did not know before because you knew them too well. With regard to the present, the past too is a way of distancing yourself" (Braudel, cited in *R&H*, 128). Hugo thus gained new perspective on his native land, and more importantly, was able to communicate his new point of view to his readers over time. At the same time, he was aided by the cyclical nature of history, as one wave of thinking replaced another in the never-ending attempt to control both the political apparatus and the national memory.

Nowhere has this vast array of cyclical events, beliefs and societal forces been more evident than in eighteenth– and nineteenth-century France, where one revolutionary cycle followed another from 1789 through 1871. As each new stage unfolded, certain individuals and groups attempted to appropriate a part of the recent past as a watchword for the present bid for power over the government and the collective consciousness of the nation. We have seen Louis-Napoléon's evocation of the spirit of the first empire in his attempt to portray his empire as legitimate. This replaying of history can be seen as tragedy or farce, depending on your point of view. For Hugo, it was a paradoxical combination of both. Hugo failed to see, however, that Louis-Napoléon was more like his uncle than Hugo would have liked. It took Karl Marx to point out the resemblances: "When Victor Hugo called the nephew 'Napoléon le Petit,' he acknowledged the greatness of the uncle. . . . It would be more useful to have the present generation admit that Napoléon le Petit figures, in fact, the pettiness of Napoléon le Grand."[19] In other words, Hugo had deliberately ignored any shortcomings of the first emperor in order to discredit the second by comparison. This was not a new strategy for any polemicist, including Marx himself, but it showed the willingness of Hugo to distort the past upon which he directly depended in his condemnation of Louis-Napoléon.

Marx is very clear about how he sees the relationship between past and present: "Men make their own history, but they do not make it as they please, under circumstances chosen by themselves; they do so under conditions directly encountered, given, and transmitted from the past."[20] Making history is not the same as writing it, however. The historian can indeed write history as he pleases, under conditions he has chosen. He can choose the parameters of the discussion and the style in which he will write. He can even choose his audience by writing in one style or another. He can manipulate the narration, as Hugo did, by omitting or distorting facts. While historical events may be cyclical, the reporting of them can be less dependent on past influence.

While Marx emphasizes the effect of the past on present events, he also acknowledges the importance of forgetting the past in order to achieve any progress in the future. He makes the analogy between moving ahead in history with the learning of a second language. One must forget the mother tongue in order to learn the new one. Jeffrey Mehlman summarizes Marx's views: "There is thus a movement from an invocation of the ineluctable nature of history as a constraint to an active practice of forgetting. The mother tongue is to be spent utterly in the exercise of the second language: the Bonapartist move par excellence of repressing the ('constituent') mother" (R, 33). Only by forgetting can we move ahead; only by repressing aspects of the past that do not serve its purposes can a regime, or an author such as Hugo, make its voice dominant. Only by jettisoning a negative past, can an ideal be attained.

CONCLUSION

The next three chapters examine the relationship between the written word and the formation of a nation's collective memory of historical events. A number of questions come to mind related to the effect of literature on the national psyche: What is the relationship between the author and the events discussed? Was the author a participant or an observer? How close is the date of publication to the actual events? What is the author's political persuasion? Who will be the readers of the text? Did they live through the events being described? What visible effect did the text's publication have on the readers of the time? What is the text's overall contribution to the collective memory of the events it describes? Some of these questions are easy to answer, others more problematic. We can, however, study the text itself in order to find clues to how the author's memories of events, coupled with a certain distance—chronological, physical, affective—can contribute, through his text, to the ongoing collective memory of the events at hand.

In the chapters that follow, the interdependence of memory and history will come to life in Victor Hugo's writing. The historiography of the Second Empire becomes a battleground between a writer best known for his poetry and novels and a propaganda machine controlled by the emperor. While those who controlled political, economic and military power dominated the era, their legacy was formed after their departure. Throughout the period, Hugo's voice was heard clearly through his powerful critique of the empire. These works are his history of the present and his legacy to us all. Three very different texts: a political polemic, a collection of poetry, and a novel all turn their attention to history. Another common thread is memory, whether individual or collective, lived or reported, even voluntary or involuntary. Each text has a tale to tell and a wrong to right. Each uses a different genre to get the point across, but memory shines through as the way to truth.

3

Napoléon le petit: Hugo as Archivist

THIS IS WHERE IT ALL BEGINS. VICTOR HUGO WENT INTO EXILE ON December 11, 1851, just over a week after the coup d'état of December 2 had given Louis- Napoléon his new status of supreme ruler of France. In the *Constitutionnel* of January 11, 1852, we read: "In the name of the French: Louis-Napoléon, President of the Republic, decrees: 'Expelled from French territory, from Algeria and from the colonies, for reasons of general security: the former representatives of the legislative Assembly whose names follow . . .'" (January 11, 1852). One of those names was of course Victor Hugo, who took refuge in Belgium. The words "general security" (*sûreté générale*) are significant because they echoed throughout Louis' reign as president and then emperor. His regime ruled on the themes of "order" and "security," as if some imminent danger threatened the very existence of the French nation. Hugo was Louis' greatest nightmare, a purveyor of disorder, whose only goal was to disrupt the government and dethrone the emperor.

While in Brussels, Hugo wrote *Napoléon le petit*, more than two hundred pages of political polemic that represents the first salvo in the eighteen-year struggle between him and Louis-Napoléon.[1] Hugo's text is nonfictional and relates the coming to power of Louis-Napoléon in 1848 and the betrayal of his oath to defend the constitution. Louis-Napoléon's mandate as president was to run until the second Sunday in May 1852, but Louis did not keep his promise to relinquish power on that date. Instead he launched the coup d'état that would lead to his becoming emperor a year later. Hugo's premise is simple: since Louis violated the constitution at every turn after December 2, 1851, he should be ousted from power and replaced by a legitimate republican government.[2] The rhetoric, however, is far from simplified; it is perhaps the most fiery diatribe Hugo ever wrote and represents a sharp departure from anything he had previously produced. Throughout these pages, Hugo makes sure his reader feels the agony of betrayal, the baseness of deceit, and the loneliness of exile. *Napoléon le petit* represents more than a political critique; it is a cry from the wilderness of the exalted poet extolling his readers to avenge the usurpation of their freedom by an imposter. Published in Brussels in 1852, *Napoléon le petit* had to be smuggled into France a few copies at a time. While such restrictions prevented the text from becoming a bestseller, it captured the imagination of a segment of the French population and came to represent an appeal for resistance along the lines of De Gaulle's radio address of June 18, 1940. In this chapter we shall see Hugo at his vituperative best as he sets the stage for his even more powerful appeals in *Les Châtiments* and *Les Misérables*.

THE EYEWITNESS (*BOOK 1: MAN*)

Throughout all the texts that Hugo writes against Louis-Napoléon, the first emperor will be a constant reminder that the second does not live up to the name. From the outset of *Napoléon le petit*, Hugo compares Louis to his uncle Napoléon Bonaparte, and the nephew does not come off favorably. Hugo describes him at his swearing in as president in 1848 as having small eyes, a timid and worried manner, and no resemblance whatsoever to the great emperor. The specter of the past works on the national consciousness as a reminder of what they have lost and of the mediocrity of that for which they have settled. In 1848, the country turned to Louis-Napoléon in hopes that his famous name could help solidify the new Second Republic. The future under the Second Republic seemed bright: "Pour tous, pour ses amis comme pour ses adversaires, c'était l'avenir qui entrait, un avenir inconnu" (4) [For everyone, friends as well as adversaries, the future was beginning, and that future was unknown.][3] This last phrase is a deliberate foreshadowing of what is to come. Louis ironically becomes an emperor unworthy of both his uncle and of the future of the French nation. Hugo presents in these opening pages the major thrust of his argument that the present ruler is not a fit representative of either the past or the future.

A further irony is that Louis has been an exile, following aborted attempts to overthrow the July Monarchy in 1836 and 1840. Louis and Hugo should share a common bond and want the same things for the future of the country, but while one continually fights for democracy, the other thinks only of his self-interest. This first chapter of *Napoléon le petit* will detail all the money Louis appropriates himself as well as the silencing of his critics. The former exile imprisons or exiles those who would criticize him, and he muzzles all newspapers that are not favorable to him. This is particularly galling to Hugo, for in the Presidential Oath, Louis had sworn to be a servant of the people. Instead he has placed himself above them, in an untouchable position of power.

Hugo was an eyewitness to the events of 1848 as well as those of December 2, 1851, and as such had a privileged position in the historical narrative of the events. Hugo had also been present the day of the swearing in, and he claimed right from the start his privileged position as eyewitness to events. As a member of the national assembly, Hugo was particularly appalled by Louis' abrogation of his Oath as President of the Republic when he engineers the coup d'état. The two men were thus squared off against one another, one the attacker, the other the target; one the revered poet in exile, the other the ruler comfortably ensconced in power. Only history would decide the victor. Hugo's graphic description of soldiers killing people in the streets is testimony to the horror he felt at the time. His recording in *Napoléon le petit* of the events he had seen represent the first stage of Paul Ricœur's notion of historical knowledge (*la connaissance historique*), as an eyewitness begins the narrative of what he has seen.[4] Hugo's observations were supported by the evidence given by other witnesses, and the beginnings of an archive took place. The resulting text was Hugo's first attack in his crusade against Louis-Napoléon and the Second Empire.

The intention of any historian is to present the past as it happened. In order to do so, he must first establish the proof of what he will be writing as his final narrative, and the archives relevant to the events at hand constitute a sort of first draft of the final product. Between the two written records, documentation and narration, the historian will pass through the stage of explanation/comprehension, in which the documentation will be analyzed so as to give analytical grounding to the final narrative. The first stage of documentation is critical to the whole process, because the historian's readers must be convinced that he is telling them the truth. This is the stage at which memory plays its most crucial role. Without the memories of the eyewitnesses, the first narrative providing fodder for the archive would be impossible. The witnesses must be credible and must be backed up by corroborating evidence from other witnesses. Hugo provides all of this evidence and corroboration, and

his status as a famous writer gives his documentation a sense of legitimacy right from the beginning. Hugo the eyewitness becomes Hugo
the repository of memory, and the beginning of an archive takes
place. Because he was there and because he knows the constitution
so well, he can remind us of what exactly Louis swore: "Art. 68.
Toute mesure par laquelle le président de la République dissout
l'Assemblée nationale, la proroge ou met obstacle à l'exercice de
son mandat, est un crime de haute trahison. Par ce seul fait, le président est déchu de ses fonctions, les citoyens sont tenus de lui refuser
obéissance" (6). [Article 68. Every measure by which the President
of the Republic dissolves the National Assembly, adjourns it, or ob-
structs its function, is a crime of high treason. For this reason alone,
the president will be stripped of his powers, and the citizens will owe
him no loyalty.] The new emperor will attempt to make the French
nation forget that when he became president in 1848, he swore to
give up the post in 1852. Hugo will do everything he can to make
them recall it. This struggle for the high ground of memory will be
at the heart of the conflict between the two men. Whoever controls
the collective memory of the nation will ultimately decide the way
the history of the period will be written.

As a self-appointed representative of the people, Hugo has sworn
to perform two basic duties: to offer himself as a protector of the
people in case of treason and to combat the traitor at every turn:
"Celui qui écrit ces lignes est de ceux qui n'ont reculé devant rien,
le 2 décembre, pour accomplir le premier de ces deux grands devoirs; en publiant ce livre, il remplit le second" (8). [He who writes
these lines is one of those who feared nothing, on December 2, to
accomplish the first of these duties; by publishing this book he fulfills the second.] He will continue taking on this second duty, as he
writes *Les Châtiments* and *Les Misérables*. All of these texts have one
target and one goal: by ridding France of an illegitimate emperor,
France will be able to return to a peaceful and just republic, one
based on the ideals of the Revolution of 1789.

Another section of this first chapter is an excerpt from what will
become *Histoire d'un crime*, a detailed picture of the events of December 4. Hugo immediately sees himself as an historian: "L'auteur se
rend cette justice qu'en écrivant cette narration, austère occupation
de son exil, il a sans cesse présente à l'esprit la haute responsabilité
de l'historien" (46). [The author gives himself this much, that in
writing this narrative, the austere undertaking of his exile, he is always conscious of the crucial responsibility of the historian.] This is

a significant admission so early in the game. Hugo's exile is less than a year old, and he already sees himself as having a role in the writing of the history of his time. At the same time, he predicts that his text will cause a large reaction: "Quand elle paraîtra, cette narration soulèvera certainement de nombreuses et violentes réclamations" (46). [When this narrative appears, it will certainly cause numerous and violent protests.] Unfortunately for Hugo, *Napoléon le petit*, while engendering significant discussion, did not have a wide enough readership to cause any concrete reaction to the regime, and *Histoire d'un crime* was not published until 1877, long after Louis' demise.

Hugo goes even further and calls himself "le juge d'instruction de l'histoire," [the examining magistrate of history] one who elicits testimony from "chaque acteur du drame, chaque combattant, chaque victime, chaque témoin" (46) [each actor of the drama, each combatant, each victim, each witness]. Unlike the traditional historian who deals only with facts that are "dead," Hugo will be writing a living history: "En général, les historiens parlent aux faits morts; ils les touchent dans la tombe de leurs verges de juges, les font lever et les interrogent. Lui, c'est aux faits vivants qu'il a parlé" (46). [In general, historians concern themselves with dead facts; they touch them in the tomb with their judicial wands, make them rise and question them. He has addressed himself to living facts.] These "living facts" will be the stuff of which Hugo will write throughout his exile and will form the evidence upon which he will condemn, again and again, Louis Napoléon. The role of the professional historian who comes after him will be to "compléter ce récit, mais non l'infirmer" (46) [to complete but not weaken this narrative]. His narration will not be contradicted by the historian and his documentation because it is the truth, as seen through the eyes of people who were there on the streets of Paris December 2 to 4, 1851. Hugo's writings represent thus the first building block in the construction of history. They will not, in themselves, succeed in dethroning the emperor, but they will have an immense impact on the professional historian and therefore on the collective memory of the time.

As a conscientious historian, Hugo collected almost two hundred testimonies from eyewitnesses to the coup d'état. While the "historiographes officiels" (46) [official historiographers] remain reticent about the events, Hugo does not. He does not claim to be impartial because impartiality does not necessarily lead to the truth. Only the truly impassioned historian will see the difference between right and

wrong: "Malheur à qui resterait impartial devant les plaies saig-
nantes de la liberté! . . . [Chez l'auteur] la passion pour la vérité
égale la passion pour le droit. L'homme indigné ne ment pas. Cette
histoire du 2 décembre donc . . . aura été écrite . . . dans les conditions de la réalité absolue" (46). [Woe to he who would remain impartial faced with the bleeding wounds of liberty! . . . For the author
the passion for truth equals the passion for right. The indignant
man does not lie. This history of December 2, then, will have been
written with the utmost regard for fact.] While the concept of absolute reality is one that could fill many philosophical treatises, Hugo
takes it to mean an eyewitness account of events. For him, there is
nothing more accurate, and when reported by a committed journal-
ist/historian, these accounts become the equivalent of the lived experience itself. These accounts then strike a chord with those who
are reading them because only reality can have such a profound impact. Once the French people take stock of their situation and pon-
der the brutality of the regime, they will be prodded into action.

Hugo presents some very interesting documentation to support
his cause. Jérome Bonaparte, brother of Napoléon, writes to his
nephew to caution him about his course of action: "C'est au nom
de la mémoire de mon frère, et en partageant son horreur pour la
guerre civile, que je vous écris; croyez-en ma vieille expérience, et
songez que la France, l'Europe et la postérité seront appelés à juger
votre conduite" (49). [I write to you in the name of my brother's
memory, and sharing his horror of civil war. I speak from experience
when I ask you to remember that France, Europe, and posterity will
be called on to judge your conduct.] The aging uncle was, of course,
correct. It did not take long for Hugo to take up his pen against the
nephew. History begins such a judgment quickly, even if the acceptance of the historian's account takes longer.

Hugo sees a deliberate cover-up in the accounts of the events surrounding the coup d'état, and he will set the record straight: "Nous
allons dévoiler la plus sinistre des préméditations de Louis Bonaparte; nous allons révéler, dire, détailler, raconter ce que tous les
historiographes du 2 décembre ont caché. . . . Nous entrons dans
l'horrible" (50). [We are going to unveil the most sinister of Louis
Bonaparte's premeditations; we are going to reveal, tell, detail, and
recount that which all the historiographers of December 2 have hidden. . . . We are entering the horrible.] While the "official historians" have obvious reasons for covering up the actions of the military
and the number of dead, even those who lived through the events

are reluctant to see the truth. For a nation to accept something into its collective memory, it must be able to get beyond the horror, and this is a process of healing that takes time. Examples throughout history abound, from the Terror to Waterloo to the German occupation of the Second World War to the Algerian War. Hugo wants to speed the process along by forcing his readers to confront the horrible reality.

While at times vaunting his role of historian, Hugo occasionally takes a back seat and calls himself a simple recorder of testimony: "En présence de ces faits sans nom, moi qui écris ces lignes, je le déclare, je suis un greffier, j'enregistre le crime; j'appelle la cause. Là est toute ma fonction" (55). [In the presence of these deeds without a name, I who write these lines proclaim myself the recording officer who registers the crime; I bring the cause before the court. That is my only function.] If it were only he who was speaking out against these crimes, people might pay no attention, so he turns the tale over to other eyewitnesses: "Le narrateur seul, quel qu'il fût, on ne le croirait pas. Donnons donc la parole aux faits vivants, aux faits saignants. Ecoutons les témoignages" (55). [The narrator alone, whoever he may be, would not be believed. Then let living, bleeding facts speak. Let us listen to the evidence.] Of course Hugo's witnesses confirm his own vision of events, that a virtual slaughter took place on December 2 to 4, 1851.

Eyewitness accounts are, for better or worse, the best and most trustworthy evidence that assure us that an event has actually taken place. We know, for example, that Louis-Napoléon was sworn in as President of France on December 20, 1848 because numerous eyewitnesses, including Hugo, were present at the time. The event became part of the official governmental history only after the official scribe witnessed and recorded the event. And so historiography begins by the archiving of memories (*MHF*, 148).

Each documented occurrence begins at a given date that becomes the reference point for the rest of the narrative. *Napoléon le petit* begins with the swearing in of Louis as president in 1848 and continues through the coup d'état and its aftermath. Ricœur cites Benveniste's definition of the "chronical time": "1) the reference of every event to a founding event that defines the axis of time; 2) the possibility of traversing the intervals of time in terms of the two opposed directions of anteriority and posteriority in relation to the zero date; and 3) the constitution of the repertory of units serving to name recurring intervals: day, month, year, and so on" (*MHF*, 154).[5] Hugo constantly refers back to Louis' coming to the presidency as the beginning of the treachery that led to the coup d'état. After swearing allegiance to the constitution, Louis set about to destroy it, and Hugo will not let us forget that oath.

The formation of the archive by the accumulation of eyewitness narratives has as its goal the creation of a body of evidence that can be consulted by professional historians who will then do the analysis necessary to write their account of the events (*MHF*, 161). These eyewitness documents take many forms besides a written narrative such as *Napoléon le petit*, including genres that are not literary, such as pictorial images. Some of these resist explanation, representation, and therefore archivization, staying deliberately on the margins of historiography (*MHF*, 161). Yet each eyewitness's story leaves its trace, and the accumulation of such traces results in the archive.

At each stage in the journey from event to historical account, suspicion grows as to the reliability of the evidence. Ricœur breaks these stages down into three distinct performances: the perception of the event; the memory of what one has seen; and the declarative and narrative restitution of the events that have been witnessed (*MHF*, 162). The first action taken to counteract these suspicions is the assertion of the factual reality of the reported event (*MHF*, 163). The witness makes his claim that what he has seen is true according to his experience of it. While this type of evidence is the most reliable because it is the most directly related to lived experience, it immediately causes suspicion on the part of the auditor because we do not know the witness's point of view concerning the events or his reliability as a narrator of them. While the witness maintains the authority of the first-person narration ("I was there. I saw."), his interlocutor might not ascribe the same importance to the events. This dialogic stage between witness and his audience represents the witness's attempt to be believed. The narrative can only be authenticated when his audience accepts it. Here again, the narrator's reputation comes in to play, as the audience will react with more or less suspicion depending on their attitude toward the speaker (*MHF*, 164).

A major obstacle presents itself to the eyewitness if someone else's version does not correspond to his. In the next chapters of his text, Hugo rectifies what he sees as a huge information gap concerning the events of December 2 to 4, 1851. The French people have never been told the truth about the coup d'état and the violence in the streets that resulted from it.[6] He will inform them in great detail of what happened, based on his own observations and those of a host of witnesses he has been able to locate. In addition, several opposition publications have furnished him with information, and thanks to all of this information, "les faits commencent à percer . . . Il importe qu'on sache ce que c'est que M. Bonaparte" (10). [The facts are becoming known. . . . It is important that we know what Monsieur Bonaparte is.] Hugo will try to prove to his readers that his versions of the facts are true and that Louis has betrayed them through a series of cover-ups and lies.

In one of the most remarkable passages of *Napoléon le petit,* Hugo spells out how Louis-Napoléon has manipulated language in order to present himself and his actions in a light that will be acceptable to the French as a whole:

> Aucune chose, aucun homme, aucun fait n'ont leur vraie figure et ne portent leur vrai nom; le crime de M. Bonaparte n'est pas un crime, il s'appelle nécessité; le guet-apens de M. Bonaparte n'est pas guet-apens, il s'appelle défense de l'ordre; les vols de M. Bonaparte ne sont pas vols, ils s'appellent mesures d'État; les meurtres de M. Bonaparte ne sont pas meurtres, ils s'appellent salut public; les complices de M. Bonaparte ne sont pas des malfaiteurs, ils s'appellent magistrats, sénateurs et conseillers d'État; les adversaires de M. Bonaparte ne sont pas les soldats de la loi et du droit, ils s'appellent jacques, démagogues et partageux (10).

> [No thing, no man, no deed appears as its real form and bears its real name. The crime of Monsieur Bonaparte is not a crime, it is called necessity; the ambush of Monsieur Bonaparte is not an ambush, it is called the defense of order; the robberies of Monsieur Bonaparte are not robberies, they are called acts of the state; the murders of Monsieur Bonaparte are not murders, they are called public safety; the accomplices of Monsieur Bonaparte are not evildoers, they are called magistrates, senators, and councilors of State; the adversaries of Monsieur Bonaparte are not soldiers of law and right, they are called peasants and power hungry demagogues.]

All of Europe is in the dark about the truth of how Louis took power, and Hugo intends to unmask him and his associates while rectifying the false language that keeps them in power.

Once competing narratives are in play, the recounting of the event enters "l'espace public" (*MHF,* 164). At this point, each witness needs to garner corroboration for his own account, and he does this by asking his audience to test his narrative by asking someone else if he is right. "If you don't believe me, ask someone else" (*MHF*, 164–65). When corroborative evidence is found, the account receives more credibility. A certain moral dimension is evident here, as the witness promises to stick to his story over a length of time. By remaining available to tell his story again and again, the narrator decreases suspicions that he is lying or distorting the facts (*MHF*, 165).

As time passes and more corroborative evidence adds itself to the original statement, the witness's narrative becomes part of an institution of memory, in the form of an archive. The institution arises from the stability of the eyewitness account and its repetition, and its link to others who acknowledge and confirm its importance (*MHF*, 165). Ricœur calls the process "a competence of the capable human being" (*MHF*, 165) because the establishment of the archive depends on having "confidence in what other people say" (*MHF*, 165).[7] While the audience must first have confidence that what they are being told is true, their skepticism must be overcome over the long run. When the narrative has become part of the accepted norms of the community in which it resides, then it will have a place in the archives of that community.

This sense of community acceptance is undermined when unscrupulous political forces conspire to destroy the social trust that has led to its establishment. They can do so through mutual surveillance or untruthful practices that lead one community member to doubt another. Such subversive tactics are an example of manipulated memory at its most pernicious (*MHF*, 166). Communities are made up of people who are similar, and a common archive gives people a sense that they belong together. A campaign of separation created through untruths can lead to distrust and the destruction of community unity (*MHF*, 166). Louis-Napoléon uses the language of the strongman to justify his coup d'état. Portraying France as a nation in chaos after the revolution of 1848 and the ensuing installation of the Second Republic, he claims that the takeover was "necessary" and that he should be absolved of any blame for violating the Constitution (*Napoléon le petit*, 8). For Hugo, these words harken back to 1793, when watchwords such as "order" and "security" led to the Terror. From this moment on, Hugo dedicates himself to showing how a call for order is an appeal to passivity. His goal is to awaken the French people from the slumber that the emperor has induced in them through his claims to be the savior of France from the riotous face of democracy. Hugo saw his role as a community rebuilder, someone who had to reconstruct the damage done by Louis-Napoléon's campaign of untruthful propaganda.

History provides examples of witnesses whose testimony is so extraordinary that their audience is unable to corroborate and therefore to fully believe them. These "historical witnesses" (*MHF*, 166) have seen things that the ordinary person cannot comprehend, because the experience is outside the realm of the normal. These witnesses live in a tragic state of solitude brought on by the incomprehension of their audience. The twentieth century gave us far too many instances of horror where the witnesses' accounts were filled with gruesome details that defied comprehension by anyone who had not been there. Hugo risked falling into the category of "historical witness" because of his status as a writer/historian in exile. His renown paradoxically conferred respect and distance on him. He was no longer physically a member of the French community, and his words were in direct conflict with the official governmental version of events, so a measure of distrust was inevitable. He was saved from the solitude of the "historical witness" by his status as the greatest poet of his generation.

The Archive

When an eyewitness account enters an archive, it does so as a written document. The original testimony gave life in narrative form to a specific memory. The writing down of the account creates a certain rupture in the continuity of the remembrance, but it is a necessary step in the historiographical process (*MHF*, 166). The archive is not just a physical space where people, particularly historians, can come and consult the documentation, but a social space. Here the sense of community is enhanced as each written account takes its place with others that respond to similar societal needs. Bringing the document to the archive represents the first step in the epistemology of "historical knowledge" (*MHF*, 167). Here the road to documentary proof takes a significant step, as documents become available as verifiable testimonies.

The archivist is an important figure because he must preserve and organize the documents that represent a community's past. Ricœur identifies three moments of activity in the archives: organization, classification and consultation (*MHF*, 168). The archivist is responsible for the first two, the historian for the third. Hugo performs all three functions in *Napoléon le petit*. He is first of all an eyewitness; then a reporter who collects evidence from other witnesses; then a writer, organizer, and classifier who amasses as much evidence as he can find to support his campaign against Louis-Napoléon; and finally, he is a historian who reads French history and makes comparisons between his era and the ones that have come before. By performing all these tasks, Hugo becomes a true historian of his present.

By being placed in an archive, a document takes on a new public role because of its relation to its audience. An eyewitness account has a specific, limited audience; an archived document does not. The document becomes more vulnerable to contradiction, and a change in its status as a reliable document can create a mutation in the historical record of a community (*MHF*, 168). If the greater public acknowledges its authenticity, however, the testimony's status as documentary proof is enhanced.

What then are the goals of history, and how can archives help us arrive at them? Marc Bloch's conception of history is one centered on the people who make events happen. "That history should have recourse to testimony is not fortuitous. It is grounded in the very definition of the object of history. This is not the past, nor is it time, it is 'men in time.'"[8] By focusing on the human element, we can better "understand the present by the past" and "'understand the past by the present" (*MHF*, 170). For Bloch, the notion of "trace" is at the heart of all historiography because it represents the evidence an historian uses to construct his narrative.[9] The accumulation of traces results in an historical document that concentrates on the history of individuals and has as its goal the fight against incredulity on one hand and the will to forget on the other (*MHF*, 176).

How does one "prove" the validity of an historical document? The historian approaches it with questions and hypotheses. "The documents do not speak unless someone asks them to verify, that is, to make true, some hypothesis. Therefore there is an interdependence among facts, documents, and questions. . . . Trace, document, and question thus form the tripod base of historical knowledge" (*MHF*, 177). As the historian goes about searching for answers to his questions, the document gets further and further away from the original eyewitness testimony (*MHF*, 177). We can certainly see this process at work in *Napoléon le petit*, as the precise eyewitness account is followed by the narratives of other witnesses and then by Hugo's reaction to all that has happened. Eventually, this distancing will lead to another stage in which the original witnesses will question the validity of the document to make sure that it has not strayed too far from objective reality. The eyewitness accounts and the historical document coexist therefore in an uneasy space in which "history reinforces spontaneous testimony through the criticism of all testimony" (*MHF,* 181). A historical document, which *Napoléon le petit* most certainly is, deepens our understanding of the events at hand by adding the historian's questions—and sometimes answers—to the original eyewitness testimony. The combination of witnessing and analysis is Hugo's greatest arm in the fight against Louis-Napoléon for the truth of the events of December, 1851. We arrive now at Ricœur's second category of "historical knowledge," that of explanation and comprehension.

While the entire population remained virtually silent as Louis took control, Hugo does not blame the poor but the bourgeois, the ones with the education and power to do something about what is happening. After the coup d'état, this large and ever more powerful group has been content to return to business: "Depuis le 2 décembre, il n'y a plus en France de fonctionnaires, il n'y a que des complices" (9). [Since December 2, there are no more functionaries in France; there are only accomplices.] This is a powerful accusation, and we can see it in all its force, as the word accomplice has resonances of the past (the Terror) and the future (the German occupation during the Second World War). For Hugo's present, these accomplices will be the ones to whom he addresses his writings from exile.

While he does not expect the bourgeoisie to rise up in armed rebellion against the new regime, he does have confidence that he can get them to see his version of the truth: "Qu'on le sache donc, et qu'on se hâte, et, du moins, qu'on brise les chaînes, qu'on tire les verrous, qu'on vide les pontons, qu'on ouvre les geôles, puisqu'on n'a pas le courage de saisir l'épée! Allons, consciences, debout! éveillez-vous, il est temps!" (9). [Let every one, then, know this, and at least hurry to break the chains, draw the bolts, empty the prison ships, since no one has the courage to seize the sword. Come on, consciences, stand up! Wake up! It is time!] These words will echo throughout Hugo's works from exile, but their true effect will not become evident until after the fall of the empire in 1870. Only when history begins its judgment of the period will Hugo's prescience become apparent.

Hugo certainly sensed that his redemption would come in the future, for he never ceased writing about and planning for a better future based on his ideals, which corresponded with many of the tenets of the French Revolution: "Si la loi, le droit, le devoir, la raison, le bon sens, l'équité, la justice, ne suffisent pas, qu'on songe à l'avenir. Si le remords se tait, que la responsabilité parle!" (9). [If law, right, duty, reason, good sense, equity and justice are not enough, let us think about the future. If remorse is silent, let responsibility speak!] If Hugo cannot win the populace over through reason, he will try to wear them down through their sense of fairness and responsibility. He knows that such an approach will take time, but he is in exile, and he will take whatever time is necessary to bring about the downfall of the emperor. And he is confident of success: "Mais cela ne sera pas; on se réveillera" (10). [But it will not be so; the people will wake up.]

The complicity of the bourgeoisie may not have been a physical one, but the moral component of their cooperation scandalizes Hugo the most. Theirs is a collaboration born of passivity and self-interest, in which going to a ball at the Elysée Palace is more important than holding a president to his oath of office. We are struck by the parallel between Hugo's view of the role of the bourgeoisie under the Second Empire and that of the bourgeoisie under the German occupation. While most people did not openly cooperate with the coup d'état or with the Germans, their passivity allowed the continuing oppression of all of French society: "Et que tous ceux qui . . . vont aux bals et aux banquets de Louis Bonaparte et ne voient pas que le drapeau noir est sur l'Elysée, que tous ceux-là sachent . . . que s'ils échappent à la complicité matérielle, ils n'échappent pas à la complicité morale" (9). [And let all who attend the balls and banquets of Louis Bonaparte, not seeing the black flag flying over the Elysée Palace, know that even though they have escaped material complicity, they have not escaped moral complicity.]

The lower classes are not spared, even if Hugo never gives them a leading role in his version of collaboration. The notion of contagion is important because it is what permits the spread of the passivity he is talking about. If you do not see your neighbor opposing tyranny, why should you risk your freedom or your life? The easy way is to continue life as it was. Indifference is lethal, and Hugo specifically states that the goal of his text is to awaken the slumbering population: "Ce livre n'a d'autre but que de secouer ce sommeil. La France ne doit pas même adhérer à ce gouvernement par le consentement de la léthargie; à de certaines heures, en de certains lieux, à de certaines ombres, dormir c'est mourir" (10). [This book has no other goal than to shake them out of their slumber. France must not obey this government through lethargy; at certain times, in certain places, in certain shadows, sleep equals death.] Hugo's role is to remind them that their lives were different before, that the republic brought them a way of life that an empire never can.

Hugo will continually compare past and present in order to keep alive the memory of the freedoms that have been lost: "Regardez donc: la tribune, la presse, l'intelligence, la parole, la pensée, tout ce qui était la liberté, a disparu. Hier cela remuait, cela vivait, aujourd'hui cela est pétrifié" (11). [Look at this: the courts, intelligence, freedom of speech, and thought, everything that constituted liberty has disappeared. Yesterday these were living, moving forces, today they are petrified.] The government wants everyone to believe that the present state of affairs is the face of the future; Hugo wants them to remember the past.

Hugo does not condemn everyone who supports the emperor. He can understand that the seeming inevitability of the empire convinces even honest people that this is the way things will be. "La société continue, et force honnêtes gens trouvent les choses bien ainsi. Pourquoi voulez-vous que cette situation change? . . . Ceci est solide, ceci est stable, ceci est le présent et l'avenir" (11). [Society goes on, and many honest people believe that things as they are, are good. Why do you want this situation to change? It is solid and stable, it is the present and the future.] All of which makes Hugo's task that much more difficult. And things will get even more difficult for him as the empire, firmly entrenched, leads France into a period of economic prosperity.

Hugo sees change emerging out of the forgotten past. In order for it to reemerge, it must have been submerged in oblivion for a certain period of time. "Non, tu ne meurs pas, liberté! un de ces jours, au moment où on s'y attendra le moins, à l'heure même où on t'aura le plus profondément oubliée, tu te lèveras" (11). [No, you are not dying, liberty! One of these days, when it is least expected, at the very hour when you are most forgotten, you will rise up.] This resurrection will not come about on its own, however. It will need the prodding of the keeper of the nation's memory, Hugo, to come back to the light of day.

Hugo sees Louis-Napoléon as a man entrenched in the wrong era. "Ce n'est pas un idiot. C'est un homme d'un autre temps que le nôtre" (14). [He is not an idiot. He is a man from another time.]

The danger comes from the fact that the French people do not see the difference. They hear the name Napoléon and immediately think of the uncle. This inability to differentiate between present and past will be a difficult obstacle for Hugo to overcome. The supporters of the new emperor make comparisons with the first: " 'L'un a fait le 18 Brumaire, l'autre a fait le 2 décembre: ce sont deux ambitieux' " (15). [One brought about the 18th of Brumaire, the other has brought about December 2; these are ambitious men.] Hugo sees through such favorable comparisons and knows a self-interested man of limited vision when he sees one. In fact, he sees the new emperor expanding the crime of his uncle's coup d'état: "[Le] 18 brumaire est un crime dont le 2 décembre a élargi la tache sur la mémoire de Napoléon" (15). [The 18th Brumaire is a crime whose stain on the memory of Napoléon has been magnified by December 2.] The first emperor has never been spotless in Hugo's memory, but his accomplishments are diminished by name association with his nephew. Only history will be able to judge the difference between the two men. "Il aura à démêler la chose avec l'histoire" (16). [He will have to reckon with history.]

In addition to not living up to his uncle, Louis-Napoléon is not worthy of his century. "Pourtant, ne pas confondre l'époque, la minute de Louis Bonaparte, avec le dix-neuvième siècle; le champignon vénéneux pousse au pied du chêne, mais n'est pas la chêne" (17). [However, let us not confound this era, the minute of Louis Bonaparte, with the nineteenth century; the poisonous mushroom grows at the foot of the oak, but it is not the oak.] The nineteenth century represents to Hugo all that is good about the French Revolution. Louis could never live up to those ideals.

Louis takes power by claiming to save French society from socialism. He stays in power through the use of artifice and money. The ruse is carried out by Louis' band of "panégyristes" who keep the propaganda machine well oiled. Everyone is paid off, from political cronies to soldiers in the street; and of course the emperor takes his own hefty share. The carrot and the stick take form in money and repression. Hugo sees Louis as trying to seize Charlemagne's scepter and the policeman's billy club at the same time (22). Hugo can reach far back in the national memory to create images unfavorable to Louis.

More changes in vocabulary are effected by the new regime: "Depuis trente-six ans il y avait en France toutes sortes de choses pernicieuses: cette 'sonorité', la tribune; ce vacarme, la presse; cette insolence, la pensée; cet abus criant, la liberté" (22). [For thirty-six years there had been in France all sorts of pernicious things: this loud sound, the court; this racket, the press; this insolence, freedom of thought; this crying abuse, liberty.] Once the public hears the new vocabulary enough times, the old will begin to recede in their memories. The demagogue's lexicon will replace revolutionary language. Louis will replace the forgotten institutions with his own version of how to save French society from itself: replacing the court by the Senate, a free press by censorship, intelligent thought by ineptitude, liberty by the sword (22). For this, Hugo calls him "le dernier des hommes" (22) [the last of all men].

Hugo's confidence that the current state of affairs will not last comes fundamentally from his faith in God: "Et que cela pourrait durer! Et vous dites que cela durera! non! non! . . . cela ne durera pas! Ah! si cela durait, c'est qu'en effet il n'y aurait pas de Dieu dans le ciel, ou qu'il n'y aurait plus de France sur la terre!" (22) [And this could last! And you tell me it will last! No! No! It will not last! Ah! If it were to last, that would mean that there would be no God in Heaven, nor France on earth!]

THE GOVERNMENT (*BOOK 2*)

Louis-Napoléon's most egregious crime is his abrogation of the constitution, and Hugo gives numerous examples. The ones that strike closest to Hugo's heart are the limitation of the freedom of the press and the co-opting of the courts. Hugo gives his version of Louis' new constitution: "*Article deuxième et suivants*. La tribune et la presse, qui entravaient la marche du progrès, sont remplacées par la police et la censure et par les discussions secrètes du sénat, du corps législatif et du conseil d'état" (23). [Article the Second, and Following. The assembly and the press, which were impeding the march of progress, are replaced by the police and censorship, and by the secret debates of the Senate, the legislative body, and the Council of State.] Without an open discussion or a fair judiciary, no free society can exist. Louis prefers "order" and "calm" to freedom and uses repressive means to keep the streets quiet. "Il est impossible de recevoir avec plus de chasteté et de grâce ce que M. Bonaparte, dans son style d'autocrate, appelle des 'garanties de calme,' et ce que Molière, dans sa liberté de grand écrivain, appelle des 'coups de pied.'" (26). [It is impossible to receive with a more

chaste modesty and grace what Monsieur Bonaparte, in his auto-
cratic style, calls "certain guarantees of tranquility," and what Molière, with the freedom allowed a great author, calls "kicks"] Hugo
is not averse to using literary references to activate the collective
memory of his readers. If Molière is set in opposition to Louis, the
new emperor will come off worse for the comparison.

Hugo accuses Louis of doing more than just muzzling the press:
he has closed down newspapers all over France and put journalists
in prison for their views. "A Paris, vingt journaux anéantis; dans les
départements quatrevingts" (28). [Twenty journals abolished in
Paris, eighty in the countryside.] Louis is compared with tyrants of
the past: "Qui donc règne? Est-ce Tibère? Est-ce Schahabaham?"
(28) [Who is reigning? Is it Tiberius, or is it Schahabaham?] Three
quarters of the republican journalists have been banished, the rest
sought by the government, dispersed and hidden. This is Hugo's
version of hell, in which the written word is trampled and the purveyors of ideas made to suffer the ignominy of both censorship and
imprisonment. Only a few carry on, but they do so under restrictive
conditions: "Ça et là, dans quatre ou cinq journaux survivants, dans
quatre ou cinq journaux indépendants, mais guettés . . . quinze ou
vingt écrivains courageux, sérieux, purs, honnêtes, généreux . . . écri-
vent, la chaîne au cou et le boulet au pied" (28). [Here and there,
in four or five surviving journals, in four or five journals that are
independent, but closely watched . . . fifteen or twenty courageous
writers, serious, pure, honest and generous men, still write with a
chain around their neck and a ball hanging from their leg.] If complete freedom of the press does not exist, how can freedom itself?

Hugo outlines how Louis has even tried to muzzle the foreign
press and any exiled French writers. The French government uses
economic threats to intimidate foreign newspapers that dare to
print any critical material. They threaten to expel any foreign corre-
spondents that do not toe the line. Lawsuits or arrest await any
French journalists in foreign countries who do not write the party
line. Foreign governments will be asked to extradite them. But ultimately, the empire will not be able to control them at such a distance because they will always be able to go somewhere and be free.
(Hugo himself moves from Brussels to Jersey to Guernsey during the
eighteen-year odyssey of his exile.) "[Les] proscrits iront ailleurs; ils
trouveront toujours un coin de terre libre où ils pourront parler"
(30). [The banished will go elsewhere. They will always find a corner
of some free land where they may speak freely.] Later, Louis will try

just that by passing the Faider law, outlawing any criticism of any monarchy.[10]

Hugo knows that this very text, *Napoléon le petit*, will be condemned in France, and he is not concerned about it: "Ce livre sera donc jugé en France, et l'auteur dûment condamné, je m'y attends. . . . Rien n'égalera mon dédain pour le jugement, si ce n'est mon mépris pour les juges. Ceci est mon plaidoyer" (30). [This book will be judged in France, and the author condemned accordingly. I expect it. . . . Nothing will equal my disdain for this verdict except my disdain for the judges. This is my closing argument.] In fact, Hugo's defense argument lasts eighteen years, and during that time the government is never able to silence him completely.

The government set up by Louis bears only lexical resemblance to the preceding democratically elected legislature. The new group, made up of "imbéciles" (31), is full of self-interested cowards, whose fear of the government is equaled only by their greed. The words and slogans used by the new assembly take on completely new connotations: "Humanité, lisez: Férocité; Bien-être universel, lisez: Bouleversement; République, lisez: Terrorisme; Socialisme, lisez: Pillage; Fraternité, lisez: Massacre; Evangile: lisez: Mort aux riches" (31). [Humanity actually equals Ferocity. For Universal Well Being read Upheaval. Republic equals Terrorism. Socialism equals Pillage. Fraternity equals Massacre. The Gospel equals Death to the Rich.] Such interpretation of words that have come to be hallowed in the nineteenth century is anathema to Hugo and the left. Whenever one of their causes is debated, the right has a way of twisting the meanings of the words to suit their goals: "De telle sorte que lorsqu'un orateur de la gauche disait, par exemple: 'Nous voulons la suppression de la guerre et l'abolition de la peine de mort,' une foule de pauvres gens, à droite, entendaient distinctement: 'Nous voulons tout mettre à feu et à sang'" (31). [So when an orator of the left said for example, "We want an end to war and the abolition of the penalty of death," a crowd of miserable people among the right distinctly heard: "We wish to ravage everything with fire and sword."] Repression of the freedom of the press and of free speech thus results in a loss of any real dialogue. The only exchange left is a *dialogue de sourds*, in which the side in power hears only what it wants. Hugo intends to provide the other side of the dialogue in the hopes that enough people will hear him and understand his words, so that a real dialogue will take place.

We must not lose sight of the fact that when Hugo writes *Napoléon le petit,* Louis is not yet emperor. Hugo goes so far as to ask: "Maintenant M. Bonaparte sera-t-il ou ne sera-t-il pas empereur?" (34). [Will Monsieur Bonaparte be emperor or will he not?] The implied answer is "yes." In fact, he has already taken the necessary steps to become the sole ruler of France. And he will take the elimination of revolutionary principles to an extreme unmatched even by the first emperor: "Il a effacé des murs *Liberté, Egalité, Fraternité.* Il a eu raison. Ah! Français, vous n'êtes plus ni libres, le gilet de force est là; ni égaux, l'homme de guerre est tout; ni frères, la guerre civile couve sous cette lugubre paix d'état de siège" (34). [He has erased the words *Liberty, Equality, Fraternity* from the walls. He was right. Ah! Frenchmen, you are neither free (you are in a straightjacket), nor equal (the man of war is supreme), nor brothers (civil war smolders under this dark peace of the state of siege).] Even if Louis has not yet declared himself emperor, he might as well have. Hugo is not going to worry about such distinctions; for him the damage has already been done, and his own future is clear. He will be the opposition in exile, the conscience of the French people.

On the surface, Louis does not seem to be a dangerous character, first because he is inept and second because he does not take any initiative. Hugo can almost be made to pity him: "Ces crimes exceptés, il n'a rien produit. Omnipotence, complète, initiative nulle. Il a pris la France et n'en sait rien faire. En vérité, on est tenté de plaindre cet eunuque se débattant avec la toute-puissance" (36). [These crimes excepted, he has produced nothing. Limitless power and no initiative. He has conquered France and does not know what to do with her. In truth, one is tempted to pity this eunuch struggling with his omnipotence.] Unfortunately, his power is unlimited and the potential for evil is always there. Since he is not a creative genius, he settles for making decrees, whose danger lies in their lack of creativity and initiative. Only the repressive side remains when the imagination is stripped away from any government initiative. What remains is a government that resembles the later years of the Roman empire: "S'amuser et s'enrichir, tel est leur 'socialisme'" (37). [To amuse and enrich themselves, such is their "socialism."] Hugo, a man of great imagination, will provide the counterweight to the regime's insouciance.

Louis uses his uncle's name to great advantage only when it suits him. When he needs to make himself look better in comparison, he goes so far as eliminating holidays related to the first emperor and replacing them with his own. Commemoration is essential in the development of the history of any public figure, and Hugo knows this as well as anyone. Whoever controls the signifiers of collective memory controls the discourse in this domain. Monuments, museums, parades, and other ceremonies mark important figures and dates in history, and choosing which ones to privilege is a prerogative of those in power. Hugo can only seethe as he sees Louis manipulating the collective memory in this manner.

To those who argue that Louis should be given some credit for economic prosperity as well as social and technological advances, Hugo replies that Louis had nothing to do with them: "Mais on nous dit: N'allez-vous pas un peu loin? n'êtes-vous pas injuste? concédez-lui quelque chose. N'a-t-il pas, dans une certaine mesure, 'fait du socialisme'? Et on remet sur le tapis le crédit foncier, les chemins de fer, l'abaissement de la rente, etc. Nous avons déjà apprécié ces mesures à leur juste valeur; mais en admettant que ce soit là du 'socialisme,' vous seriez simples d'en attribuer le mérite à M. Bonaparte. Ce n'est pas lui qui fait du socialisme, c'est le temps" (39–40). [But people say to us: Are you not going a little too far? Are you not unjust? Allow him something. Has he not to some extent "created socialism"? And then we are told of the *crédit foncier*, the railways, abatement of rents, etc. We have already estimated these measures at their full value; but even admitting that there was something of "socialism" in all this, you would be naive to attribute any credit for it to Monsieur Bonaparte. It is not he who brings about socialism; it is the times.] Crediting circumstance instead of the man in power is a critical distinction because it will form the basis of the argument between the supporters of the two antagonists. Can Louis take credit for the advances under his regime, or are they simply a logical outgrowth of the industrial revolution? Hugo would argue that progress is simply the result of the application of revolutionary principles, what he calls "socialism." For him, Louis has neither the intellectual capacity nor the generosity even to imagine such advances. "En somme et après tout, qu'est-ce que cela prouve? que ce courant qui s'appelle Révolution est plus fort que ce nageur qui s'appelle Despotisme" (40). [Finally, in essence, what does all this prove? That this current, whose name is Revolution, is stronger than this swimmer, whose name is Despotism.] In the grand scheme of history, Louis and his regime will be insignificant in the context of the events of the nineteenth century.

If anything, Louis is an aberration, a blight on the landscape of his time: "cet homme pèse sur l'époque entière, il défigure le dix-neuvième siècle, et il y aura peut-être dans ce siècle deux ou trois années sur lesquelles, à je ne sais quelle trace ignoble, on reconnaîtra que Louis Bonaparte s'est assis là" (42). [This man weighs on the entire era; he disfigures the nineteenth century, and there will perhaps be two or three years in this century marked by some indescribably ignoble trace of the presence of Louis Bonaparte seated there.] Louis will be a painful, but ultimately insignificant historical figure. While history may be made up of just such "traces" as Hugo mentions, the forces of history will overwhelm the smallness of Louis' historical stature. For the moment, Louis is in the spotlight. "Aujourd'hui, baisse la tête, histoire, l'univers regarde l'Elysée!" (43) [Today, bow your head, History, the universe is watching the Elysée Palace!], but his fame will not last forever, and hopefully not for very long. When Louis has disappeared from the scene, he will have no place in the pantheon of great figures of the nineteenth century.

Hugo sees the present situation as a vast misunderstanding that can be rectified by educating the people about the alternatives, including the republican years they have just lived through and the glorious era of the first empire: "Certes, il faut réveiller cette nation; il faut lui prendre le bras, le secouer, il faut lui parler. . . . [Toute] cette situation n'est autre chose qu'une immense et fatal quiproquo" (43). [Certainly this nation needs to be awakened; she needs to be taken by the arm, shaken, and spoken to. . . . The whole situation is nothing other than an immense and fatal misunderstanding.] Once the people have seen the horror of the real situation around them, they will rally to Hugo's cause. They will understand that the new emperor is not the same as the one on their wall. "Ce peuple est bon et honnête. Il comprendra. Oui, paysan, ils sont deux, le grand et le petit, l'illustre et l'infâme, Napoléon et Naboléon!" (43). [These people are good and honest. They will understand. Yes, peasant, there are two of them, the great and the little, the illustrious and the infamous, Napoléon and Naboléon!] For the next eighteen years, Hugo will try to influence these very people.

CRIMES (*BOOKS 3* AND *4*)

In this section, Hugo details the atrocities that took place in the streets of Paris after the coup d'état of December 2. Most of what he recounts took place during the day of December 4. As barricades

were being constructed to protest the takeover, the army began
shooting, supposedly because someone had shot at them. But Hugo
claims, and he uses eyewitness accounts as his evidence, that the fu-
sillade was a coordinated effort on the part of the military, that several units in different neighborhoods began shooting at the same
time. The loss of life, among the dead many who were innocent bystanders, far exceeded the 190 dead admitted by the government.
Hugo's figures, while never pinpointed for fear of inaccuracy, would
be well into the thousands. Yet after order had been restored, life
quickly went back to normal. Louis had achieved his goal of frightening the population into submission. Hugo is outraged that life
could go on as if there were not "des cadavres là-dessous" (45) [bod-
ies under there]. Once again, his job is to awaken the French people
to the reality of their situation: "Ah! Si l'on ne s'en souvient plus,
rappelons-le à ceux qui l'oublient! Réveillez-vous, gens qui dormez!
Les trépassés vont défiler devant vos yeux" (46). [Ah! If this is no
longer remembered, let us remind those who forget! Wake up, you
who are sleeping! The dead are about to parade before your eyes.]

Louis' motivation in turning loose the military was a cynical one.
In order to maintain security and crush any opposition to the coup
d'état, he had to demoralize the opposition as quickly as possible.
Once the killing had been done, he allowed the population to come
out and look at the destruction in order to press upon their imagination the seriousness of his purpose. He had not perpetrated the massacre just to cover it up: "Massacrer n'était que le moyen, terrifier
était le but" (67) [To massacre was only the means; to terrify was
the goal.] Louis had succeeded in making himself so feared that he
"ressemblait plus à rien de l'histoire. . . . La population de Paris sen-
tit qu'elle avait le pied d'un bandit sur la gorge" (67). [resembled
no one that had come before. . . . The people of Paris felt that the
foot of a bandit was on its neck.] The strategy was successful, as all
meaningful resistance disappeared, not only in the short term but
also for the duration of the empire.

This new villainy sparks comparisons in Hugo's memory with foreign invaders, who have entered Paris and declined to destroy her
or her people out of respect for her beauty and history. "Dès qu'ils
ont mis le pied sur le seuil de cette ville . . . tous, en pénétrant dans
Paris, ont entrevu dans ces murs, dans ces édifices, dans ce peuple,
quelque chose de prédestiné, de vénérable, d'auguste" (68). [No
sooner had they set foot on the threshold of the city . . . all of them,
when they had entered Paris, glimpsed in the walls, in the buildings,

in the people, something predestined, venerable and august.] Paris
is a sacred city that represents the home of all humanity. "Tous ont
senti la sainte horreur de la ville sacrée; tous ont compris qu'ils
avaient là, devant eux, non la ville d'un peuple, mais la ville du
genre humain; tous ont baissé l'épée levée!" (68) [Everyone felt a
sacred horror of the sacred city; they all understood that there, before them, was not the city of a certain people, but the city of all
mankind; all of them lowered their uplifted sword!] To violate the
sanctity of the city in the manner of Louis Napoléon's troops is to
go against historical precedent, one based on the respect for one
nation's history by its adversaries. Louis' actions are more proof that
he has no historical perspective and that his own place in history will
be a small and negative one. Louis is a "misérable," who was willing
to massacre his own people, citizens who were protected by attackers
as diverse as Wellington, Schwartzenberg, Blücher, and Platow.
Hugo gives us this historical overview in order to make his little Napoléon seem that much smaller.

The only time Louis ever thinks about history is when he needs to
justify his position or his actions. Realizing that the truth about the
events in the streets could be harmful to his new regime, he moves
to limit the damage by deflating the number of dead. "Louis Bonaparte, sentant venir l'histoire et s'imaginant que Charles IX peuvent
atténuer la Saint-Barthélemy, a publié, comme pièce *justificative*, un
état dit 'officiel des personnes décédées'" (69). [Knowing the
power of History, and imagining that Charles IX could hide the true
magnitude of the St. Bartholomew, Louis Bonaparte has published
what he calls an 'official list of the dead,' as evidence.] Louis recognizes a historical lesson only in negative terms: Charles IX might
have lessened the impact of the Saint-Barthélémy massacre with the
right public relations. Louis' propaganda machine puts the number
of dead at 191.

Hugo immediately produces eyewitnesses whose estimates of the
number of people killed on December 4 is far higher than the government's. One person claims to have seen over eight hundred
dead. Hugo himself takes the high road here in leaving the official
count to the historians. "Le nombre des victimes? On est réduit aux
conjectures. C'est là une question que l'histoire réserve. Cette question, nous prenons, quant à nous, l'engagement de l'examiner et de
l'approfondir plus tard" (70). [The number of victims? We can only
guess. It is a question reserved for history. We swear to examine the
question and to better understand it later.] But his object is clear:
he shows through his witnesses that Louis's estimate is ridiculously

low. Even a military officer guesses that there were twelve hundred dead.

Because of the distortion of facts and the repression of the press, Hugo despairs of ever knowing the truth of the matter. "Quels que soient les efforts de l'histoire, le 2 décembre plongera peut-être longtemps encore dans une sorte d'affreux crépuscule" (70). [Whatever be the efforts of history, December 2 will, for a long time, perhaps, be bathed in a sort of awful twilight.] Louis Bonaparte, "l'homme de silence et de nuit" (70) [the man of silence and night], has put the reality of events into shadows from where the historians will have a very difficult time extracting it. Hugo's account, supported by his eyewitnesses, will remain one of the best records, albeit a biased one.

Hugo sees the coup d'état as only the first in a series of crimes to be committed by Louis because "un crime appelle l'autre" (71) [one crime calls for another]. History is again our guide here, as we remember the famous criminal rulers of history. Once justice and freedom have been repressed, the tyrant must continue to press on the jugular of the people in order to keep them in a state of submissive ignorance. "La loi est comme le voile du temple: quand elle se déchire, c'est du haut en bas" (71). [The law is like the veil of the temple; when it is torn, it is from top to bottom.] This is Hugo at his most pessimistic. He sees Louis' apparent ignorance of historical precedence and predicts brutal acts to come.

Louis will have to rely of course on collaboration from key sectors of society in order to remain in power, the judiciary and the legislature foremost among them. Once the power brokers in the three branches of government have decided the form of such collaboration, those in the lower ranks will carry out their decisions. "En haut, des hommes atroces ont donné des ordres qui ont été exécutés en bas par des hommes féroces. La férocité garde le secret à l'atrocité" (71). [Atrocious men on high have given orders that have been executed by ferocious men below. Ferocity keeps the secret of atrocity.] This collaboration between the higher and lower echelons of society results in the repression of information. No one wants his crime revealed, and he will go along with the party line in order to conceal it. "De là ce silence hideux" (71). [Hence this hideous silence.]

Fortunately for Hugo, time will eventually get the better of the cover-up. While the entire truth may never be known, posterity will not accept Louis' version of history. "L'avenir ne voudra pas croire à ces prodiges d'acharnement" (71). [The future will not believe

these relentlessness acts of horror.] The atrocities were too great to
be hidden under the cover of darkness. At some point the truth will
come out, and Hugo will do his best to make it happen sooner
rather than later.

Hugo sees the coup d'état as the beginning of a theater piece that
has the face of both farce and tragedy. Buffoons hiding behind
masks terrorize an unsuspecting crowd. "Maintenant, le carnaval
impérial danse" (72). [Now the imperial carnival is dancing.] But
one day, the tables will turn, and the dancers will not be the perpetrators of the crime but their victims. "Quelque jour, sous les pieds
de Bonaparte . . . cette fosse se rouvrira brusquement, et l'on verra
sortir l'un après l'autre chaque cadavre avec sa plaie . . . tous debout,
livides, terribles, et fixant sur leur assassin des yeux sanglants!" (72)
[Some day, under the feet of Bonaparte, that trench will open suddenly, and from it we shall see rise up one after another . . . every
corpse with its wound . . . all livid and terrible, and fixing on their
assassin their blood-shot eyes.] The ghosts of December 4 will dance
on the grave of the new regime. Hugo does not know when this day
will come, but he predicts that the full force of history will come to
bear on the final judgment of Louis. "En attendant ce jour, et dès à
présent, l'histoire commence votre procès, Louis Bonaparte. L'histoire rejette votre liste officielle des morts et vos '*pièces justificatives.*'
L'histoire dit qu'elles mentent et que vous mentez" (72). [Waiting
for that day, history begins your trial now, Louis Bonaparte. It rejects
your official list of the dead and your evidence. History says that they
lie and that you lie.] For the moment, Hugo is witness, prosecutor,
judge, and historian, but he is confident that the forces of history
will take his side.

We have seen the importance in history of the person who dares
to say "No." Hugo turns the formulation on its head by making
Louis the man of denial. Faced with the accusations of Hugo, Louis
would naturally deny them. "Vous dites que non. Je dis que si" (72).
[You say, no. I say, yes.] Hugo becomes the man who says "Yes,"
yes to the accusations and yes to the final judgment that history will
render.

The final arbiter of the dispute between Louis and the lovers of
freedom will be the French people. They are the ultimate authors of
history, "car le peuple, c'est la réalité" (73) [because the people are
reality]. No matter what propaganda they believe, they will eventually see the light because they are eternal and a political regime is
not. Hugo hopes that he will be around long enough to see the re-

versal and to be its historian. "A ce que nous venons de raconter, ajoutez tous les autres crimes sur lesquels nous aurons plus d'une occasion de revenir et dont, si Dieu nous prête la vie, nous raconterons l'histoire en détail" (73). [To what we have just said, add all the other crimes to which we shall have more than one opportunity to return, and which, if God spares us our life, we shall relate in detail.] While the events and consequences he has seen can be compared to history's worst calamities "cette épouvantable proscription, comparable aux plus tragiques désolations de l'histoire" (74) [this frightful lawlessness, comparable to the most tragic devastation of history], Hugo is sure that his, and the French people's, day will come.

Another of Hugo's grievances against the emperor is his reinstitution of the death penalty. The great crusader against capital punishment sees this move as further proof of Louis' depravity. He goes so far as to envisage another Terror. "A moins qu'un universel cri d'horreur n'arrête à temps cet homme, toutes ces têtes tomberont" (77). [Unless a universal cry of horror stops this man in time, all these heads will fall.] The executions Hugo describes are fresh in his memory, some of them only days past, and this gives his account the power of immediacy that he wants to convey to his readers. This parody of the legal system makes honest, respectable citizens shudder. Ironically, Louis himself might have been subjected to the same fate had he lost his bid for power, and he may still be the guillotine's victim in the future.

The only thing holding Louis back from being a true butcher is the enlightenment of the nineteenth century. "Ce n'est pas sa faute; c'est que le siècle s'y refuse obstinément. . . . Le dix-neuvième siècle, siècle de douceur" (80) [It is not his fault; it is because the age is obstinately opposed. . . . The nineteenth century, a century of gentleness], which puts limits on Louis' cruelty. Otherwise he would become a tyrant to equal history's worst. Even the most violent despots would restrain themselves "devant la force invisible du progrès accompli, devant le formidable et mystérieux refus de tout un siècle qui se lève . . . autour des tyrans, et qui leur dit non!" (80) [faced with the invisible force of progress accomplished, with the formidable and mysterious refusal of a whole century rising before tyrants, and saying to them, "no!"]. Here it is not an individual, such as Hugo, who takes a stand against inhumanity, but an entire era.

Hugo continually calls Louis' regime the "party of the past." "Le parti du passé, sous le nom de l'ordre, résistait à la République, en

d'autres termes résistait à l'avenir" (81) [The party of the past, in
the name of order, resisted the Republic, in other words resisted the
future.] For Hugo, the reinstallation of a republic is the inevitable
future, and there are two ways of arriving there: by progress, the
means favored by democrats; or by armed struggle, where the forces
of repression think they have an advantage (81). Hugo believes that
God is on his side, that France's destiny is to be a republic, and that
what comes from resisting such a destiny is chaos and injustice. "Ce
qui doit être sera; il faut que ce qui doit couler coule; que ce qui
doit tomber tombe; que ce qui doit naître naisse; que ce qui doit
croître croisse; mais faites obstacle à ces lois naturelles, le trouble
survient, le désordre commence. Chose triste, c'est ce désordre
qu'on avait appelé l'ordre" (81). [What must be will be, what must
flow must flow, what must fall must fall, what must be born must be
born, what must grow must grow; but place an obstacle in the way of
these natural laws and trouble arises, disorder begins. A sad thing,
this disorder that has been called order.] Clinging to the past leads
only to moral sickness, a "choléra moral" that infects the entire society. If Louis had restrained himself and contented himself with
being president for four years, the natural order of things would
have played itself out slowly. Instead, Louis instigated a series of
crimes that created a sickness only time will heal.

Louis not only rigged his election by frightening people with images of what socialism would bring them, but he went about debas-
ing the reputation of his uncle, the first emperor. Hugo's texts
written in exile are replete with comparisons of the two men, but
one of the most forceful appears in this section of *Napoléon le petit.*
"Voici l'impopularité qui monte autour de la grande figure, et c'est
ce fatal neveu qui a posé l'échelle! Voici les grands souvenirs qui
s'effacent et les mauvais souvenirs qui reviennent. . . . On oublie le
héros, et l'on ne voit que le despote. La caricature commence à
tourmenter le profil de César. Et puis quel personnage à côté de
lui!" (86). [Now unpopularity mounts around that great figure, and
it is this fatal nephew who has placed the ladder! Now the great
memories are all erased and all the evil ones return. . . . the hero is
forgotten, and only the despot is visible. Caricature is beginning to
torment the profile of Caesar. And then what a figure beside him!]
The mask has been placed over the face of France's glorious past;
the carnival has replaced the empire.

PARLIAMENTARISM AND ABSOLUTION (*BOOKS 5 AND 6*)

Hugo launches into a long defense of "la tribune française," the court system that guarantees the freedoms won through combat and revolution. "Cette tribune, c'était la terreur de toutes les tyrannies et de tous les fanatismes, c'était l'espoir de tout ce qui est opprimé sous le ciel" (92). [This tribunal was the terror of all tyrannies and of all fanaticisms, it was the hope of all oppressed under heaven.] Hugo sees a free judicial system as a universal concept that will protect liberty even if it is continuously threatened by those who would control it for their own ends. Its greatest weapon is what Hugo calls "le Verbe" (92). Any decision rendered by the court is more than just a collection of words, it is a set of principles that will influence the future of the nation. "Un mot tombé de la tribune prend toujours racine quelque part et devient une chose. . . . C'est un avenir qui germe; c'est un monde qui éclot" (93). [A word fallen from the tribunal always takes root somewhere, and becomes a thing. . . . It is a future germinating; it is a world dawning.] This is why it is so devastating when Louis replaces justices with political hacks ready to do his bidding. The courts, representing both "conquest" and "ideas," are able to resolve the great contemporary problems, but if they are not free to do so, chaos and/or tyranny will result.

The French judicial system is based on a history of ideas that has been further developed since 1789. The English court established principles of "affaires," while the French was a court of ideas. "La tribune française avait élaboré dès '89 tous les principes qui sont l'absolu politique, et elle avait commencé à élaborer depuis 1848 tous les principes de l'absolu social" (93). [The French tribunal had elaborated since '89 all the principles that form the political absolute; and they had begun since 1848 to formulate all the principles of the social absolute.] These principles ruled both the nation and its imagination. To reject them now would mean rejecting the collective memory of a time of enlightened justice.

With the demise of the free judicial system comes a whole series of consequences. Lost are freedom of discussion, of the press, of the individual; control of taxation and open financial records; freedom of beliefs; the security of every citizen; the dignity of the nation; the reputation of France; public initiative; movement; and life itself. The individual is reduced to nothing but a part of the applause ma-

chine for the emperor who has taken away the basic rights that the
nation had secured at a heavy cost.

Hugo is at his cynical best when he discusses Louis' justification
for the coup d'état and the subsequent plebiscite that gave Louis
seven and one-half million votes out of ten million cast. He outlines
the three conditions for a fair vote: it must be free of any constraint,
it must be open and strictly regulated, and the final tally must be
honest. Any republic would uphold these conditions, but Louis of
course subverted them at every turn. There could be no honest election without freedom of the press. If the public did not know what
choice they had, how could they make an informed choice? Without
regulation of the votes, the government was free to announce any
figure they wished. For Hugo, "Ce vote est l'excuse des lâches; ce
vote est le bouclier des consciences déshonorées" (102). [This vote
is the excuse of cowards; this vote is the shield of dishonored consciences.] While the result of the vote is Louis' only justification for
remaining in power, it becomes a powerful tool in the hands of
Louis' propagandists. Who would dare argue against such an over-
whelming majority?

In this vote, Hugo sees a great irony of the bourgeois mentality:
they vote for a man they would not have as their checkout boy.

> "Vous avez nommé Louis Bonaparte Président de la République?"
> "Oui."
> "Le prendriez-vous pour garçon de caisse?"
> "Non, certes!" (104–5)

> ["You have voted for Louis Bonaparte to be President of the Republic?"
> "Yes."
> "Would you take him for your cashier?"
> "No, certainly not!]

"Disons-le, l'intelligence humaine, et l'intellect bourgeois en parti-
culier, ont de singulières énigmes" (104). [Let us say at once that
the human intellect, and the bourgeois intellect in particular, contain some curious enigmas.] Fully able to judge the capacities of a
clerk, the bourgeois is unable, or more likely unwilling, to see the
truth behind the coup d'état. His greatest fear is disruption, and
Louis has promised to restore "order." For Hugo, this attitude
means that Louis' only rival in this election was the French nation
itself, for it was in the immediate past that Louis went searching for
the disorder that he wanted so passionately to extinguish.

In this chapter, Hugo approaches the identification between himself and the conscience of the nation. The nation has been subju-
gated and silenced, and it is now up to him to begin the long process
of recovery. "Quelqu'un qui est perdu dans l'obscurité, un passant,
un inconnu se dresse devant vous et vous dit: 'Tu ne feras pas cela'"
(107). [Someone who is lost in the dark, an unfamiliar passerby,
rises up before you and says, "You will not do that."] We, the readers, are not fooled by the supposed "inconnu." We can read into
the word "obscurité" another more powerful word, "exil." Hugo
may be out of the picture physically, but he is always present in the
French consciousness and conscience. "Ce quelqu'un, cette bouche
qui parle de l'ombre, qu'on ne voit pas, mais qu'on entend, ce passant, cet inconnu, cet insolent, c'est la conscience humaine" (107).
[This someone, this mouth speaking from the shadows, whom we
hear but do not see, this unknown person, this insolent person, is
the human conscience.] Hugo is in the shadows of exile, but he is
rising up against injustice by appealing to a conscience higher even
than the national one. By equating his voice with the conscience of
all humanity, Hugo has given himself a universality that cannot, in
the end, be defeated.

As the voice of the human condition, Hugo proposes himself as
an opposition candidate for the hearts and minds of the French people. His argument is based on morality. Those who support him understand the difference between the animal who is complete
because all his needs are provided for on earth, and the human
being, who recognizes the existence of the metaphysical. Because of
such awareness, the human knows the difference between right and
wrong, and with that comes his sense of responsibility. "De là, en
l'homme, ce grand et double sentiment de sa liberté et de sa responsabilité. Il lui est donné d'être bon ou d'être méchant" (108).
[Hence the great twofold sentiment in man of his liberty and of his
responsibility. He can be good or he can be wicked.] This Christian
existentialist view of the world forms the basis of Hugo's candidacy
to overthrow the illegally elected Louis, whose egotistic—read ani-
malistic—instincts are all the more evident to us after we have read
a passage such as this: "Monsieur Louis Bonaparte, la notion du
bien et du mal, vous ne l'avez pas. Vous êtes le seul homme peut-
être dans l'humanité tout entière qui n'ait pas cette notion" (108).
[Monsieur Louis Bonaparte, you do not have any notion of good
and evil. You are perhaps the only man in all humanity who does
not have this notion.]

Louis tries to use the election as evidence of his place in history, but history is not convinced. "Le crime essaye de tromper l'histoire sur son vrai nom; il vient et dit: 'Je suis le succès.' Tu es le crime" (109). [Crime tries to deceive history as to its true name; it comes and says, "I am success." You are crime.] History will be the final judge. No vote can decide the moral high ground. "La notion du bien et du mal est insoluble au suffrage universel. Il n'est pas donné à un scrutin de faire que le faux soit le vrai et que l'injuste soit le juste. On ne met pas la conscience humaine aux voix" (110). [The notion of good and evil cannot be resolved by universal suffrage. It is not given to a ballot to make false become true and the unjust the just. The human conscience cannot be put to a vote.] By awarding himself the moral high ground, Hugo has taken the dispute between the two men out of the realm of the political and into the moral. He thus gives himself time to work on the psyche of the French people, to convince them that he is right and Louis is wrong. He allies himself with history and memory in the fight for a moral victory.

In the next section, Hugo spells out his political agenda in order to contrast it with Louis'. These ideas will never change over the course of Hugo's exile:

> Le suffrage universel vrai, libre, pur, réel . . . les journaux dans toutes les mains . . . les affiches couvrant les murailles, la parole partout, la lumière partout! Eh bien, à ce suffrage universel, soumettez-lui la paix et la guerre, l'effectif de l'armée, le crédit, le budget, l'assistance publique, la peine de mort, l'inamovibilité des juges, l'indissolubilité du mariage, le divorce, l'état civil et politique de la femme, la gratuité de l'enseignement, la constitution de la commune, les droits du travail, le salaire du clergé, le libre échange, les chemins de fer, la circulation, la colonisation, la fiscalité. . . . [Soumettez]-les-lui, il les résoudra. (111)

> [Universal suffrage must be, true, free, pure, real . . . newspapers in every hand . . . posters covering the walls, free speech everywhere, light everywhere! Well, to such universal suffrage as this submit peace and war, the size of the army, public credit, the budget, public relief, the death penalty, the irrevocability of judges, the indissolubility of marriage, divorce, the civil and political status of women, free education, the constitution of the commune, the rights of labor, the salary of the clergy, free trade, railroads, the currency, colonization, fiscal questions. . . . Submit these to it, and it will resolve them.]

Hugo is confident that if his agenda is put to a vote, most of his proposals will be approved. "La vérité morale" (112) [moral truth] will win the day.

At the end of the chapter, Hugo explicitly identifies himself as the voice that cries "No." Now he takes us back to Rome and says that if one person had stood up against Nero, the course of history would have been different. He is determined to be that voice for France: "Eh bien! Cette voix qui proteste dans l'ombre, c'est la mienne" (112). [Well, this voice uttering its protest in the shadows is mine.] Hugo could not make his case in any stronger terms. By equating himself with all other humans, he excludes Louis from the human race.

The Oath and Progress in the Coup d'État (*Books 7* and *8*)

Hugo is outraged that Louis, who broke his presidential oath by refusing to relinquish power at the end of his four-year term, has required a loyalty oath of the French public. This "farce" represents another example of how the forces in power can manipulate memory and, in this case, forgetting. By renouncing his own oath, Louis invalidates the one that he is now demanding from the French people. He makes his demand out of fear. "Le bourreau a une secrète peur de la victime" (118). [The executioner has a secret fear of his victim.] Louis is afraid of what the future holds and of how history will judge him. By asking for the people to legitimize his coup d'état, he is asking for absolution. But Hugo knows that history has something else in mind for Louis. "Il espère ainsi donner le change à la France qui, elle aussi, est une conscience vivante et un tribunal attentif, et que, le jour de la sentence venu, le voyant absous par ses victimes, elle lui fera grâce. Il se trompe. Qu'il perce le mur d'un autre côté, ce n'est pas par là qu'il échappera" (119). [He thus hopes to deceive France, who also is a living conscience and an attentive tribunal; and that when the day for the sentence comes, seeing him absolved by his victims, she too will pardon him. He is mistaken. Let him break through a wall in some other direction, he will not escape this way.] Louis is trapped by his own actions and no oath will eliminate them from the collective memory.

The requirement of the loyalty oath creates a number of ironies that Hugo would find comic if they were not so serious. "Parmi ces

premiers présidents qui juraient fidélité à Louis Bonaparte, il y avait
un certain nombre d'anciens pairs de France qui, comme pairs,
avaient condamné Louis Bonaparte à la prison perpétuelle" (119).
[Among these first presidents who swore fidelity to Louis Bonaparte,
there were a certain number of ex-peers of France, who, as peers,
had condemned Louis Bonaparte to life in prison.] Louis is hoping
that his failed invasion of France and his subsequent prison term will
be forgotten in his sweep to power. Hugo will make sure that it remains in the memory of the people.

Hugo shocks his reader by beginning this chapter by pronounc-
ing himself satisfied with the coup d'état. What is he up to? How can
he write such a statement after all the insults he has been hurling at
Louis? Like a good suspense novelist, Hugo will reveal his intentions
as the chapter progresses. "Il y a des moments où, en présence du
Deux-Décembre, je me déclare satisfait" (123). [There are moments
when, faced with December 2, I declare myself satisfied.] "Je suis
toujours de ceux que le Deux-Décembre indigne, je ne suis plus de
ceux qu'il afflige." (123) [I am always one of those in whom the
December 2 rouses indignation, but I am no longer one of those
whom it grieves.] "L'œil fixé sur certains côtés de l'avenir, j'en viens
à me dire: 'L'acte est infâme, mais le fait est bon'" (123). [With my
eyes fixed on certain aspects of the future, I arrive at this conclusion:
"the act is infamous, but the fact is good."] What Hugo means, of
course, is that the long-term consequences of the coup d'état may
be beneficial to French society because it may speed up the rate of
change. "Sous cette victoire monstrueuse et à son ombre, un immense et définitif progrès s'accomplit" (124). [Beneath this monstrous victory and in its shadow, a vast and certain progress is being
accomplished.] Hugo is less interested in the cause—in which he
sees the hand of Providence—than in the effect. The "orgie de l'ordre" (124) will bring about the downfall of the dictator and the beginning of a new age. "Quel est l'avenir de la France? Est-ce
l'empire? Non, c'est la République" (124). [What is the future of
France? Is it the Empire? No! it is the Republic.]

Hugo sees the coup d'état as a speeding up of the historical process. Because Louis has so blatantly usurped both power and his uncle's memory, he has overloaded the circuits of France's collective
memory. The people will not accept the complete annihilation of
their republican past. "On n'aperçoit plus '93 qu'à travers sa justification, et Napoléon qu'à travers sa caricature; la folle peur de la
guillotine se dissipe, la vaine popularité impériale s'évanouit. Grâce

à 1848, la République n'épouvante plus. L'avenir est devenu possible" (124). [No longer is '93 seen except through its justification, and Napoléon is seen no longer except through his caricature; the senseless dread of the guillotine is dissipated, the vain popularity of the Empire has vanished. Thanks to 1848, the Republic no longer makes people afraid. The future has become possible.] Hugo is willing to let go of his reverence for Napoléon in order to banish Louis from the political landscape. For the moment, all Hugo has is the word "République," but he knows that the republic is inevitable (125). "Ce sont les secrets de Dieu" (125), [These are the secrets of God] and of history.

Having relegated the empire to oblivion, Hugo is free to focus on the specifics of his future republic, "la fédération démocratique du continent" (125) [the democratic federation of the continent]. In one paragraph he proposes universal suffrage, elected judges, priests limited to their role in the Church, war limited to the defense of the nation, with the army reduced to a national guard. "La loi toujours, le droit toujours, le vote toujours; le sabre nulle part" (125). [The law everywhere, the right everywhere, the vote everywhere; the saber nowhere.] There will be formidable obstacles of course, and Hugo lists the four principal ones:

"L'armée permanente,
"L'administration centralisée
"Le clergé fonctionnaire
"La magistrature inamovible." (125)

[A permanent army.
A centralized administration.
A paid clergy
Irremovable judges.]

The reasons for these institutions being a danger to progress are obvious; the most evident one is that these are four of the pillars of traditional French society. "C'étaient les quatre vertus de l'ordre, les quatre forces sociales, les quatre colonnes saintes de l'antique formation française" (126). [They were the four virtues of order, the four social forces, the four holy pillars of the ancient French system.] If the coup d'état had never happened, there would be even less chance of ridding the future of these obstacles to freedom and justice.

Hugo never saw the realization of his dream, and even in today's united Europe, countries still have standing armies, centralized administrations, and judges appointed for life, but he never stopped trying. "[Ce] prophète veut éclairer les hommes d'état" (127). [This prophet wants to enlighten statesmen.] He expects these institutions to autodestruct from the weight of their injustice and hypocrisy, but he is not averse to helping them on their way. In a caption under an illustration of a large hand holding Louis by the ear, we read, "L'historien ne pourra que le mener à la postérité par l'oreille" (131). [The historian can only lead him to posterity by the ear.]

CONCLUSION
FIRST PART: THE PETTINESS OF THE MASTER, THE ABJECTION OF THE SITUATION

"Soyez tranquilles, l'histoire le tient" (131). [Be still, history has him in its grip.] This phrase could certainly stand as a subtitle of the whole work. Hugo is not the one who will bring down Louis-Napoléon; history will do it for him. Louis' lack of stature in every domain will leave him in historical oblivion. As a villain, Louis does not stack up to history's worst. Even if he declares himself emperor, he will remain a buffoon. "Dictateur, il est bouffon; qu'il se fasse empereur, il sera grotesque. . . . Il sera hideux, et il restera ridicule. Voilà tout. L'histoire rit et foudroie" (131). [As a dictator he is a buffoon; as emperor, he will be grotesque. . . . He will be hideous, and he will remain ridiculous. Nothing more. History laughs and crushes him.] Hugo concludes that the title of his book is a good one.

In the next section, Hugo explicitly evokes the national conscience as a collective force. "De toute agglomération d'hommes, de toute cité, de toute nation, il se dégage fatalement une force collective" (133). [From every aggregation of men, from every city, from every nation, there evolves of necessity a collective force.] When the collective strength of a nation is put to good use, a new republic will emerge. "Mettez cette force collective au service de la liberté, faites-la régir par le suffrage universel, la cité devient commune, la nation devient république" (133). [Place this collective force in the service of liberty, let it be regulated by universal suffrage, and the city becomes a commune, the nation becomes a republic.] The people are the ultimate arbiters of history, for they are the ones who speak the loudest through their votes.

The problem with the collective conscience is that it is not an organized, consistent force. The nebulous nature of any national spirit renders it easy to influence but difficult to harness. "Cette force collective n'est pas, de sa nature, intelligente. Etant à tous, elle n'est à personne; elle flotte pour ainsi dire en dehors du peuple. . . . Elle peut être asservie par la tradition; elle peut être surprise par la ruse" (133). [This collective force is not, of its own nature, intelligent. Belonging to everyone, it belongs to no one; it floats, so to speak, outside the people. . . . It may be enslaved by tradition; it may be surprised by cunning.] This force can be harnessed by an "ennemi social" such as Louis, but the nation has more staying power than the passing tyrant. This national conscience is a historical force to which every government should be secondary. It is a moral force that can be bruised but not eliminated. "S'il n'y avait avant peu un dénouement brusque, imposant et éclatant, si la situation actuelle de la nation française se prolongeait et durait, le grand dommage, l'effrayant dommage, ce serait le dommage moral" (134). [If there were not before long an abrupt, imposing, and striking ending, if the present situation of the French nation were prolonged and extended, the great injury, the terrible injury, would be the moral injury.] Hugo's role will be to keep this moral force from being damaged any more than it has been by the injustices of dictatorship.

National doubt is Hugo's major obstacle. He sees the French people as confused and afraid to risk persecution and especially death at the hands of the dictator. "Ce qui est plus affreux encore, c'est de songer qu'à l'heure où nous sommes les peuples doutent, et que pour eux la France, cette grande splendeur morale, a disparu!" (135). [It is even more frightful to think that at the present moment people are in doubt, and that for them France, that great moral splendor, has disappeared!] The disappearance of morality leads to the disappearance of the nation itself. "Il n'y a plus de France. C'est fini" (135). [France is no more. It is finished.] Hugo despairs at the torpor and shame that he sees in France at the moment and compares it to past glory and national pride. By making his readers remember better times in the past, Hugo takes the first step in leading them back to the resumption of those honorable times.

Hugo says that he is happy to be in exile. "Oh! quel bonheur d'être banni" (136) [Oh, what happiness to be banished], because it gives him the perspective and freedom from repression that his

fellow citizens do not have. While Louis and associates render
money the new god, Hugo can remain faithful to his ideals without
any temptation of material riches coming his way from the government. Material corruption leads to moral decay, necessitating the
suppression of words that will make the people remember the past
or hope for a different future. "Les mots: indépendance, affranchis-
sement, progrès, orgueil populaire, fierté nationale, grandeur Française, on ne peut plus les prononcer en France" (137). [The words
independence, enfranchisement, progess, popular pride, patriotism
and French greatness can no longer be uttered in France.] These
are very different words from "order" and "security."

The working class lies at the heart of this national conscience, and
they are at once the strongest and the most vulnerable force therein.
Because their very existence is so tenuous, they are susceptible to
slogans and the bonds of tradition. They are tempted by the promise
of new riches and must be assisted in keeping their eyes on the
moral path. Hugo has great sympathy for this underprivileged class,
as we shall see throughout his writings and particularly in *Les Misérables*, and he sees himself as their protector. He will continually remind them of the difference between hard work and ill got gains,
between order and repression, between morality and immorality.
"Même avec ce perpétuel enseignement, à la fois divin et humain,
cette classe si digne de sympathie et de fraternité succombe souvent.
La souffrance et la tentation sont plus fortes que la vertu. Maintenant comprenez-vous les infâmes conseils que le succès de M. Bonaparte lui donne?" (138) [Even with his perpetual teaching, at once
divine and human, this class, so worthy of sympathy and brotherhood, often succumbs. Suffering and temptation are stronger than
virtue. Now do you understand the infamous advice that the success
of Monsieur Bonaparte gives to his class?] As dire as Hugo makes
things sound, we are ever conscious of the latent power of this social
class and of its place in the national conscience as a whole. Louis
may have seduced them for the moment, but they will outlive him
as a historical force.

Louis' biggest blind spot is his attitude toward the French people.
He treats them as a conquered people, instead of the powerful nation they are. "A la degradation morale se joint la dégradation politique, M. Bonaparte traite les gens de France en pays conquis"
(139). [To moral degradation is joined political degradation. Monsieur Bonaparte treats the French as a conquered country.] Once
this attitude is established between ruler and people, the inevitable

result is a relationship based on fear and distrust. Liberty must be suppressed to maintain order, and basic rights must be suspended. Just as any good resistance fighter would do, Hugo calls for leadership to oust the tyrant. "Trouvez-moi un moyen quelconque de jeter bas cet homme et délivrer ma patrie! . . . Un moyen, le premier venu, plume, épée, pavé, émeute, par le peuple, par le soldat" (139). [Find me any means whatever of removing this man and liberating my country. . . . Any means, the first at hand, pen, sword, paving-stone, riot, by the people or by the soldier.] For the first time, Hugo is not putting himself necessarily at the forefront of the resistance. He will follow anyone with the will and the power to oust the dictator. "Oui, quel qu'il soit, pourvu qu'il soit loyal et au grand jour, je le prends, nous le prenons tous, nous, proscrits, s'il peut rétablir la liberté, délivrer la République" (140). [Whatever it may be, provided it be loyal and open, I will take it, we will all take it, we the banished, if it can restore liberty and free the Republic.] When the republic is reestablished, Louis will be relegated to the forgotten. "Relever notre pays de la honte, et faire rentrer dans la poussière, dans son oubli, dans son cloaque, ce ruffian impérial" (140). [Raise our country out of shame, and send back into the dust, into oblivion, into the cesspool from which he emerged, this imperial ruffian.] Hugo's ultimate triumph would be to see Louis not only dethroned but forgotten.

CONCLUSION
SECOND PART: MOURNING AND FAITH

In order to progress, a society must forget the bulk of its past, retaining only the guiding principles upon which it is based. While societal evolution generally proceeds at its own pace and in its own inevitable way, occasionally a revolution is necessary to spur things along. Revolution represents the future as well as the whole concept of truth. When the natural evolution is disrupted by tyranny, however, the forces of the past hold sway and progress comes to a halt. History is replaced not by a new history but by repression and fear. All of the guiding principles of the society are discredited, leaving a void that no call to order can fill. Among all the peoples of Europe, the French have always been the first to revolt against injustice and the most conscious of their historical imperative. It will be up to them to lead the rest of Europe into the future. France itself becomes the prophet. "Il y avait un peuple parmi les peuples qui était une sorte d'aîné dans cette famille d'opprimés, qui était un prophète dans la tribu humaine. . . . Il allait, il disait: Venez, et on le suivait" (145–46). [There was among the peoples one people which was a sort of elder in the family of the oppressed, which was like a prophet for mankind. . . . It said, "Come" and everyone followed.] Hugo has been representing himself as the leader of the movement toward the future, but here he cedes the place of honor to the nation itself. On the grand scale of human progress, even the great poet is just one member of the national conscience.

The most important principle as the nation moves toward the future is faith, a concept that ties in with Hugo's political and religious beliefs. In a time when all seems lost, faith is necessary to continue, and in a society that devalues religious principles, faith is necessary to maintain belief in a better future. "Ayons foi. Non, ne nous laissons pas abattre. Désespérer, c'est déserter. Regardons l'avenir" (147). [Let us have faith. Let us not be defeated. To despair is to desert. Let us look to the future.] Not everyone can be a revolutionary, and times occasionally demand a certain stoicism based on faith, even for intellectuals such as Hugo whose instinct is to call for action. "Le penseur doit accepter avec simplicité et calme le milieu où la Providence le place. La splendeur de l'intelligence humaine, la hauteur du génie n'éclate pas moins par le contraste que par l'harmonie avec les temps. L'homme stoïque et profond n'est pas diminué par l'abjection extérieure" (147). [The thinker must accept with simplicity and calm the environment in which Providence has placed him. The splendor of human intelligence, the elevation of genius, is not less striking by contrast than by harmony with the times. A stoic and thoughtful man is not lessened by external degradation.] Patience and faith will sustain the thinker while history runs its natural course. If the occasion for revolutionary action presents itself, so be it. Hugo finds his most useful role in stimulating discussion, thought and faith in the future.

Hugo puts his faith in the moderation he sees as the greatest strength of the nineteenth century. "Ce siècle est le plus grand des siècles; et vous savez pourquoi? Parce qu'il est le plus doux" (147). [This century is the greatest of all; and do you know why? Because it is the most gentle.] This century, "immédiatement issu de la Révolution française" (147) [coming directly from out of the French Revolution], freed the slaves in America, gave new dignity to women, replaced the rights of the strong with those of the just, eliminated piracy, lessened prison sentences, cleaned up prison camps, condemned the death penalty, deemphasized war, and lessened the power of tyrants. "Ce siècle proclame la souveraineté du citoyen et l'inviolabilité de la vie; il couronne le peuple et sacre l'homme" (147). [This century proclaims the sovereignty of the citizen and the inviolability of life; it crowns the people and consecrates man.] The nineteenth century values its artists and "la majesté, la grâce, la puissance, la force, l'éclat, la profondeur, la couleur, la forme, le style; il se retrempe à la fois dans le réel et dans l'idéal, et porte à la main les deux foudres, le vrai et le beau" (148) [majesty, grace, power, strength, splendor, depth, color, form and style. It steeps itself in both the real and the ideal, and carries in its hands the two thunderbolts, truth and beauty.] Some of this is idealism, particularly since slavery had not been abolished in 1852 and since Louis is still in power, but Hugo never varies from these themes as he promotes his vision of the future. "Est-ce que vous ne sentez pas que le vieux monde avait fatalement une vieille âme, la tyrannie, et que dans le monde nouveau va descendre nécessairement, irrésistiblement, divinement, une jeune âme, la liberté?" (149) [Do you not feel that the old world had of necessity an old soul, tyranny, and that on the new world a young soul is about to descend necessarily, irresistibly, divinely, a young soul, liberty?]

Hugo has faith that the enlightened century will eventually turn all the people against the despot. While they are silent for the moment, their resignation will not last long. "Te voilà sans mouvement. Les hommes de despotisme et d'oppression rient et savourent l'illusion orgueilleuse de ne plus te craindre. Rapides joies. Les peuples qui sont dans les ténèbres oublient le passé et ne voient que le présent et te méprisent" (150). [There you are, motionless. The men of despotism and oppression laugh, and delight in the haughty delusion that you are to be feared no more. Their joy will be fleeting. The nations who are in darkness forget the past and see only the present and despise you.] Hugo sets the present against the past, but the French people have come to a better understanding of the present through the education that their recent history has provided them. They have learned well lessons that "les hommes du passé" [men of the past] have forgotten.

Hugo closes by reminding the reader that Louis' reign is shrouded in lies (152). In one day, the dictator managed to turn the nation upside down. "Tout ce qui était axiome est devenu chimère. Tout ce qui était mensonge est devenu fait vivant. . . . La civilisation, le progrès, l'intelligence, la révolution, la liberté, il a arrêté cela un beau matin, purement et simplement, tout net, lui, ce masque, ce nain" (152). [Axioms have become illusions. Everything that was a lie has become a living fact. . . . Civilization, progress, intelligence, revolution and liberty have been brought to an end, purely and simply, at a moment's notice, by this mask, this dwarf.] But such illusions cannot last long. "[Vous] ne voyez donc pas que le Deux-Décembre n'est qu'une immense illusion, une pause, un temps d'arrêt, une sorte de toile de manœuvre derrière laquelle Dieu, ce machiniste merveilleux, prépare et construit le dernier acte suprême et triomphal de la Révolution française!" (152) [You do not see, then, that December 2 is only an immense illusion, a pause, a halt, a sort of stage curtain behind which God, that wonderful machinist, is preparing and building up the last act, the supreme and triomphal act of the French Revolution!] We have seen these themes throughout *Napoléon le petit*, and Hugo repeats them here to maximum effect in the final paragraph.

   In the end, Hugo turned out to be right. The Second Empire lasted only eighteen years and the republic was restored. Yet in 1852, such a future was envisioned by only one man, a poet with a mighty pen and a reputation to match, but who was in exile, far from the center of political power. *Napoléon le petit*, coming from anyone else, would probably have been largely ignored. Since Hugo was the author, however, the work received a fairly wide readership, although the government restricted its distribution. Circulating under cover, the text was widely discussed and certainly gave hope to the left, particularly to the intellectuals for whom socialism was a goal. A great many people shared Hugo's ideals, but they would have to wait for their time to come. In the meantime, Hugo continued to rail against the emperor in *Les Châtiments* and less directly in *Les Misérables*. When he returned to Paris in 1870, he could rightly claim to have foreseen the events that had unfolded. The prophet had become the historian. The collective memory of the French nation would be forever influenced by the texts he wrote while in exile. The historical view of Louis-Napoléon and the whole Second Empire would be revised, with Hugo leading the way. Today, as we look back on this period, we see Louis more as an opportunist who played on his famous name to acquire wealth and power for himself and a small group of friends. While the period was one of prosperity and of social progress, Louis is not given all the credit for bringing them about. Rather they were a byproduct of the momentum built up earlier in the century, Hugo's enlightened century of goodness and progress.

Karl Marx criticized *Napoléon le petit* as "a bitter and witty invective" against "the violent act of a single individual," and Pierre Albouy goes even further: "If one could choose a single emblem of Hugo's unreadability it would be the prophetic bombast which led him to cast himself as a beacon to humanity."[11] While I agree with the notion that Hugo's attack is personal and seemingly limited, I see *Napoléon le petit* as a much more significant text than do the two critics cited above. First, it is only the initial text in a series of attacks on the emperor, each one more sophisticated than the one before; second, it reveals Hugo's talent as a political critic; third, it represents a call for goodness, and this can never be limited to the personal struggle between two men; finally, it is a text with basic tenets that are alive and well today. The significance of *Napoléon le petit* lies in its unwillingness to compromise. His view of the future, accurate in many ways, has helped shape our vision of Europe today. Hugo's prescience worked on the collective conscience of his fellow citizens and continues to color the way all of us view France in the nineteenth century.

One year later, *Les Châtiments* built upon the archival base provided by *Napoléon le petit* by placing the events and Hugo's critique of them in poetic form. Ricœur's explanation/comprehension phase of historical writing comes to life in the emotional power of Hugo's verse. Moving from the factual toward the metaphorical allows the reader a certain physical and temporal distance from the events of December, 1851, while deepening their affective involvement in Hugo's project of redemption. Concepts such as freedom and justice are given life through mythical imagery, while the emperor and his henchmen are portrayed as the most heinous figures of the underworld. The following chapter analyses Hugo's poems and shows them to be another significant step in his historiographical project.

4

Les Châtiments: Poetry as Historical Metaphor

IN THE FIRST TWO YEARS OF HIS EXILE, HUGO WROTE A COMPANION PIECE
to *Napoléon le petit* in verse form, *Les Châtiments*. Published in Brussels
in 1853, the collection did not elicit the immediate popular interest
as its prose equivalent. Seventeen years later, however, it was reissued
to a triumphant reception. The times had changed, and the victory
predicted in the pages of this volume had come to pass. The inherent nature of poetry—a certain delay between the writing, the reception and the reaction—as opposed to the immediacy of a call for
resistance such as *Napoléon le petit*, allowed events to catch up with
the predictions of the poet and readied the public for Hugo's return
to France in 1870.[1] In these ninety poems, we have evidence of the
poet at his most vituperative and most powerful, and at the same
time, we see the *mise en littérature* of his furor. This is a work that had
the time to mature before reaching the public as a justification of all
that Hugo had been saying over the past seventeen years. It is precisely this delay, this *mise en mémoire* that shows the influence of literature on the writing of history.[2] By entering the public conscience
seventeen years after its conception, *Les Châtiments* worked on the
collective memory of the French public instead of on the battered
and fearful conscience of the populace in 1853. Here is a good example of Braudel's long duration (*longue durée*); as the Second Empire ran its course, the French were able to see the ramifications of
Louis' policies that further enriched the bourgeoisie while repressing basic freedoms in the name of order. Seventeen years after the
fact, the coup d'état no longer looked like the beginning of a glorious new era.

Hugo's goal in writing these poems is as clear as it was for *Napoléon
le petit*: reduce the government of December 2 to historical oblivion.
A lofty goal, to be sure, but one that Hugo is confident will eventually come to pass. He will replace lies with the truth, myth with reality. The poet in exile is in a privileged position. He can see what the

110

people cannot. He is not blinded by fear nor influenced by propaganda nor burdened by crushing poverty and a lack of education. He has the knowledge, distance, leisure, and passion to write about what really happened in December of 1851 and subsequent months, and can create a counter-discourse to the one coming from the official mouthpieces in Paris. He is not fooled by the usurpation of the myth of Napoléon I by his nephew, and he will not be intimidated by the Faider law that banned all works critical of those in power. The social and political movement necessary for the reception of his work will take place over the next seventeen years.

Poetry is an ideal genre for a work that needs the time and attention of a vast readership. As the verses roll along, they enter the minds of the readers on the waves of rhythm, sound, refrain, and metaphor. Each section of the book responds to the others and connects them in the reader's memory, reminding them of the horror and proposing a counter-discourse as well as a new world in a new republic.[3] The poems have at their core the tradition of the philosophy of history, and this grounding gives the work a seriousness that will ensure its long life. This is not just any poet. Hugo is the prophet of a better future and counts on his fame and respect among all French readers to carry his message beyond the years. The poet is the interpreter of both history and the word of God, and his voice unmasks scandal in the manner of the prophet announcing the future (Chamarat, *Nommer l'innommable,* 12–13). It is this future that informs the whole collection, as Hugo steadfastly points to it as a goal of "progress." As long as the betterment of the populace as a whole comes before that of the individual, the salvation of all the French people will be assured. In order for that to happen, the empire must go the way of all corrupt administrations and give France back to the ideals of the Revolution.

Hugo establishes here a new role for the poet. No longer aloof, distanced from the whirlwind of history, he is engaged, in the French sense of *engagé.* For Hugo, poetry always already emanated from a moral, political, and social conscience, but until *Les Châtiments,* his poetry was hardly polemical. In this volume, he intensifies the political process, as the ideas find full voice in the poems. By alerting his readers to the possibility of a new world order, far removed from the current corruption, Hugo awakens the collective conscience. He becomes the mouthpiece of a movement, both political and social. He has taken action by exiling himself and by writing his counter-discourse. He calls on his readers for resistance to the dominant discourse and to the myth it is creating. He knows that a new revolution will not take place, at least not in 1853, but he is also sure that the future holds progress and a new republic in its hands.

THE EXPLANATION/COMPREHENSION OF HISTORY

Les Châtiments represents Hugo's explanation/comprehension stage of his history of the events of December, 1851. After the initial phase of documentation (*Napoléon le petit*), in which eyewitness accounts are compiled and formed into documents that make up the archive pertaining to certain historical events, Hugo, as any good historian would do, attempted to place the documents in the overall scheme of the history of the people affected by the events. Memory and history begin to separate in this stage into distinctly different entities, as the historian gathers and rearranges the material at hand. We have already seen the beginnings of this split in the documentary stage because of the inconclusiveness of eyewitness testimony, which renders every bit of evidence susceptible to interpretation (*MHF*, 182). The originality of the explanation/comprehension stage lies in the way in which it strings together the evidence recorded in the documentary stage (*MHF*, 182). To explain something generally means to answer the question "why" with a series of answers beginning with "because" (*MHF*, 182). This type of analysis is far from the realm of individual memory, which is far more likely to try to answer the question "what happened?" The extreme of the explanation/comprehension stage is Fernand Braudel's long duration, in which patterns emerge over long periods of time. Eyewitness accounts become documents in a number of archives until a pattern of repetition begins to establish itself. These patterns can be analyzed structurally and quantitatively in a way no single document ever could.[4] While *Napoléon le petit* was the documentation of eyewitness accounts, the poems of *Les Châtiments* represent Hugo's working through of the implication of the events he has witnessed.

Les Châtiments represents a new stage in the representation of the history of the present. No matter that the poems repeat many of the same themes expressed in the earlier work; they are works of art that rely as much on metaphor as memory to get their point across. Paradoxically, it is precisely this move toward metaphor that confers upon *Les Châtiments* its status as analytical document as it moves away from witnessing and toward a more reflective view of the events at hand. In this context, versification becomes a form of verification.

As the writing of history moves into the realm of literature, questions are inevitably raised about its authenticity as a historical document. Where does history leave off and fiction begin? Can a work of fiction tell us anything about historical events?[5] Questions of reliability arise as soon as the first eyewitness tells his tale, and I discussed these questions in the previous chapter as they related to the formation of the document and the archive. Here, however, it is not just the reliability of the narrative that is in question but also the intention of the historian. The fictional nature of the text raises questions of authenticity and authorial intentionality that are central to this intermediary stage between documentation and representation. As Hugo examines the ramifications of the coup d'état and expresses his frustration and outrage to his readers, poetry allows him to shed some of the limits of historical representation present in a narrative such as *Napoléon le petit* which strives for believability at all times. In *Les Châtiments* the individual events are still at the heart of the matter, but the poet is allowed a freedom of expression and an increasing distance from the actual eyewitness accounts that he did not have in the earlier work. The result is a collection of reflections that put forth not only what happened but why, and what might be done to remedy the situation.

Once the author is able to shed the strictures of the document, he can bring into play a whole host of elements that will enrich his narration and lead to a better explanation of the historical context and outcomes. Robert Mandrou lists some of these tools: "representations and images, myths and values, recognized by groups or by society as a whole, and which constitute the elements of collective psychology."[6] With each step away from individual memory, historical perspective grows and we approach Braudel's conception of long duration or what Elias and Mandrou call "l'histoire des mentalités."[7] In so doing, we also approach the notion of collective memory, as it is formed from all the societal memories of a given era. We thus have a view of events that is more global and more able to give the author and his readers a better understanding of the implications of what has taken place.[8]

By writing history, the author seeks a societal norm against which he can compare the events that he is recounting. He is constantly balancing the legal with the illegal, the accepted with the taboo. Inevitably, this comparison will revolve around the just and the unjust as they determine the legitimacy of the person or institution in question. Between the extremes of right, represented for Hugo by the ideals of the French Revolution, and wrong, represented by the tyranny of Louis-Napoléon, there must be a space of what Ricœur calls "adjustment" (*MHF*, 221), in which one searches for that which fits the circumstances. The development of a societal norm is thus crucial for the establishment of an historical judgment. In order for Hugo's denunciation of Louis-Napoléon to have any lasting credibility, the emperor must be judged, over a certain period of time, by the people who make and suffer through their shared history.

In this epic battle between poet and emperor, the people will eventually have to choose sides. Ricœur establishes a way for them to do this by imagining a hierarchy of legitimacy, what he calls "the scale of degrees of legitimation" (*MHF*, 221). In this construct, the degree to which someone is believed depends on his standing in the community's opinion. A person's conduct ultimately determines his reputation and thus his credibility.[9] If a person feels justified in undertaking an action, and if the community at large agrees with the action, then the credibility of the person is increased. In a public dispute, the question of credibility is crucial, for a community must decide; it cannot stay on the sideline or the historical process will lose all meaning and the society will plunge into chaos. Hugo and Louis-Napoléon are the combatants here, and the collective memory of the years 1848–70 will ultimately decide whose version of events will be the lasting one. Louis counts on his position as emperor and his control of the sources of information to provide him the necessary advantage. Hugo relies on his stature as the greatest living poet and, more importantly, on the forces of time to readjust the memories that Louis has distorted. While most disputes are resolved through compromise or "adjustment," such is not the case here, for the emotions are too raw and the stakes too high. No reconciliation will be possible during the affixed time period; only the steady progress of time and the development of the collective memory will bring about a verdict.

Hugo will attempt once again, however, in *Les Châtiments*, to show that his view is the legitimate one. For this, he counts on a weapon that is crucial in such a debate: intelligibility (*MHF*, 221). It is not enough to be great; one must put forth a convincing argument.[10] Each element of a society has its priorities, and a rhetorician must always seek to strike the right chord. What is important to a merchant is less so to an artist, and so on. While Hugo and Louis represent different domains—literature and politics—Hugo is enough of a politician to know the language common to both. His advantage lies in his literary experience, his high standing with the French people and his absolute faith that he has right and justice on his side. Hugo shows himself to be, in the long run, the more intelligible of the two rivals because his ideals have deeper roots in the French psyche and because they are closer to what he believes the people of his time really want. He becomes a historian of the present not by emphasizing short term hierarchies, but by constantly bringing the reader back to his fundamental beliefs in freedom and justice, beliefs that create and maintain the equilibrium of a democratic society (*MHF*, 226).

Hugo does not have all the cards, however. The notion of societal norm is closely linked to the habits and the security of a community, and it is here that Louis can emphasize the power of the state to protect the traditions ingrained in the fabric of the group. Louis' incessant boasting of how he restored order to a nation in political and social chaos rings true because security is one of a society's most pressing needs. Without it, a state of constant conflict replaces the norm of stability, and the state plays the key role in preserving the safety of the people in a modern society. Yet as Camus will point out a century later, a regime that comes to power claiming to have restored order has taken the first step toward tyranny, and Hugo will attack the ruthless nature of the coup d'état and the repressive measures that followed as tyrannical rather than palliative.

While he may be the philosopher and historian who is expounding on his fundamental beliefs and exhorting his reader to agree with him, he cannot succeed without establishing a dialogue with his reader. This dialogic exchange is representative of the writing of the history of the present because there are no truths yet about what has just occurred in the society. The different phases of the writing of history have not had time to run their course. The historian of the present must therefore present a convincing case that he is telling the truth. "In this moment of literary expression, the historian's discourse declares its ambition, its claim to represent the past *in truth*" (*MHF*, 228). In a situation such as Hugo's where two versions are competing for the status of historical truth, the people will ultimately decide. This call for readers to believe his version mirrors, yet always follows, the call for them to believe the testimony of eyewitnesses. A parallel dialectic is always present between memory and history, and the voice that offers the most credible version of both memory and history will prevail.

Historians of the present find their mirror image in social agents who narrate their social links and their contribution to such links. These historians become implicitly readers of their place (being and acting) in society, and it is this link between history and society that makes them historians of the present. Hugo had always had one foot in history and the other in his society, so this role fits him perfectly. Who better to ferret out the truth of contemporary events than the poet/philosopher/historian?

Hugo calls repeatedly to the French people from exile. He exhorts, cajoles, and harangues them; first to action, then to caution, then to envisioning a better future. We should pause here to inquire about who these people are. Is Hugo a true democrat in the sense that he includes all of the French people, or is he appealing to those who will see his point of view, a group that was certainly in the minority in 1853? Instead of speaking specifically to the French, is he reaching out to democrats from around Europe who themselves are fighting for new republics? Yves Gohin thinks this is the case: "How could Hugo have accepted the law of the majority of French citizens who supported 'Napoléon le petit'? It was simply the amalgamation of a satisfied bourgeoisie and a meek proletariat. There remained a few French people, like him, to preserve the honor of exile. But above all, he felt more and more solidarity with efforts for independence, which is to say democracy, that developed among European nationalists."[11] Hugo's worldwide prestige, particularly after the publication of *Les Misérables* in 1862, contributed to the power of this appeal.

The future of the country cannot, therefore, be left solely to the whim of the people because they cannot be trusted to reject someone as clearly fraudulent as Louis-Napoléon. Hugo must lead them in the right direction, and for that he needs the support of intellectuals and politicians who think as he does, no matter what country they come from. Hugo's vision of the French people united in harmony will not come to pass until a new republic is in place.[12] Hugo desires to be the conscience of his entire century, not just of the majority of the French people. His goals are lofty: to rise above the mud and stench of the Second Empire and to bring the whole continent into his "United States of Europe."

Even during his years in exile, Hugo considers himself a kind of conqueror. He has risen above the riffraff who have decided to follow a false emperor. His triumph is of the enlightened elite over the ignorant.[13] He has the ability to elevate himself above corruption because he has the power of poetry in his hands and because he knows that he has right on his side.[14] Hugo's elevation to the status of prophet comes from his negative portrayal of the emperor, as well as from the positive force of his poetry.

Poetry in the hands of a prophet becomes superhuman by going beyond the boundaries of the real. Hugo's project in *Les Châtiments* is not simply a practical, political one; he intends to surpass the everyday and bring his ideal to the fore through the blending of realism and mythology, with himself as the pied piper leading the parade. It is not enough to oust the emperor and punish his followers; poetry must be a beacon for a better universe.[15] In order to lead the people out of the darkness, Hugo must be completely convinced that he is right. His confidence "is the consciousness of being right on a superior plane, of being, in the absolute, on the side of goodness, of progress, of light" (*C*, 160). *Les Châtiments* are another compelling argument in Hugo's crusade to turn the French people against the emperor.

Hugo's writings from exile that directly attack Louis-Napoléon have a commonality of style, even if they are composed as different genres. Hugo takes the popularity of caricature and turns it into a literary genre all its own. The visual nature of caricature strikes more directly, but literature can develop its own ways of accomplishing similar goals.[16] Such manipulation results in what Gaudon calls "réalisme lyrique."[17] The combination of grotesque imagery and mythological symbolism gives Hugo's poetry the power to surpass the banality of the everyday. By rejecting common language, Hugo does not allow his poetry to become outdated. Even though Hugo has elevated the style, the essential elements of caricature in *Napoléon le petit* are still in evidence in *Les Châtiments*. This literary caricature has the power to strike at its adversary in ways that even the illustrated caricatures did not because it provides the reader with a dizzying array of images with which to imagine the perfidy of those being satirized.

Les Châtiments may be a weaker attack than *Napoléon le petit* because of its elevated tone, but by giving Louis-Napoléon a stature he did not have in the previous text, the poems render him more universal and in that way broaden the appeal of Hugo's call for justice. While Hugo can certainly be accused of excess in these texts because of the power of the feeling behind the words, the poet can be excused for such excess because of the quality of his vision and the strength of his belief in his ideals.[18] Hugo's philosophy of history and art gives him the means to satisfy the obligations that it creates for him.[19] Like Eisenstein and *Potemkin*, Hugo creates a text that becomes the legitimate representation of the real, more real than the actual events which have faded into the historical record. He accomplishes this through his style that elevates the whole sordid mess that is the Second Empire and through the force of his message that the poet will lead the people to a better world.

Hugo the prophet uses a style that is worthy of one of such stature. He, in his elevated position, will find the words to make the people follow him. His source of inspiration is divine. He does not require acceptance from his readers at large; he is above such considerations.[20] Hugo the famous poet transforms himself into Hugo the prophet through his poetry, through the images of the real that he makes into images of permanence and of transcendent truth and beauty.

The ultimate effect of the style of *Les Châtiments* is to contribute to the delay in its acceptance. This rejection is perhaps inevitable in a text that is both satiric and lyric. The relative failure of *Les Châtiments* in 1853 does not in any way diminish its later success. It simply makes us wonder. We generally assume that topical literature almost immediately loses its effectiveness, but the lot of satiric literature generally proves the opposite, as its effect is felt more strongly over time.[21] The delayed success of *Les Châtiments* becomes one of the factors in its continued popularity throughout the nineteenth and twentieth centuries.[22] The import of the poems will thus be felt in the collective memory of its readers, those who chose to ignore it in 1853 as well as those who read it with fascination in 1870.

As a poet in exile, Hugo is in a privileged position. From this distance, the poet becomes the mouthpiece of both history and God, and his voice can rail against scandal, like the prophet denouncing the present and announcing a greater future.

The Poems

In *Les Châtiments*, Hugo plays upon the memory of his readers and anticipates the memories of future readers. While the events of the coup d'état are still fresh in 1853, the themes related to the corruption of the empire remain valid when the revised edition appears in 1870. The poems speak eloquently for themselves of all that concerns Hugo during his exile, so I will limit my analysis to specific passages from selected poems in order to discover the flavor of Hugo's passion for progress through remembering.

In the edition of 1870, which I use here, Hugo writes a short preface beginning with the following passage: "Il a été publié, à Bruxelles, une édition tronquée de ce livre, précédée des lignes que voici":

> Le faux-serment est un crime.
> Le guet-apens est un crime.
> La séquestration arbitraire est un crime.
> La subornation de fonctionnaires publics est un crime.
> La subornation de juges est un crime.
> Le vol est un crime.
> Le meurtre est un crime."
>
> (23)

[A shortened version of this book, published in Brussels, was preceded by the following lines:

> False testimony is a crime.
> Entrapment is a crime.
> Arbitrary imprisonment is a crime.
> Bribery of civil servants is a crime.
> Bribery of judges is a crime.
> Theft is a crime.
> Murder is a crime.]

These lines introduce the accusation that Hugo presents against Louis-Napoléon. Yet, rather than dwelling on the seriousness of these crimes, he quickly switches to a forward-looking register, as he encourages his readers to look for redemption in the future. Such a reversal is inevitable because, as he concludes this preface, "Rien ne dompte la conscience de l'homme, car la conscience de l'homme, c'est la pensée de Dieu" (24). [Nothing can subdue the human conscience, because the human conscience is the thought of God.]

"Nox"

In the first poem of the volume, Hugo recounts the events of the coup d'état and places them in their historical context. From the very outset, it is clear that memory will play a role on several different fronts for Hugo as well as the current regime. The first is the necessity for Louis-Napoléon to get the coup d'état over with and forgotten before proceeding to a vote:

> Soldats, mitraillez-moi toute cette canaille!
> Feu! Feu! Tu voteras ensuite, ô peuple roi!
>
> (28)

> [Soldiers, shoot to pieces for me all of this rabble!
> Fire! Fire! Then you'll vote, oh people, the king!]

The richness of the choice of vocabulary is striking. The populace is at once "rabble" and "king," indicating Louis' contempt for both the people and the monarchy. They will vote for him or he will have them all shot . . . again. "Then you'll vote" clearly indicates the temporal disconnect between the coup d'état and the election. The second cannot take place before the first has been forgotten, or at least repressed by fear and a sense of self-preservation.

Hugo imagines Louis deepening the historical perspective by bringing his uncle into the picture:

> Nous nous partagerons, mon oncle et moi, l'histoire;
>   Le plus intelligent,
> C'est moi, certes! Il aura la fanfare de gloire,
>   J'aurai le sac d'argent.
>
> (30)

> [We'll share between us, my uncle and I, history;
>   I am the cleverer,
> Certainly! He shall have the fanfare of glory,
>   I the sack of silver.]

Louis is confident that his priority, money, is the one that counts. He has neither the intelligence nor the passion of the hero, and his designs are more worldly and more individually satisfying. He is happy to use his uncle's name but only so he can profit from it:

> Je me sers de son nom, splendide et vain tapage,
>   Tombé dans mon berceau.
> Le nain grimpe au géant. Je lui laisse sa page,
>   Mais j'en prends le verso.
>
> (30)

[I make use of his name, splendid and vain outrage,
  In my crib fell the curse.
The dwarf crawls to the giant. I'll leave him his page,
  But I'll take the reverse.]

Incapable of understanding or caring about what his uncle's myth represents for the country, Louis thinks only of what he has to gain from associating himself with it.

As the poem progresses, the images assigned to Louis become more grotesque and his crimes more severe:

> Cet infâme apportait à Dieu son attentat.
> Comme un loup qui se lèche après qu'il vient de mordre,
> Caressant sa moustache, il dit: J'ai sauvé l'ordre!
> Anges, recevez-moi dans votre légion!
> J'ai sauvé la famille et la religion!

(35)

> [This despicable creature brought his crime to God.
> Like a wolf who, having murdered, licks his paws.
> Stroking his whiskers he says: to save order was my cause!
> Angels, accept me as one of your legion!
> I've saved family and with it religion!]

Here Hugo contrasts his view of events with the emperor's. The use of the present tense by the narrator indicates the immediacy of the danger, while the *passé composé* of the following lines emphasizes the completed nature of the events at hand. The coup d'état has reestablished order, the watchword of tyrannical regimes. The emperor would have the people forget the violence and think only of the ordered society he has restored, one based on traditional values of family and religion. Hugo is having none of it, of course, and despite the sea's attempts to calm him, he insists on expressing his "bitter thoughts" (*âpre pensée*).

Hugo then turns to his ultimate weapon, the comparison between Louis-Napoléon and the Revolution that has enlightened the years leading up to the coup d'état. The poet even tries, in vain, to oust images of the Second Empire from his mind:

> Oh! Ne revenez pas, lugubres visions!
> Ciel! Nous allions en paix devant nous, nous faisions
> Chacun notre travail dans le siècle où nous sommes,

Le poète chantait l'œuvre immense des hommes,
La tribune parlait avec sa grande voix,
On brisait des échafauds, trônes, carcans, pavois,
Chaque jour décroissaient la haine et la souffrance,
Le genre humain suivait le progrès saint, la France
Marchait devant avec sa flamme sur le front,
Ces hommes sont venus! Lui, ce vivant affront,
Lui, ce bandit qu'on lave avec l'huile du sacre!
Ils sont venus, portant le deuil et le massacre,
Le meurtre, les linceuls, le fer, le sang, le feu;
Ils ont semé cela sur l'avenir, grand Dieu!

(38)

[Oh! Lugubrious visions, do not return!
Heavens! We went before us, each doing in turn
His own work in the century that is ours at present,
The poet sang mankind's immense achievement,
The forum conversed in redoubtable tones,
We shattered the scaffolds, pedestals, yokes, thrones,
Each day diminished suffering and abhorrence,
The human race followed holy progress, and France
Walked ever forward, her flame's light on her face,
Those men came then! Him, the living disgrace,
Him, the bandit they washed with holy water,
They came bringing with them mourning and slaughter,
Murder, death shrouds, iron, fire and blood;
That is what they have sewn the future with, great God!]

The poem becomes a battleground in which images of peace brought about by the Revolution contrast with the violence of the Second Empire. Louis is reduced to a bandit who has stolen the country from its people. The future in this first poem is not a bright one, and only God will be able to change the course of history that these scoundrels have set in motion.

There is great irony in some of the passages set forth in "Nox." When Hugo describes the Revolution as:

Toi qui par la terreur sauvas la liberté
Toi qui porte ce nom sombre: "Nécessité . . ."

(39)

[You who by terror saved liberty
You who bear the dark name: "Necessity."]

he uses some of the same terms found in his condemnations of
Louis-Napoléon. Is there a great deal of difference between the Revolution using the Terror in the name of Necessity and Louis-
Napoléon's use of military force in the name of Order? For Hugo,
the difference lies in the stature of the people and ideals involved:

> Reste seul à jamais, Titan quatre-vingt-treize!
> Rien d'aussi grand que toi ne viendrait après toi.
>
> (39)

> [Remain alone forever, Titan ninety-three!
> Nothing as great as you shall ever come after you.]

Here we see the mythological terminology so prevalent in *Les Châtiments.* Louis-Napoléon is clearly not a Titan, and therefore he has
no right to resort to violence to secure his ultimate goal of order
and empire.

Hugo speaks, in the name of all the French, on behalf of a Christian ideal based on love:

> Ce que la France veut pour toujours désormais,
> C'est l'amour rayonnant sur ses calmes sommets,
> La loi sainte du Christ, la fraternité pure.
>
> (39)

> [What France desires forever from now on,
> Is for love to shine over her calm mountainsides,
> The holy law of Christ, purest brotherhood.]

Only through a rejection of violence and tyranny can France pros-
per. Only through the embrace of Christian notions of love and
peace can the country return to living the ideals of the Revolution.
Hugo will return to these themes throughout the work, as he calls
more and more specifically for a return to democracy in the form of
a republic. He wants to win this Titanic struggle, but he wants to do
so with dignity:

"Etre vainqueurs, c'est peu, mais rester grands, c'est tout" (40). / [To
be conqueror is little, to remain great is everything.]

The first poem of *Les Châtiments* contains all the elements of
Hugo's political and poetic project: rejection of the emperor, com-

parison of the glory of the Revolution and Napoléon I with the corruption of the Second Empire, and a call for a new France, based on Christian and democratic ideology. In these ideas, we see the crucial role played by memory. As Hugo looks back on the coup d'état that has led to his exile, he then projects his thoughts further into the past in order to construct the comparison between the Revolution and the Second Empire. His vision of the future of France is based solidly on the past, both revolutionary and Christian. Only by destroying the immediate past will France be able to achieve Hugo's beloved *progress* toward a republic. But France will never be able to destroy the empire if she forgets how that regime took power. Hugo is there to remind them, hammering away at his reader's imagination ultimately in order to rewrite collective memory.

Evil

Louis-Napoléon represents for Hugo all that is evil in the world. The nephew's attempt to emulate his uncle, first by attempting to overthrow the government by an invasion from outside the country and later by trying to recreate the empire, render him the most dangerous sort of threat to Hugo's ideals. Louis is a liar (renunciation of the presidential oath), a thief (appropriation of government funds for his personal use), a murderer (the coup d'état cost scores of lives) and a megalomaniac who will lead France into disastrous foreign campaigns. The poems of *Les Châtiments* relentlessly remind the reader of Louis' perfidy.

In the third poem of the collection, Hugo attacks the press loyal to the new emperor, calling them a "tas de dévots" [bunch of worshipers]. In doing so, he establishes the parameters of a battle of words that will last through much of Hugo's exile. As the emperor's mouthpiece, *Le Moniteur,* launches broadsides against the exiled poet, Hugo responds in kind. Here he presents his case against the official *gazettes*:

> Cela hurle en grinçant un *benedicat vos*;
> C'est laid, c'est vieux, c'est noir.
>
> (47)

> [It screams, while hissing a *benedicat vos;* (may the Lord be with you);
> It's ugly, it's old, it's black.]

Hugo uses an interesting tactic, assigning religious appellations to Louis-Napoléon's followers. Hugo will use such irony throughout these poems in order to show the heresy of such worship of the emperor.

According to Hugo, the greatest crime committed in these publications, apart from the outright distortion of the truth, is the limits put on the imagination, particularly on poets and writers such as himself. These *gazettes* are as adept at their use of the past as Hugo. By citing writers known to all French readers, Molière, Pascal, Rousseau, Voltaire, and Diderot, the papers have appropriated France's literary history and stifled independent thought. Propaganda replaces logic, and people of *esprit* such as Hugo, who represent a threat to such complacency, are sent into exile and/or silenced. The dominant voice is the only one to be heard, "la seule qui soit reçue au paradis [the only one that will be welcome in paradise]."

The emperor's mouthpieces have not only silenced contemporary critics, they have eliminated all references to the roots of western classical society, and even treated God as a servant:

> Ils écrivent à Dieu comme à leur intendant
> Critiquant, gourmandant, et lui demandant compte . . .
> Ils ont supprimé Rome, ils auraient détruit Sparte.
> Ces drôles sont charmés de Monsieur Bonaparte.
>
> (48)

> [They write to God as if to an employee
> Criticizing, demanding answers, openly greedy . . .
> They've eliminated Rome, they'd've destroyed Sparta.
> These fellows are charmed by Monsieur Bonaparte.]

The battle is not solely between Hugo and Louis-Napoléon, each one using the images of the past that suit his purpose. An ideological war is fought with words culled from the collective conscience, images constructed from fragments of the historical past. Each combatant selects the memories that will best serve him, in order to create a narrative that will achieve lasting power. Hugo remains supremely confident throughout that on this kind of battlefield he will emerge victorious.

In "A Juvénal" (6–13) Hugo explains how the empire's propaganda machine has managed to transform its crimes into good works. They have succeeded in making the people forget the bloody events that took place in the streets of Paris and concentrate only on how much money they stand to earn under the empire. Philosophical and ethical connections between the past and present are corrupted by the promise of a materially better future. Collective memory can be easily manipulated if you know the right words to use:

> . . . Lorsqu'un peu de temps sur le sang a passé,
> Après un an ou deux, c'est une découverte,
> Quoi qu'en disent les morts avec leur bouche verte,
> Le meurtre n'est plus meurtre et le vol n'est plus vol.
>
> (246)

> [. . . Once a little time has passed through the blood,
> After one year or two, a discovery's released,
> Despite what may say the green lips of the deceased.
> Murder is no longer murder, theft no longer theft.]

The dominant discourse has convinced the people to ignore voices of discord:

> O miracle! Entouré de croyants et d'apôtres,
> En dépit des rêveurs, en dépit de nous autres
> Noirs poètes bourrus qui n'y comprenons rien,
> Le mal prend tout à coup la figure du bien.
>
> (246)

> [O miracle! Surrounded by apostles and believers,
> In spite of us poets, in spite of dream weavers,
> Thick-headed, by whom nothing is understood,
> Evil suddenly wears the face of good.]

The moral here is that time changes any story into a completely different history. "En vieillissant, le crime devient beau," [As it ages, crime becomes beautiful] symbolizes not just Louis-Napoléon's hold on power, but the vital tool necessary for all governments to convince the people that their discourse is the valid one.

Louis Napoléon had for the moment the ultimate weapon, censorship. For a writer such as Hugo, the greatest danger was the Faider law, enacted December 20, 1852, which criminalized those who committed the least offense against a monarch (*Préface*, 6–7). Hugo and Louis-Napoléon fought their battles with words, the former attacking, while the latter defended by attempting to silence criticism. The Faider law was the most blatant attempt by the government to eliminate attacks by critics, most especially, Hugo. We know that Hugo continued his diatribes from exile, but the law had the effect of making diffusion of his works extremely difficult. *Napoléon le petit* was published openly in Brussels but had to be smuggled into France. *Les Châtiments* proved to have an even smaller readership. Yet Hugo went on fighting, and his poems show the clarity with which he saw his situation.

In protesting the Faider law, Hugo goes straight to the idea of the constitution as the guarantor of freedom of speech (3–14: "A propos de la Loi Faider"). The people, in their wisdom, adopt the constitution and then proceed to live happily by its tenets. The problem comes later, when the people take freedom for granted and allow evildoers to usurp its power:

> Un beau matin, le peuple en s'éveillant va voir
> Sa constitution, temple de son pouvoir;
> Hélas! De l'antre auguste on a fait une niche.
> Il y mit un lion, il y trouve une caniche.

(135)

> [One lovely morning, the people rising go to find
> His constitution: his power enshrined;
> Alas, of the great lair they've made a kennel.
> He left a lion there, but there he finds a poodle.]

By forgetting to appreciate the source of their freedom, the people have allowed the constitution to be debased. Without a written guarantee of freedom, no one will remember what those specific freedoms were supposed to be. These freedoms are protected only through the filter of national conscience, and by neglecting to remember, the people allow usurpers to rewrite the cherished words of the Revolution. Hugo is here to remind them of their forgetfulness, to exhort them never to be negligent again, once the tide has turned and a new constitution is in place.

Censorship results in the strengthening of the press favorable to Louis-Napoléon. The owners of newspapers are members of the bourgeoisie, with whom Hugo is particularly unhappy. They are the ones who helped Louis-Napoléon take power, all in a self-interested grab for money and power. Even those not directly implicated in the coup d'état are accused of complacency. In "Un Bon Bourgeois dans sa maison" [A Good Bourgeois in his House] he clarifies his

image of these happy few by comparing them with a prosperous man
from China. Again, he begins the piece with a quotation in prose,
this time in the form of a letter:

"Mais que je suis heureux d'être né en Chine! Je possède une maison pour m'abriter, j'ai de quoi manger et boire, j'ai toutes les com-
modités de l'existence, j'ai des habits, des bonnets et une multitude
d'agréments; en vérité la félicité la plus grande est mon partage!"
(115). [How happy I am to have been born in China! I have a house
to shelter me, plenty to eat and drink, I have all the conveniences of
existence, I have clothes, hats, and a multitude of luxuries; in truth,
the greatest happiness is my share!] Hugo accuses the bourgeoisie
of both demagogy and cowardice.

The cowardice of the bourgeoisie, their inability to see beyond the
material comforts afforded them under the new empire, angers
Hugo beyond any point we have seen before. For him, Louis' actions
are crimes that must be punished and then forgotten, but the complicity of the bourgeoisie is something he will never forget. Not only
did they not prevent the coup d'état, but they also refuse now to
listen to Hugo's calls for justice. Even if they have read *Napoléon le
petit*, which many of them undoubtedly have, they are not ready or
willing to take any action against the bandits in power. They are
warm and well fed; they are not going to risk the loss of material
comfort for the vague promise of some future paradise. They have
seen the disorder of the Second Republic and, consequently, are
happy to have calm restored to the society that affords them this
comfortable way of life. While Hugo calls for them to be judged at
the same time as the perpetrators of the coup d'état, he does not
have the same assurance that the memory of their cowardice will be
so easily washed away.

Hugo often places this depressing contemporary situation in a setting that is lower, more base, more vile than the rest of recorded
history: "L'histoire a pour égout des temps comme les nôtres"(3–
12, 134). [Times like ours are the sewers of history.] These locales
can take the form of caves, basements, hell, or here, a sewer. Such
an image speaks for itself, as the reader immediately conjures up
the sights, sounds and especially the smell of a sewer. Here is where
revolutionary ideals have been soiled and debased beyond the point
of human tolerance. Louis-Napoléon and his men have filtered out
all that is pure, leaving only the waste behind. The just and the wise
are hanging from gallows that no one dares approach. The women
have become lascivious, the men gluttonous sharks. The poet estab-

lishes a dichotomy represented by freedom and justice on the heights and evil down below. His role will be continually to call attention to the ideal that has been forgotten by contemporary society.

Hugo returns in "L'Egout de Rome" (7–13) [The Sewers of Rome] to some of his favorite themes: the sewer that France has become during the empire, opposed to the glory of Rome. Even that great republic was led to ruin by the corruption of her rulers, and Hugo sees the same process happening in France. All that was positive about the previous regime has been forgotten:

"Ici, l'oubli, la peste et la nuit font leurs œuvres" (274). / [Here, oblivion, plague and night do their work.]

The sewer is the antithesis of the morning star; while the former is a place of darkness, forgetting and filth, the latter represents a new awakening in the crisp air of dawn.

The morning star is not the only image of nature that Hugo uses in order to contrast the purity of the natural world with the filth of the corrupted society of man. He often shows the poet retiring to the countryside in order to escape the horrors of the town. In this poem, he has just been informed of Louis' "meurtre juridique" [a legal murder] of some of his enemies, and he can no longer stand the misery of the city. Only the fresh air of the countryside can change his state of mind:

Je m'enfuis dans les champs paisibles et dorés;
O contre-coups du crime au fond de l'âme humaine.

(7:5:276)

[I shall flee to the golden and peaceful fields;
O consequence of the crime in the depths of the human soul.]

The human soul has come to represent all that is criminal in this world. Only the countryside and his faith in God can restore the poet to a state of calm. As we have seen throughout these poems, Hugo's faith in his fellow man never wavers. If criminality resides in the human mind, so does the capacity to rectify their wrongs and to forget the wrongs of the recent emperor in order to return to a state of grace, represented by his uncle and a not so distant memory of freedom and justice.

References to Louis' inferiority compared to his uncle and other revolutionary figures abound and become more explicit as the volume progresses. Hugo compares Louis' naïveté to the glorious revolutionary past (3–12):

> Te figures-tu donc que ceci durera?
> Prends-tu pour du granit ce décor d'opéra?
> Paris dompté! Par toi! Dans quelle apocalypse
> Lit-on que le géant devant le nain s'éclipse?
>
> (133)

> [You imagine, then, do you, that this will endure?
> Do you take for real granite the opera's décor?
> Paris subdued! By you! In what apocalypse
> Does one read that the giant by the dwarf is eclipsed?]

History will eventually be the judge, and Hugo knows what it will say.

Hugo waits until this sixth book to entitle a poem "Napoléon III" (6–1). Having established his major arguments in the preceding poems, he unleashes his wrath in a scathing comparison between Napoléon I and the current emperor. In so doing, he directly recalls all the great names of the Revolution, including his own father and uncles who served in the fight for freedom. Louis is once again portrayed as a pretender who does not measure up to his uncle:

> Faquin! Tu t'es soudé, chargé d'un vil butin,
> Toi, l'homme du hasard, à l'homme du destin!
> Tu fourres, impudent, ton front dans ses couronnes!
>
> (216)

> [Scoundrel! You've bound yourself, vile loot in hand,
> You, the man of chance, to destiny's man!
> You shamelessly shove your forehead into his crowns!]

Napoléon I is associated with destiny, always advancing toward a brighter future. His nephew represents the whims of history, the weak man who inherited power by chance and uses it only for personal gain. His view is always toward the past, his only strength lying in the fortuitous occasion of his birth into the family of a true hero, while the world advances toward the brighter future Hugo foresees, one based on true achievement and courage.

Like the tide, Louis-Napoléon's power and then his legacy will recede. No matter how hard he tries to "cacher son carcan à l'histoire" [to hide his yoke from history], posterity will assign him a negative role (7–2: "La Reculade"). He has been unable to take the place of his uncle, and the memory of the first emperor will forever doom the second to inferior status:

> Et dans sa sombre plaine, ô douleur, j'entends rire
> Le noir lion de Waterloo!
>
> (269)

> [And in his dark plain, oh despair, I hear laughing
> The black lion of Waterloo!]

The ever-present image of the lion reinforces Louis' secondary status, his role as a vile dog ("chien avili").

One final comparison between uncle and nephew shows Hugo's absolute faith in the destruction of the memory of Louis-Napoléon. In *Chanson* (6) Hugo writes of Napoléon I: "Sa grandeur éblouit l'histoire" (278). / [His greatness dazzles history.]

And of Louis-Napoléon:

> Toi, son singe, marche derrière,
> Petit, petit
>
> (278).

> [You, his monkey, walk behind,
> Little, little.]

This last line becomes the refrain of the poem and of this collection of poems. The nephew will never measure up to the uncle, and his memory will sink into the mud:

> Toi, tu te noiras dans la fange,
> Petit, petit.
>
> (279)

> [You will drown yourself in the mire,
> Little, little.]

Such destruction of memory is Hugo's ultimate goal because by forgetting the emperor, the people will be able to move forward.

According to Hugo, Louis-Napoléon will have no place at all in the annals of history. His lot deserves the ultimate punishment,

oblivion. Hugo's writings all work toward this end. By constantly attacking the emperor during the present day of his reign, Hugo is
working toward revising and then destroying memories of the emperor and his regime.

> Tu dis ton orgueil: je vais être historique.
> Non, coquin! Le charnier des rois t'est interdit;
> Non, tu n'entreras point dans l'histoire, bandit!
>
> (7–10: 290)

> [You state your arrogance: I will be historical.
> No, you rascal! From the king's crypt you are banned;
> Never shall you enter into history, you brigand.]

Hugo sees such a fate as worse than death, for the death of remembrance would mean the end of Louis' aspirations to immortality.
This desire to make the people forget Louis is as strong as Hugo's
wish to make them remember revolutionary ideals.

THE DIFFERENT ROLES OF THE POET

Hugo sees himself as a, or perhaps the, savior of the French people. In this first poem of the First Book (*La Société est sauvée* I),
Hugo's words become an instrument of salvation and even military
power:

> France! à l'heure où tu te prosternes . . .
> Le banni, debout sur la grève . . .
> Parlera dans l'ombre tout haut;
> Et ses paroles, qui menacent,
> Ses paroles, dont l'éclair luit,
> Seront comme des mains qui passent
> Tenant des glaives dans la nuit.

> [France! In the hour where you bow down . . .
> The banished one, standing on the bank . . .
> Will speak aloud in the shadows;
> And his words, a looming menace,
> His words that glow with lightning's might,
> Will be akin to hands that pass
> Carrying broadswords in the night.]

His words take on superhuman qualities:

> Elles feront frémir les marbres . . .
> Elles seront l'airain qui sonne . . .
>
> (41)

> [They will make marble shake . . .
> They will be the brass that sounds . . .]

in order to appeal to the French people, who have been lulled to sleep by the Emperor's propaganda.

> Sur les races qui se transforment,
> Sombre orage, elles planeront;
> Et si ceux qui vivent s'endorment,
> Ceux qui sont morts se réveilleront.

> [Over the transforming numbers,
> Lightless storm, aloft they will glide;
> And if those who live do slumber,
> Those who are dead will arise.]

The emphasis on the power of the poet's words to effect actual change in the psyche of the French people is of capital importance. This is Hugo's driving force in exile, his way of taking an active part in resisting tyranny. The last line of the poem points out the major effect his words will have: they will reach into the past (French history) to awaken the dead (the spirit of the Revolution).

Hugo patiently begins to construct the image of himself as a prophet, and more specifically, as a man of God. In "A un martyr" (1–8) [To a martyr] he contrasts the good priest with the bad, and the good priest bears a striking resemblance to the poet:

> Il s'est dit qu'il est bon d'éclairer dans leur nuit
> Ces peuples, égarés loin du progrès qui luit.
>
> (60)

> [He's decided it's good to illume in their night
> These people, distraught, far from progress's light.]

The wicked priests, who espouse the doctrine of the emperor, are seen as willing to sell their souls, along with their God: "Ils vendent

Jésus-Christ! ils vendent Jésus-Christ!'' (61). / [They sell Jesus Christ! they sell Jesus Christ!] Hugo will expose the truth that these priests have sold, if the people will listen to his version of it. Visions of a past in which truth and justice reigned compete with those of the present discourse, dominated by the emperor's propaganda, the institution most antithetical to the dissemination of truth.

The source of the power of art lies in the talent of the artist and in the willingness of the reader or spectator to believe the message being communicated. Only the harmonious working together of these two can bring about change, peace, justice, and truth. All of these ideals are based on a common heritage, a common memory that determines the mores and traditions of a society. When any force attempts to subvert these memories, tyranny results. Then it is up to the artist to remind the people of their forgotten antecedent, in this case the Revolution.

"L'Art et le peuple" (1–9) [Art and the people] is Hugo's attempt to make the French people see that art is as powerful as any other weapon against the forces of tyranny.

> L'art, c'est la pensée humaine
> Qui va brisant toute chaîne!
> L'art, c'est le doux conquérant!
> A lui le Rhin et le Tibre!
> Peuple esclave, il te fait libre;
> Peuple libre, il te fait grand!
>
> (64)

> [Art is humanity's thought
> That goes breaking every bond!
> The gentle subduer is he!
> To him the Tiber and Rhine!
> He sets free the confined!
> He makes great the free.]

One might leave the analysis of this quite simple poem at this point, but what strikes the reader is the date noted at the end of the piece: 6 November 1851. The poem was thus written *before* the coup d'état of December. Hugo already sees the French people as enslaved by the dominant discourse that is leading them toward disaster. His voice is raised in protest well before his exile. He is prescient, as always, and takes the lead in criticizing individuals and contemporary events that are undermining the Second Republic. It is fitting that the poem finds its way into a collection of pieces written many months later, for the idea that art can set you free is even more telling after the republic has given way to the Second Empire.

The poet's voice is not the only one to be heard; the people must break into song to reaffirm their ancient beliefs in freedom and peace:

> Ta voix joyeuse et profonde
> Est l'espérance du monde,
> O grand peuple fraternel!
>
> (65)

> [Your voice joyful and deep
> Is the world's strongest hope,
> O great fraternal people!]

The song of the people is equated to the lion's roar, a symbol of the power of the voice and of its song. The importance of song can be seen throughout this volume, as Hugo entitles a number of his poems "Chanson" [Song]. The feeling of fraternity comes through each of these poems. Hugo the exile does not suffer alone. His fellow French citizens are equally exiled in their own homes, and only a common voice can save them. The poet, and by implication other artists, can set them free.

Hugo is the avenging poet who will never relent until his appetite for justice has been sated. In the end he will become the jailer of those who imposed their lies on the French people. He has refused their version of history and will tolerate nothing but the truth:

> J'ai mis des verrous à l'histoire;
> L'histoire est un bagne aujourd'hui.
>
> (1–11, 68)

> [I've put locks on history;
> History is a prison today.]

As the tramps, beggars, and vile rascals try to make the people forget their revolutionary past in favor of the imperial version, the poet will rise up and cry "Memento!" The poet will be the "esprit vengeur" [vengeful spirit] who ousts the demons and sets the people free. Conversely, Hugo urges the people to oust the emperor from their memories. Only then will they be able to move forward.

In "L'Autre Président" (2–6) [The Other President], Hugo repeats this idea.

> Que ce vil souvenir soit à jamais détruit!
> Qu'il se dissolve là! Qu'il y devienne informe,
>   Et pareil à la nuit!

> [May the vile memory into oblivion take flight!
> May it dissipate there! May it become formless,
>   And the same as the night!]

Once the memory has been expunged, history will take over the cleansing process:

> Et que l'histoire un jour ne s'en rende plus compte,
> Et dise en le voyant dans la fange étendue:
> —On ne sait ce que c'est. C'est quelque vieille honte
>   Dont le nom s'est perdu!

(89)

> [And that one day history, from which he'll be erased,
> Will say upon seeing him in the gutter tossed:
> —We don't know what this is. It is some old disgrace
>   Whose name has been lost!]

The perpetrators of the tyranny will be sent to oblivion, and it will be up to the poets to keep them there:

> Poètes qui, portant dans vos mains des massues,
>   Gardez ce sombre seuil . . .

> [Poets who, carrying clubs in your hands,
>   Guard this dark threshold. . . .]

The duty of the poet is forever taking clearer shape in these poems. From protester to judge, his role increases in importance and ferocity. One constant is the role of memory, individual and collective, in remembering the republican past and in forgetting the present of the empire. This combination, spurred on by the poet, is the only way toward progress.

Hugo steps out of verse for a moment to cite a newspaper article that had lasting consequences for his future works:

M. Victor Hugo vient de publier à Bruxelles un livre qui a pour titre: *Napoléon le petit,* et qui renferme les calomnies les plus odieuses contre le prince-président.

On raconte, qu'un des jours de la semaine dernière, un fonctionnaire apporta ce libelle à Saint-Cloud. Lorsque Louis-Napoléon le vit, il le prit, l'examina, un instant avec le sourire du mépris sur ses lèvres; puis, s'adressant aux personnes qui l'entouraient, il dit, en leur montrant le pamphlet: "Voyez, messieurs, voici Napoléon-le-petit, par Victor Hugo-le-grand" (*Journaux Elyséens,* août 1852, 106.)

[Mr. Victor Hugo has just published, in Brussels, a book whose title is *Napoléon the Little,* and which levels the most odious slander against the prince-president.

It is said that one day last week, a civil servant brought this document to Saint-Cloud. When Louis-Napoléon saw it, he took it, examined it for a moment with a hateful smile on his lips; then, addressing the persons around him, he said, indicating the pamphlet: "You see here, sirs, Napoléon-the-Little, by Victor-Hugo-the-Great."]

Hugo will create from this episode his *L'Homme qui rit* (1869) [*The Man Who Laughs*]. Here he makes a first riposte by once again enlisting history on his side:

> Ah! tu finiras bien par hurler, misérable! . . .
> L'histoire à mes côtés met à nu ton épaule.
>
> (3–2; 106)

[Ah! You'll certainly end up screaming, wretched man! . . .
History at my side exposes your shoulder.]

Images such as "le fer rouge" [the red iron] render the poet executioner as well as judge. History will diminish Louis's legacy and place the instrument of revenge in the hand of the poet as representative of the French people.

We have seen the critical role played in history by those who have had the courage to say "no." In "Non" Hugo gives explicit voice to this concept, but it is not the simple rejection of the emperor we have seen up to this point. Hugo is now asking the people to abstain from taking immediate action, to wait until the moment is right, to wait and remember all that is being done to them and their freedom.

> Jamais au criminel son crime ne pardonne;
> Mais gardez, croyez-moi, la vengeance au fourreau;

Attendez; ayez foi dans les ordres que donne
Dieu, juge patient, au temps, tardif bourreau!

(3–16: 140)

[Never forgive the criminal for his crime;
But keep, believe me, vengeance in its cover;
Wait; have faith in God's instructions to time,
From Him, patient judge, to the executioner.]

Memory now takes on a new role, that of executioner, albeit a delayed one. To assassinate Louis now would mean lowering the people to his level of crime and indecency. His entry into hell will be that much clearer after he has had time to accumulate his evil doings.

Laissons vivre le traître en sa honte insondable.
Ce sang humilierait même le vil couteau.
Laissons venir le temps, l'inconnu formidable
Qui tient le châtiment sous son manteau.

(140)

[Let the traitor live in his unfathomable shame.
The vilest dagger would take offense to his blood.
Let us let time advance, the great unnamed
Which holds the punishment under its hood.]

Only by letting the empire run its course will the ouster of the emperor have the power to rejuvenate French society.

At first glance, this would seem to be a curious attitude for Hugo to take. One would imagine him to be looking forward to some sort of popular uprising against the emperor, and an assassination would seem to be the ultimate remedy for all the wrongs against which Hugo has been declaiming. On the other hand, Hugo shows throughout his writing, and particularly in *Les Misérables* that he is not a revolutionary. He writes here that he sees the reality of the situation, that even a successful attempt on Louis' life would not yield the desired results. Public opinion is not ready for such an act of violence, and the men taking power would act in the same repressive fashion as the emperor. He has understood that his power lies in the written word that must be digested over a longer period of time. When historical events give the people the opportunity, they will use Hugo's words as inspiration in their fight to restore their rights under the constitution.

Hugo cannot resist the urge to compare himself, the exiled and persecuted poet, to Jesus Christ. He does so through contemporary images of political subterfuge and intolerance, but the implications are clear. He gives us a representative of the ruling group, no matter the nationality or time period. In "Paroles d'un conservateur à propos d'un perturbateur" [A conservative's words about a troublemaker], this orator is defending the punishment of a rebel who dared to speak against the forces of order:

> Il faut que l'ordre et que l'autorité
> Se défendent. Comment souffrir qu'on les discute?
> D'ailleurs les lois sont là pour qu'on les exécute.
>
> (7–11: 291)

> [It must be that order and authority
> Defend themselves. How can discussion be allowed?
> Besides, the laws exist so as to be carried out.]

It is the language of the rebel that the orator finds most disturbing:

> Ce novateur prêchait une philosophie:
> Amour, progrès, mots creux, et dont je me défie.
>
> (291)

> [This innovator a philosophy did cite:
> Love, progress, hollow words, against which I fight.]

Condemnation of Hugo's most cherished ideals is tantamount to the Romans' rejection of the teachings of Christ. Later on, the orator accuses the rebel: "Il égarait les masses" (291). [He misled the masses]. Now Hugo's goal in the poem becomes clear. The rebel is the poet who uses words to convince the masses that the forces of order and authority are the voices of tyranny. The reaction of these forces is swift: the poet is exiled, Christ is crucified. We do not need the final stanza's identification of the rebel to know that Hugo is comparing himself to Christ; we have known it all along. The prophet has come to the people and delivered his sermon. It is up to them to follow his preaching and make sure words such as "love" and "progress" become the dominant philosophy of the times.

In "Ultima Verba" (7–14), Hugo reiterates the notion of the poet who says "no." Despite his status as an exile, he will continue to call out for justice:

> Je serai, sous le sac de cendre qui me couvre,
> La voix qui dit: malheur! La bouche qui dit: non!

> [I will be, under the sack of ashes that covers me,
> The voice that says: misfortune! The mouth that says: no!]

Even as the memory of the physical world he left behind fades, his sense of duty will never waver:

> Je ne reverrai pas ta rive qui nous tente,
> France! Hors le devoir, hélas! J'oublierai tout.
>
> (306)

> [I will no longer see your shore that tempts us,
> France! Except for duty, alas! I'll forget it all.]

The forgetting that is natural over time does not overwhelm the poet. His sights are fixed on the future, and he will stay the course. He does not even spend much energy attacking his fellow exiles who have not remained faithful to the cause. If he remains the only re-sister, so be it:

> Si l'on n'est plus que mille, eh bien, j'en suis! Si même
> Ils ne sont plus que cent, je brave encor Sylla;
> S'il en demeure dix, je serai le dixième;
> Et s'il n'en reste qu'un, je serai celui-là!
>
> (307)

> [If they're only a thousand, well then I'm there! And if
> Just one hundred remain, I'll still take Sylla on;
> If only ten stay behind, I will be the tenth.
> And if just one remains, I will be that one.]

While Hugo was not the only voice of protest heard throughout the empire, his was certainly the most important and the most strident. From his exile, he must have assuredly felt alone in his quest for a return to the light.

After preaching patience and a slow vengeance aided by unfold-ing events, Hugo finally unleashes an unbridled call for action. He

appeals to the French people to awaken and strike back at the op-
pressor. Their incentive will come from their memory of the tyranny
that has been imposed on them:

> Vous n'êtes pas armés? Qu'importe!
> Prends ta fourche, prends ton marteau!
> Délivrez, frémissant de rage,
> Votre pays de l'esclavage,
> Votre mémoire du mépris!
>
> (6–6: 231–32)

> [You're not armed? No matter!
> Take your pitchfork, take your hammer!
> Deliver, trembling with rage,
> Your country from bondage,
> Your memory from hate!]

These are the words he has wanted to say all along. Having constructed an argument for why vengeance will only come slowly, he
can contain himself no longer. Only action will suffice now. He has
taken the first step by going into exile. It is up to the people, now
that they have had time to see the tenor of this emperor's reign, to
rise up against him in any way they can.

The question remains, however, as to how effective this kind of
call to action can be. It is all well and good to ask a peasant to attack
the empire with his hammer; it is another matter to have him actually do it, much less succeed. We must see then this poem as an expression of Hugo's frustration. He does not realistically expect, or
even want, the people to revolt, but he proposes it here as an ideal.
His true feelings may be better represented by a sentence in the
"Déclaration des proscrits républicains de Jersey" (31 October
1852) [Declaration of Exiled Republicans of Jersey]: "En présence
de M. Bonaparte et de son gouvernement, le citoyen, digne de ce
nom, ne fait qu'une chose et n'a qu'une chose à faire: charger son
fusil et attendre l'heure" (239). [In the presence of M. Bonaparte
and his government, the citizen worthy of his name only does one
thing and only has one thing to do: load his gun and wait for the
time to come.] The last part of this phrase is absent from the poem
calling for immediate action, but its implication is there. Action, yes,
but at the right time.

As Hugo approaches the end of this collection, the tone becomes
increasingly optimistic. Images of horror and hell are replaced by

hope and visions of a better world to come, a world based on the memory of what once was. "Stella" (6–15) represents the morning star, his companion ("ma sœur") [my sister] as he gazes out to sea just before dawn. She is the agent of morning, of rebirth:

> Je suis l'astre qui vient d'abord.
> Je suis celle qu'on croit dans la tombe et qui sort.
>
> (258)

> [I am the star that comes before.
> I am she they believe in the tomb, who's not there anymore.]

There is a distinct flavor of memory here, as the star takes the poet back to the beginning of civilization. She is the fruit of the rebuilding of a destroyed world. Her power lies in poetry ("la poésie ardente"), and she has inspired both Moses and Dante.

The morning star uses her poetic powers of persuasion to make a call to action:

> J'arrive. Levez-vous, vertu, courage, foi!
> Penseurs, esprits! montez sur la tour, sentinelles!
>
> (258)

> [I'm coming. Get up, virtue, courage, faith!
> Thinkers, spirits! go up on the tower, sentinels!]

The people, who have slept through this time of trouble, must now awake and take action to rebuild society:

> Debout, vous qui dormez;—car celui qui me suit,
> Car celui qui m'envoie en avant la première,
> C'est l'ange Liberté, c'est le géant Lumière!
>
> (258)

> [Get up, you who sleep;—because he who follows me,
> Because he who sends me before the fight,
> Is the angel Liberty, is the giant Light!]

Through identification with the morning star, Hugo sets himself up as the guiding light that the French people must follow toward freedom; toward the knowledge necessary to re-create the republican ideal that they knew before the empire. The poet has this privileged place because he has the power of the word; the voice to make the call to action. And his call relies on his powers of recall to instill in the collective memory images of what has been lost. Only then can it be regained.

PROGRESS

The ultimate force in Hugo's universe is his notion of progress. From the darkness of the present a better future will emerge. In "La Force des choses" (7–12) [The Power of Things], Hugo gives us the image of liberty growing as the grass on the plains, slowly, patiently. The emergence of the republican ideal will evolve naturally, as the old system sheds its shell to emerge as a new being:

> Du vieil univers mort briser la carapace . . .
> Le passé n'est que l'œuf d'où tu sors, Légion!
>
> (300–301)

> [From the old dead universe shatter the shell . . .
> The past is only the egg from which you hatch, Legion!]

The role of the poet is to see these future events and communicate them to his readers. He has the power of foresight because he has not been lulled to sleep by promises of riches or by slogans promoting order and stability. He is already living the future because of his fidelity to the ideal. With the help of the natural world and the evolution of political events, the poet will see his readers through the darkness and into the light.

It is, in fact, when Hugo turns his sights on the future, rather than another condemnation of the events of December 1851, that he does some of his most effective writing. In 4–13 ("On loge la nuit") [We stay the night] he writes: "Arrive l'avenir, le gendarme de Dieu" (172) [Come, future, policeman of God]. The future is now a policeman as well as the executioner. Even the emperor will realize that his legacy has been soiled by his unjust actions:

> Regarde en frémissant dans la postérité
> Ta mémoire difforme.
>
> (5–10, 195)

[Look trembling upon posterity
At your deformed memory.]

In "A quatre prisonniers (après leur condamnation)" (4–12) [To four prisoners (after their condemnation)] the poet clearly shows his reliance on the future to avenge the injustices of the present. "Ils vous ont condamnés, que l'avenir les juge!" (167) [They've condemned you, may the future be their judge!] This poem shows all of the major themes of Hugo's protest writing from exile: persecution, silenced voices, and hope for the future based on religious belief. He calls the four prisoners "mes fils," [my sons] as if he were the father of all of them instead of just his two sons, Charles and François-Victor. Hugo opposes the prisoners' honor to the vile judges, "an abject and stupid group." The more he paints the regime as representative of the anti-Christ, the greater his intended effect on the reader.

The shorter lines at the end of each stanza accentuate descriptions of the prisoners ("ta douceur intrépide . . . ton sourire indigné") [your intrepid gentleness . . . your indignant smile] or negative images of the consequences of repression ("dans l'ombre, Douze sépulcres rangés) [in the shadow, Twelve sepulchers lined up] or even the crimes of which they are accused, and of which Hugo approves ("Insulté la guillotine, Et vengé le crucifix!" [167] [The guillotine insulted, And the crucifix avenged!])

The most telling phrase however is one that is seen throughout Hugo's writing from exile: "Ils vous ont condamnés, que l'avenir les juge!" [They've condemned you, may the future be their judge!] There is no question about who will prevail in the long run. The meek will prevail, the condemned will be justified and poets will be heard again. Just as Jesus's persecution and crucifixion liberated all Christians, these prisoners'—and by extension, Hugo's—suffering will liberate France from the clutches of evil.

We have seen elsewhere Hugo's view that retribution will come slowly and that great patience is required to make it come to pass. He repeats that idea in a short but explicit poem (5–12):

> Dès que ce grand forfait est commis, point de grâce;
> La Peine au fond des cieux, lente, mais jamais lasse,
> Se met en marche, et vient; son regard est serein.
> Elle tient sous son bras son fouet aux clos d'airain.

(201)

[As soon as this great crime takes place, no forgiveness;
Penalty on the skyline, slow, never listless,
Begins to move, and comes; her gaze is serene.
Under her arm, her brass-tipped whip can be seen.]

The imagery seen here picks up on many themes common to this volume: crime, vengeance and the inexorable progress toward the day when the criminal will be punished.

Hugo increases the pressure on the French people to remember. They have been lulled to sleep by the emperor's propaganda and have even prostituted themselves for their own gain ("Tu t'es prostitué à ce misérable homme!") [You've sold yourself to this wretched man!] In "Applaudissement" (6–16) ["Applause"] the accusatory tone continues, as he says that they have thrown away their memories of the Revolution:

> Tes propres souvenirs, folle, tu les lapides,
> La Marseillaise est morte à tes lèvres stupides.
>
> (260)

[You stone your own memories to death, insane one,
The Marseillaise is dead on your stupid lips.]

Forgetting brings about the worst abuses of freedom in a return to the prerevolutionary tyranny.

As we have seen before, however, forgetting can be turned into a positive. By setting aside their recent memories, the French people can move into a new, brighter future:

> Oui, nous verrons, ainsi va le progrès humain,
> De ce vil aujourd'hui naître un fier lendemain,
> Et tu rachèteras, ô prêtresse, ô guerrière,
> Par cent pas en avant chaque pas en arrière!
>
> (261)

[Yes, we will see, so goes human progress,
From this vile today a proud tomorrow emerges,
And you will buy back, o priestess, o soldier,
By one hundred steps forward, each step in reverse.]

This last image is striking because it represents everything Hugo has been saying about the power of memory to spur the people into action in order to create a new society. The synchronicity of certain forces—forgetting the empire and remembrance of the republic, their faith in him and his faith in God—will produce the desired result.

Hugo returns to his cherished notion of progress through the image of a caravan, moving slowly through all kinds of territory to arrive at its final destination. This journey takes on a religious connotation in "La Caravane" (7) : "Ce saint voyage a nom Progrès." (280) [This holy voyage whose name is Progress]. The route is long and slow, and at times they must stop and regroup, find the energy necessary to keep going. They are spurred on by their ideals: Liberté, Paix, Idéal, and Foi [Liberty, Peace, Ideal, and Faith].

Ironically, one of their greatest obstacles is memory. As they try to flee memories of the recent past, these images reach out in an attempt to bring them back into the world of evil they are escaping:

> C'est l'heure où le Passé, qu'ils laissent derrière eux,
> Voyant dans chacun d'eux une proie échappée,
> Surprend la caravane assoupie et campée,
> Et, surtout hors de l'ombre et du néant profond,
> Tâche de ressaisir ces esprits qui s'en vont.
>
> (281)

> [It's at this time that the Past, which they leave behind,
> Seeing each one of them as prey that has escaped,
> Surprises the caravan relaxed and encamped,
> And above all, out of the deep void's shadow,
> Attempts to recapture these spirits who are leaving.]

In the end, the caravan will arrive at its destination because the combination of its ideals is stronger than the past's pull on them. The lion of progress will make his voice heard above all others: "Ta grande voix monter vers les cieux étoilés!" (285) [Your great voice rises toward the starry skies!] The morning star is there again to receive progress's call. It will lead the caravan to the final destination, the site of liberty and freedom.

There remains the question of what form the destruction of the empire will take. Hugo does not take a stand on the matter until almost the end of the collection. Then he clearly delineates how he sees the triumph of the people: by rejecting the culture of violence they have witnessed during the empire, they will be free. In order to accomplish this rejection, they must stifle their urge for vengeance.

Hugo is talking, of course, about himself and his own urges. He would happily throw Louis-Napoléon to the lions, but he must remain above his baser instincts in order to keep the people focused on the ideals he proposes. And so in this poem, he calls for restraint. When the people have their moment of triumphant return to power, no one must die:

> Mais ces jours effrayants seront des jours sublimes.
> Tu feras expier à ces hommes leurs crimes,
> O peuple généreux, ô peuple frémissant,
> Sans glaive, sans verser une goutte de sang,
> Par la loi: sans pardon, sans fureur, sans tempête
> Non, que pas un cheveu ne tombe d'une tête.
>
> (7–9, 287)

> [But these horrifying days will turn to days sublime.
> You will make these men atone for their crimes,
> Oh trembling people, oh people filled with good,
> Without the sword, without one drop of blood,
> By the law: without forgiveness, fury or squall
> No, may not one strand of hair from one head fall.]

In the supreme sacrifice, the poet even proposes to spare his mortal enemy: "Tous ces hommes vivront. Peuple, pas même lui!" (287) [All these men will live. People, not even him!] Hugo cannot foresee, of course, how events will unfold, but he is certain of how they should go if there is to be stability again in the halls of government. He does not want a return of the Terror but an orderly transition. He hopes the empire will die through its own corruption and leave an open door for the people to recover peacefully their republic.

"Lux"

"Lux," the companion piece to the opening poem, "Nox," presents Hugo's vision of the world. All of the images he has created in the collection come to the fore at the end in order to summarize Hugo's project. Primary among them is the paradoxical relationship between present and past. He calls for the people to forget one era in order to remember another. At the same time, we see the ever-present urging to look toward the future:

> Car le passé se nomme haine
> Et l'avenir s'appelle amour!
>
> (311)

> [Because the past is called hate
> And the future is called love!]

Progress, in harmony with the natural world, will lead to happiness:

> Le progrès, ténébreuse abeille,
> Fait du bonheur avec nos maux.
>
> (311)

> [Progress, tenebrous honey bee,
> Makes happiness out of our pain.]

Hugo presents a vision of rebirth that adumbrates Zola's *Germinal* and portrays a world eerily similar to our ideal of modern Europe:

> Tout renaît. Le bonheur de chacun est accru
> De la félicité des nations entières.
> Plus de soldats l'épée au poing, plus de frontières,
> Plus de fisc, plus de glaive ayant forme de croix.
>
> (312)

> [All is reborn. Each one's happiness is drawn
> From the felicity of entire lands.
> No more borders, no more soldiers, weapons in hands,
> No more tax, no more sword in the shape of a cross.]

No more borders, a common currency. The only unfulfilled prophecy is the laying down of the sword.

Hugo never abandons the spiritual side of his ideal. His future is not just a political and social ideal, it is universal in nature:

> Radieux avenir. Essor universel!
> Epanouissement de l'homme sous le ciel!
>
> (313)

> [Radiant future. Universal growth flies!
> The blooming of man under the skies!]

The road to this better future will be long and tortuous, and great patience is required of those who take it:

Dieu nous essaie, amis. Ayons foi, soyons calmes . . .
Parce qu'il ne fait pas son œuvre tout de suite . . .

(315)

[God is testing us, friends. Have faith, let us be calm . . .
Because he does not complete his work right away . . .]

His will be a true republic where all voices will be heard: "O proscrits, l'avenir est aux peoples" (317) [Oh banished ones, the future
belongs to the people]. Not just the people of France, but all peoples. This idea is reminiscent of his call for a "United States of Europe," again prescient of the twenty-first century.

The tortured present will recede into oblivion, and the exiled will
return in triumph. Those who have died in exile will be martyrs for
the cause. They, not Louis, will be honored in the memories of the
people:

Et nous qui serons morts dans l'exil peut-être,
Martyrs saignants, pendant que les hommes, sans maître,
    Vivront, plus fiers, plus beaux,
Sous ce grand arbre, amour des cieux qu'il avoisine,
Nous nous réveillerons pour baiser sa racine
    Au fond de nos tombeaux.

(318)

[And we who shall die in exile may be,
Martyrs bleeding, while men with no masters, who are free,
    Will live, more beautiful and brave,
Under this great tree, beloved of heavenly space,
We will wake up, its sprawling roots to embrace,
    At the bottom of our graves.]

It is sometimes easy to forget that Hugo wrote most of these
poems between 1851 and 1853. At that time, no one, except Hugo,
could have predicted what would happen in 1870. Hugo had the
good fortune to survive his exile and see his future, or at least part
of it, come to pass.

"Lux" concludes *Les Châtiments*, a work in which Hugo confronts
and enhances reality through metaphor ("l'homme sépulcre" [the
man of the tomb] designates Napoléon III), personification ("Cette
chauve-souris qui sort des noirs marais" [This bat that emerges from
the black swamps]) and mythological imagery (Hugo, as Titan, op-

poses Louis, as mythological monster), in short, through the beauty of the poems themselves. The appeal of Hugo's vision comes from these literary techniques and opposes itself to the purely political power of Louis-Napoléon. The text transforms historical events into a new reality revealing the illusion of permanence embodied by the government in power. In Hugo's poems, words reclaim meanings they had in the more progressive periods predating Louis' rise to power. As the producer of beauty, the poet acts as a god who has the prophetic mission of leading the nation to a better future. The truths he expounds are eternal and cannot be subverted by the whims of the current power structure.

Hugo's poems become his historical vision, and in the following chapter we shall see how he develops it in *Les Misérables*, the novel that becomes the most powerful narrative of the time. The metaphorization of the narrative is completed in a work that touches the imagination of each reader through a combination of powerful imagery and an appeal to the reader's memory of historical events. Memory, history, and literature come together to correct the perception of recent history while calling for a better future.

5

Les Misérables : The Novel as Historical Allegory

LES MISÉRABLES MOVES THE METAPHORIC PROCESS ONE STEP FURTHER. The events of the novel take place earlier than the 1850s, yet they afford Hugo the vast fresco necessary to describe, analyze, conclude, and propose remedies for the injustice perpetrated on the people by Louis-Napoléon. The novel was an instant phenomenon because Hugo struck the right chord with the French populace; they were willing to be touched by the tribulations of Jean Valjean and Cosette, characters whose goodness shines through their troubled lives. The nineteenth-century realistic novel here meets the Romantic novel at its height, and the result is a work that gives full voice to Hugo's revolt.

By transcending the narrative limits of autobiography and poetry, Hugo the novelist becomes the recorder of his era in a more profound way. His characters take on the role of quasi-mythical figures representing universal truths such as freedom and justice, while still strongly rooted in the specific history of the nineteenth century. By setting the novel between 1815 and 1832, Hugo appeals to the reader's remembrances of Napoléon I and then of the freedoms won in the ensuing years to fashion his call for a return to a republican form of government. No longer tied directly to the specific events of 1851 to 1852, Hugo is freer to criticize through suggestion and metaphor. His story becomes more allegorical but more firmly entrenched in the sphere of memory. His readers have definite views on these years because they have had time to digest them and to see their effect on the present. Such reflection would not have been possible if Hugo had set the novel in the 1850s; this chronological distance, coupled with the narrative form of the novel, brings together the disparate discourses of memory, history, and fiction. It is here in the realm of the novel that Hugo emerges as one of the most significant historians of the French nineteenth century.

While *Napoléon le petit* and *Les Châtiments* attack Louis-Napoléon directly, *Les Misérables* shows the power of fiction to be just as effective in presenting Hugo's side of the story. It is not my intention here to do another detailed analysis of *Les Misérables*, but to look at ways in which Hugo manipulates the collective memory of his readers in order to gain their support, an endeavor that was highly successful.[1] His manipulation is most evident in the numerous digressions throughout the novel, flights of rhetoric that are as much a fabric of the work as the characters and plot.

The novel plays a special role in the representation of history, both as a reorganization of the historical narrative and as a purveyor of a different message. In *Les Misérables*, the richness of Hugo's style renders his calls for justice as powerful as do the images he creates. A description of Fantine captures in miniature Hugo's literary and historical project. "Cette fille de l'ombre avait de la race. Elle était belle sous les deux espèces, qui sont le style et le rythme. Le style est la forme de l'idéal; le rythme en est le mouvement" (134). [This daughter of the shadows had character. She possessed both types of beauty, style and rhythm. Style is the form of the ideal, rhythm is its movement.] While a novel is of course style and rhythm, so is history; each era has a style, and the movement through time represents the rhythm of history. By seizing, through memory, both the style and rhythm of a past era, Hugo helped his readers understand their present and lead them toward the future.

Hugo writes the history of his present by examining various aspects of the historical past: Paris, the system of justice, the sewers, and even France itself. Each of these worlds is represented by certain characters: Paris by "les misérables" and the bourgeois, the sewers by Thénardier, France by Marius and Cosette, the justice system by Javert and the judge who originally sentenced Jean Valjean.[2] Hugo brings to life in the text events of the first half of the century and, allegorically, events of the 1850s. While *Les Misérables* never explicitly refers to the Second Empire, the reader can easily identify concepts of revolt that Hugo had been making clear in other works since 1851. This is Hugo's "shadow history," in which Louis-Napoléon's reign is seen through "the language of symbol, character and topography" (*FT*, 224). Hugo shows to full advantage the powers of historical fiction that historiography does not have.

While documented history is read by and affects a more limited readership, fiction is accessible to all through the potent combination of memory and imagination. What reader of *Les Misérables* could deny the righteousness of Hugo's appeal for justice and freedom?

Yet these were the same calls he was making ten years earlier with less success; the difference here is that he has found a medium that touches people without threatening their need for stability in everyday life. Because the novel is set in the past, the reader is free to imagine those times without immediately inferring criticisms to his present. Yet those criticisms are ubiquitous, even in allegorical form, and the reader's affective distance shrinks in comparison with the temporal. If the novel's success was due to this connection with the reader's memory and his present, it was also due to timing. Had Hugo published the novel immediately upon going into exile, it would not have had the same effect because the upheaval of the coup d'état was too recent. The connections between 1832 and 1851 would have been too raw, and the reader would not have had the necessary distance to understand Hugo's project or fully appreciate the ideals being proposed.

Hugo recognizes that a certain distance is necessary for the historian to understand better the ramifications of the events that have taken place. "Cette remarquable époque est assez circonscrite et commence à s'éloigner assez de nous pour qu'on puisse en saisir dès à présent les lignes principales" (*LM*, 837). [This remarkable era is fairly short and is beginning to distance itself from us enough that we can now distinguish its major principles.] He can place events in their historical context by comparing them with other eras that have gone before and by analyzing the consequences that have resulted from them. The role of memory becomes primary here, as the poet becomes historian through the use of his own memories and the documentation available to him.

Historical Representation

This third and final stage in Paul Ricœur's "historical knowledge" is more complex than simple historiography.[3] Not simply the writing of ideas already formed, historical representation is more accurately the continuation of the process of interpretation of history begun in the previous two phases: documentation and explanation/comprehension. At this stage, the historian is ready to write that which has been documented and analyzed. The rhetoric that he uses to explain and ultimately to convince is more closely linked to argumentation than to historiography because its goal is to create a convincing case, not an objective overview. In *Les Misérables,* Hugo uses fiction as a weapon against the emperor. History as representation here becomes an active agent of change in the attitudes of the people toward their past.

Ricœur sees the writing of history as a "putting into literature" (*mise en littérature*) through narrative, rhetoric and imagination (*MHF*, 275). The novelist or historian overcomes skepticism that his version of events does not represent what truly happened through a combination of "*scripturalité*," comprehensive explanation and documentary proof (*MHF*, 278). In a novel such as *Les Misérables*, we see these processes at work, as Hugo takes advantage of the reader's suspension of disbelief to weave a tale that strikes us as true to life. Our belief in his story lies in his ability to convince us of its authenticity. Just as we saw that the best way to verify an eyewitness's testimony was to solicit other testimonies, the best way to accredit historical representation is through eyewitness documentation and its critique (*MHF*, 278). In the novel, the final representation of events may not resemble the historical events themselves, but it remains faithful to the spirit of the events, characters, and era. Hugo's narrative represents both a time that has passed and the present of his exile, as the ideals he fights for remain the same throughout.

In *Les Misérables*, Hugo shows that fiction has its place in the historiographical process. Just as historical events are the result of various interactive forces, the writing of history must incorporate different genres in order to reflect the diversity of these influences. "Great stories and histories must draw as much on imaginative insight as on the reports of eyewitnesses. They must contain drama and poetry alike" (*FT*, 202). Hugo appeals to his reader's memory through the inclusion of historical material, hoping that the reader will then extrapolate from his own personal memories images of the lost republican life that Hugo is proposing be restored.

It is important to Ricœur that this phase called historical representation not be seen as a distinct practice that attaches itself to the first two phases of historical knowledge. "Representation in its narrative aspect, as in the others I shall speak of, does not add something coming from the outside to the documentary and explanatory phases, but rather accompanies and supports them. . . . We ought not to expect from narrativity that it fill some lacuna in explanation/understanding" (*MHF*, 238). Ricœur's conception of historical representation is closely linked here with Braudel's long duration. *Les Misérables* is more a work of social than political history, as it leaves behind concerns of heads of state and delves into the tendencies and eccentricities of a community over a period of time.

In the novel, Hugo makes a clear comparison between the professional historian and the Foucault-like observer of a society's mores and ideas. "L'historien des mœurs et des idées n'a pas une mission moins austère que l'historien des événements" (*LM*, 1006). [The historian of values and ideas has a mission no less austere than that of the historian of events.] He argues that the former is just as important as the latter, and he would certainly place himself among the ranks of the historians of ideas. Hugo often comments on the role of these two fundamentally different types of historians. "L'historien des événements a la surface de la civilisation . . . l'autre historien a l'intérieur, le fond, le peuple qui travaille, qui souffre et qui attend. . . . Il faut qu'il descende le cœur plein de charité et de sévérité à la fois, comme un frère et comme un juge" (*LM*, 1006). [The historian of events has civilization's surface . . . the other historian has its interior, its depths, its working people who suffer and wait. . . . He must descend with his heart full of both charity and severity, like a brother and a judge.] While the people may not particularly want Hugo as their judge, they can certainly use the force of his words to help them interact with the events that shape their world.

The worlds of the two historians are not separate: "L'histoire des mœurs et des idées pénètre l'histoire des événements, et réciproquement" (*LM*, 1007). [The history of values and ideas penetrates the history of events, and vice versa.] Hugo can thus circulate between the two realms: "La vraie histoire étant mêlée à tout, le véritable historien se mêle de tout" (*LM*, 1007). [True history being involved with everything, the true historian involves himself with everything.] He may do so at his peril, however, because the historian of mores and ideas is far less likely to be objective about the history he is writing. Hugo, never careful about objectivity, would argue that the final goal of progress must be served and that the best way to do so is to enlighten the people. As a historian not only of ideas from the past but of the present, Hugo has a far richer collection of material upon which to draw than does the professional historian who must content himself with documentation of past events.

No historian can do anything more than sketch the outline of the events he describes, and in so doing he must make choices about the events to be covered and the point of view from which to cover them. The historian and the novelist converge as purveyors of subjective information. "Chaque historien trace un peu le linéament qui lui plaît dans ces pêle-mêle. . . . L'historien, en ce cas, a le droit évident de résumé. Il ne peut que saisir les contours principaux de la lutte, et il n'est donné à aucun narrateur, si consciencieux qu'il soit, de fixer absolument la forme de ce nuage qu'on appelle une bataille" (329). [Each historian traces the particular feature that pleases him in this confusion. . . . The historian, in this case, obviously has the right to summarize. He can only grasp the principal contours of the struggle, and it is given to no narrator, however conscientious he may be, to establish absolutely the form of this cloud we call a battle.] While Hugo is writing here specifically about the historiography of battles, his words can be extrapolated to the larger context of history in general.

Novelists are not professional historians but more like what Ricœur calls "engaged spectators" (*MHF*, 259). Their involvement in historical events takes place, as in Hugo's case, on the level of individual and collective memory, through eyewitness accounts. "Les petits détails . . . sont . . . le feuillage des grands événements et se perdent dans le lointain de l'histoire" (*LM*, 1081). [Small incidents . . . are . . . the foliage of great events and are lost in the remoteness of history.] By bringing certain of these details out of the oblivion of the forgotten, Hugo will provide the human side of history, and he will do so from the privileged position of the eyewitness, a stance that most historians cannot take. "Ce que nous raconterons, nous pourrons dire: nous l'avons vu. . . . Nous ne montrerons qu'un côté et qu'un épisode, et à coup sûr le moins connu, des journées des 5 et 6 juin 1832; mais nous ferons en sorte que le lecteur entrevoie, sous le sombre voile que nous allons soulever, la figure réelle de cette effrayante aventure publique" (*LM*, 1081). [What we shall tell, we can say: we saw it. . . . We shall only show one side and one episode, and surely the least known, of the days of the 5 and 6 June 1832; but we shall do it in such a way that the reader may catch a glimpse, under the dark veil which we are about to lift, of the real face of that frightening public debacle.] Hugo is not reticent about admitting that his history will not be a comprehensive one. No eyewitness account could ever be such. Yet it can provide what an overall history cannot: the humanity of the situation, the reality of real people during a real drama. The distance is ripped away, leaving only the observations of one who was there.

The "engaged spectator" is implicated in the past through memory much more than through the historian's discourse. This distinction between professional and amateur historian is part of the pact that develops between author and reader but does nothing to diminish the author's authority as historian of the present. While he may have a different language from the professional historian, he has complete control of the "world of the text" (*MHF,* 262). The dialectic between the "reality" of history and the "unreality" of fiction sets up an intersection (*entrecroisement*) that enriches the reader's understanding of the historical events being recounted.[4] What could once have been called fictionalization of historical discourse can be reformulated as the intersection of readability and visibility within historical discourse (*MHF,* 262). The existence of characters in the novel gives it its visibility and adds to the readability created by the narration of events. The "engaged spectator" can thus become an historian of the present through the dialectic of the visual nature of fiction and the discursive force of history.

Les Misérables proves itself to be an excellent indicator of Hugo's shift in priorities, as he moves from a direct frontal assault on Louis and his policies to a fictionalized account of an era that is not even the Second Empire, yet the societal movements and upheavals of Hugo's chosen setting profoundly affected the French psyche of the mid-nineteenth century. This larger view of the events that separate Hugo and Louis is what gives Hugo his final advantage: he is able to represent the power of long duration and of problematization in the structure of his novel. "Les faits qui vont être racontés appartiennent à cette réalité dramatique et vivante que l'historien néglige quelquefois, faute de temps et d'espace. Là pourtant . . . est la vie, la palpitation, le frémissement humain" (*LM,* 1081). [The facts that are about to be described belong to that dramatic and living reality which the historian sometimes neglects, for lack of time and space. There, however, is found the life, the palpitation, the shuddering of humanity.] Hugo makes his case for problematization as a complement to documentation. By describing a segment of the events that occurred, the novelist can be as effective at portraying what actually happened as can the professional historian. In addition, he can breathe new life into the story through the use of detail.

In conjunction with this idea of the novelist's limited scope, Ricœur points out one more fundamental difference between fiction and history, "the claim to truth on the side of history and the 'voluntary suspension of disbelief' on that of fiction" (*MHF,* 242).[5] The writer of fiction does not have to show that what he writes is true or, in the modern era, even realistic (*vraisemblable*). The reader needs only to believe in the coherence of the narrative (*MHF,* 243).

Each event is a variable of the plot, as it represents a step forward in the action. Characters have an equally important role, as they act out the events created for them. Their moral character comes into play in the dialogue between novelist and reader, as the reader wonders whether or not to identify with the character. The structure of the novel, as a phenomenon of long duration, is the condition of possibility of the event. The significance of the framework of the novel becomes clear only after the events have been recounted. The structure corresponds to social history, taking into account changes in a community over a long period of time.

Another difference between a work of fiction and the outside world to which it refers is the tendency of the novel to work toward closure, while history is an ongoing enterprise (*MHF*, 248). What makes the Hugo versus Louis encounter so fascinating is that it does have an ending, the fall of the Second Empire. Unlike history as long duration, this battle royal could be said to resemble fiction, as Hugo rode triumphantly into Paris in 1870. It will be up to Hugo's works to continue the battle for control of the collective memory of the period because the historical events have come to an end.

By writing a work of narrative fiction, Hugo creates a work of historical imagination "through a form that comes from rhetoric and more precisely from the rhetoric of tropes. This verbal form of the historical imagination is the emplotment" (*MHF*, 251). While historical narrative and fiction are both "verbal fictions" (*MHF*, 251), fiction adds the dimension of *story* to that of *history*. This distancing from the real world gives the novel its social dimension and creates the conditions necessary for the insertion of ideological implications, moral and political engagements that move the novel toward its status as a history of the present.[6] In *Les Misérables,* Hugo touches on every social class in order to distance the text from the short term history of individual events. While great men (Napoléon) and great events (Waterloo) can be found in the novel, it is the unknown characters (Jean Valjean) and events (Jean Valjean's status as fugitive) that give the work its power as social history.

Ricœur discusses at length the relationship between fiction and rhetoric, and his analysis is especially pertinent to this study of Hugo because of the persuasive nature of Hugo's works written in exile. The fundamental goal of rhetoric is to persuade one's audience. The creation of visual images supporting one's arguments is a key to persuading the reader/spectator of the validity of one's position. Ricœur uses the example of the absolute monarch whose absolute power resides in the images created of him.[7] The representation of power becomes the actual source of power, and this function is especially salient in the political realm where the desire for power is absolute (*MHF*, 264). Louis-Napoléon immediately recognized the importance of visual representation, particularly since he had his uncle's example to follow, and he set about establishing appropriate images of himself in art, sculpture, and whatever other media he could control. Hugo had, however, the advantage when it came to images created in the imagination of the reader, and it is this domain, characterized by the slow formation of more lasting images, that proves to be the more influential in the conflict over the historical reputation of the emperor.

The novelist's role is to bring collective memory into accord with the truth in order to make possible a sublime future. Hugo recognizes that memory can be falsified, that the past can seem to be something that it was not. He wants to strip away hypocrisy and falsehood in order not to repeat the mistakes of the past. The only way to do so is to defy those who would rewrite history to suit their own goals for the present or future. "En attendant, étudions les choses qui ne sont plus. Il est nécessaire de les connaître, ne fût-ce que pour les éviter. . . . Défions-nous. Le passé a un visage, la superstition, et un masque, l'hypocrisie. Dénonçons le visage et arrachons le masque" (*LM*, 525). [In the meantime let us study the things that no longer exist. It is necessary to recognize them, if only to avoid them. . . . Let us be vigilant. The past has a face, superstition, and a mask, hypocrisy. Let us denounce the face and rip off the mask.] The past, like anything in Hugo's Romantic universe, has a "sublime aspect" and a "hideous side" (*LM*, 443).

When the historians and philosophers do not do their job of denouncing injustice, someone has to step into the breach. Hugo proposes his services. "L'histoire et la philosophie ont d'éternels devoirs qui sont en même temps des devoirs simples; combattre Caïphe évêque, Dracon juge, Trimalcion législateur, Tibère empereur; cela est clair, direct et limpide, et n'offre aucune obscurité" (536). [History and philosophy have eternal duties that are also simple duties: to fight Caiaphas the bishop, Draco the judge, Trimalcion the legislator, and Tiberius the emperor. This is clear, direct, and limpid, and presents no obscurity.] Hugo certainly sees himself as a philosopher poet. "La philosophie doit être une énergie; elle doit avoir pour effort et pour effet d'améliorer l'homme" (*LM*, 535). [Philosophy must be an energy; it must have as its aim and its effect

the betterment of mankind.] As part of his task, he will enlighten
the reader in order to make him a better person. By correcting his
memory of historical events, Hugo contributes to the betterment of
the complete person; by increasing individual perception, he is
building a stronger society.

Since the failure of the barricades to stop the coup d'état, Hugo
has had no means of taking direct action against the emperor. He
must resort then to persuade the reader to join him in opposition
to the regime in power. "Rien n'est stupide comme vaincre; la vraie
gloire est convaincre" (*LM*, 681). [Nothing is as stupid as conquer-
ing; the real glory is convincing.] From the point of view of the exile,
the pen seems mightier than the sword, but given the actual choice,
Hugo would be torn. His call to action would be similar to the novel's young ideologue, Enjolras's: practical action to achieve a specific goal, with no thought of personal glory. His glory seems to
reside more in the guise of the poet/prophet who leads the people
out of darkness.

Freedom from the constraints of ego building provides the novelist a freedom of style that permits him to counteract attempts to cen-
sor him.

> Comme les Nérons règnent à la manière noire, ils doivent être peints de
> même. . . . Les despotes sont pour quelque chose dans les penseurs. Pa-
> role enchâinée, c'est parole terrible. L'écrivain double et triple son style
> quand le silence est imposé par un maître au peuple. Il sort de ce silence
> une certaine plénitude mystérieuse qui filtre et se fige en airain dans la
> pensée. La compression dans l'histoire produit la concision dans l'hist-
> orien. (*LM*, 1077–78)

> [As the Neros reign darkly, they should be so described. . . . Despots
> influence thinkers. Speech enchained is powerful speech. The writer
> doubles and triples his style when silence is imposed by a master upon
> the people. There emerges from this silence a certain mysterious fullness
> that filters and freezes into brass in one's thoughts. Compression in his-
> tory produces conciseness in the historian.]

If this is true, Hugo is the perfect writer to take up the mantle of
freedom of speech. Already intense, sometimes overblown, the Hugolian style is finely tuned to react to injustice in the form of suppression of the freedom of expression. "L'honnêteté d'un grand
cœur, condensée en justice et en vérité, foudroie" (*LM*, 1078). [The

honesty of a great heart, condensed into justice and truth, strikes like a thunderbolt.] Combined with the conviction that he is right, this intensity gives Hugo a voice as powerful as any army.

Hugo never strays from the idea that the poet is different, even mad. "Qui dit poète, dit fou" (*LM*, 1118). [He who says poet, says madman.] Hugo is referring to lovesick Marius, but the reference to the author himself is clear enough. He has been mad enough to combat the emperor, albeit from afar. He is mad enough to argue against the status quo and to propose a new way of constructing society.

Studying the details of an era uncovers the general thread of its history. The details may be forgotten by the collective memory, and it is up to the historian to bring them back to light in order to highlight the particular feature of the bygone era that will shed some light on the present. We see clearly in *Les Misérables* that no detail is superfluous to the grand historical fresco that Hugo is constructing. "Voilà, pêle-mêle, ce qui surnage confusément de l'année 1817, oubliée aujourd'hui. L'histoire néglige presque toutes ces particularités, et ne peut faire autrement; l'infini l'envahirait. Pourtant ces détails, qu'on appelle à tort petits . . . sont utiles. C'est de la physionomie des années que se compose la figure des siècles" (*LM*, 127). [That was the confusion that reigned in 1817 and has been forgotten today. History neglects almost all of these details and cannot do otherwise; infinity would overwhelm it. However, these details, which are wrongly called little . . . are useful. The face of history is composed of the physiognomy of individual years.] Hugo would seem to be applying to history St. Hilaire's positivism and to be adumbrating Zola's naturalistic view of the world, in which the accumulation of causal factors results in an image of the whole.

The causal factors at the historian's disposal are simply historical events. "Ces faits sont sortis des révolutions et des guerres, ils sont, ils vivent, ils ont droit de s'installer dans la société . . . et la plupart du temps les faits sont les maréchaux-des-logis et des fourriers qui ne font que préparer le logement aux principes" (*LM*, 838). [These facts have come from revolutions and wars; they exist, they live, they have the right to become part of society . . . and most of the time facts are pioneers and quartermasters that simply pave the way for principles.] This brilliant imagery places historical fact in relation to historiography. The facts are the basis from which rises the analysis. The facts come first, the historical perspective comes later. Memory is the agent that brings the two together.

Unlike the scientist who has a determined selection of evidence from which to work, the historian must pick and choose the historical facts he wishes to analyze, and from these choices arise the difficulties of historiography. Each historian has prejudices that affect his choice of facts and his conclusions. Hugo retains his fascination with "ce vague fourmillement qu'on nomme le passé" (612) [this vague swarming that we call the past] and acknowledges the difficulty of seizing it in its entirety. The past will not give up its secrets easily; it is up to the poet to help us all see the importance of our common past and the uses it can be put to in the present.

While a history of the present is limited in its perspective, long-term memory can incorporate truths that have come to light over the years. Nowhere is this more evident in Hugo's writing from exile than in his treatment of Napoléon I. For many years, the emperor was seen as an enlightened figure, his darker side obscured by his legend. Eventually, however, time ripped away the veil and a more reasoned image emerged.[8] "Du même homme elle fait deux fantômes différents, et l'un attaque l'autre, et en fait justice, et les ténèbres du despote luttent avec l'éblouissement du capitaine" (*LM*, 327). [Of the same man it makes two different phantoms, and one attacks the other, and metes out justice to him, and the darkness of the despot struggles with the dazzling sight of the captain.] In admitting the shortcomings of his hero, the first and legitimate emperor, Hugo is describing the strength of historiography. Only by looking back at a person or an era can we see the truth because the forces—political, social, and historical—at work during the intervening years have obfuscated short-term memory. Hugo's definitive judgment (*appréciation définitive*) is what I have been calling the collective memory of the people. Theirs will be the final word, but they must be given all the facts by the novelist/historian.

The battlefields of history are replayed in the pages written by the historian, and just as in life, history reveals the winners and losers. In Hugo's time, the real losers are the forces that cling to the past.

La famille Bourbon crut qu'elle avait des racines parce qu'elle était le passé. Elle se trompait; elle faisait partie du passé, mais tout le passé c'était la France. Les racines de la société française n'étaient point dans les Bourbons, mais dans la nation. Ces obscures et vivaces racines ne constituaient point le droit d'une famille, mais l'histoire d'un peuple. (*LM*, 839)

[The Bourbons believed that they had roots because they were the past. They were wrong; they were part of the past, but the whole past was

France. The roots of French society were not in Bourbons but in the nation. These obscure and living roots did not constitute the right of a family, but the history of a people.]

The past is a world that must be contested by the various elements residing therein. Each has a certain claim to historical legitimacy, but eventually the primacy of one over the other comes to the fore. This privileging happens through the passage of time and through the coming to light of the various aspects of the different claims. Hugo in this case does not need much historical perspective to see that the French nation is a more powerful historical force than the Bourbon family, but the example leads us to think of other competing forces such as the Second Republic and the Second Empire, where the memories of the French people render their decision of whom to support much more difficult.

In a short chapter entitled "A quelle condition on peut respecter le passé" (529) [On what condition we can respect the past], Hugo begins a more systematic look at how past, present, and future interact. This will be the springboard for his evocation, in this section of the novel, of his sense of the ideal and how it can be brought to reality in the future. At the chronological center of Hugo's view of the world is of course the nineteenth century, the scene of the continuation and development of revolutionary ideals. "Il faut en ce siècle que la révolution soit partout" (635). [In this century, the revolution must be everywhere.] This phrase refers to M. Gillenormand, a hardened royalist, who is the bourgeois par excellence, but it reveals a greater feeling of Hugo's: that the nineteenth century is the century of revolution. The Revolution may have begun in the eighteenth century, but its continuation gives the nineteenth century its shape and meaning. Hugo's project of revolt comes out of his desire to understand his century instead of merely mocking it: "On raillait le siècle, ce qui dispensait de le comprendre" (636). [They ridiculed the century, which exempted them from understanding it.]

In describing the years between 1814 and 1820, Hugo identifies a basic problem of incomprehension between generations. "Jadis méconnaissait Hier. On n'avait plus le sentiment de ce qui était grand, ni le sentiment de ce qui était ridicule" (637). [Formerly misunderstood Yesterday. One no longer had a sense of what was grand nor a sense of what was ridiculous.] The ideal for one is the enemy of the other. The glorious past for one is the infamy of the other. Napoléon

I represents one thing for Hugo, another for Louis-Napoléon. Each generation or political party uses the past for its own ends. In the end, the ideas that are the most true will win out: "Quels flots que les idées! Comme elles couvrent vite tout ce qu'elles ont mission de détruire et d'ensevelir, et comme elles font promptement d'effrayantes profondeurs!" (*LM*, 637). [What floods are ideas! How quickly they cover all that they are supposed to destroy and bury, and how promptly they create frightening depths!]

Hugo gives the Restoration its due and reinforces the idea that the whole nineteenth century, not simply the Republic, is the descendant of the Revolution. "C'est sous Louis XVIII et Charles X que vint le tour de parole de l'intelligence . . . l'égalité devant la loi, la liberté de la conscience, la liberté de la parole, la liberté de la presse, l'accessibilité de toutes les aptitudes à toutes les fonctions" (840). [It was under Louis XVIII and Charles X that intelligence in its turn found speech . . . equality before the law, freedom of conscience, freedom of speech, freedom of the press, the accessibility of every function to every aptitude.] These new freedoms will come into play in Hugo's comparison of Louis-Napoléon with the rest of his century. The second emperor does not have the stature of any of his predecessors, and in order to maintain his power, he must suppress the liberties that even the monarchy could tolerate.

Paradoxically, the past can become an obstacle to moving forward into the future. Tyranny can reappear. "Le passé . . . est très fort à l'heure où nous sommes. . . . Il semble vainqueur. Il arrive avec sa légion, les superstitions, avec son épée, le despotisme, avec son drapeau, l'ignorance" (*LM*, 1023). [The past . . . is very strong at the present time. . . . It seems victorious. . . . It comes with its legion, its superstitions, with its sword, its despotism, with its flag, its ignorance.] Hugo then warns those who refuse to look forward toward the future. "Mais que ceux qui ne veulent pas de l'avenir y réfléchissent. En disant non au progrès, ce n'est point l'avenir qu'ils condamnent, c'est eux-mêmes." (*LM*, 1023). [But let those who do not want the future think of it. By saying no to progress, it is not the future they condemn, but themselves.] We have seen the irony of a statement such as this. Hugo's own attachment to the revolutionary past is given immunity to the malady described here. Only those attached to despotism will suffer from their obsession with memory.

Because it is the era of revolution, the nineteenth century is the people's century. As inheritors of the Revolution of 1789, they will establish a lasting French republic. "Le peuple, ébauché par le dix-huitième siècle, sera achevé par le dix-neuvième" (*LM*, 1023). [The people, sketched out by the eighteenth century, will be completed by the nineteenth.] Hugo calls repeatedly for a peaceful return to republican times. "La philosophie sociale est essentiellement la science de la paix" (*LM*, 1024). [Social philosophy is essentially the science of peace.] His faith in humanity to survive difficult times allows him to abandon the violent rhetoric of *Napoléon le petit* or even, at times, *Les Châtiments.* "Sous la mortalité sociale, on sent l'impérissabilité humaine" (*LM*, 1025). [Beneath social mortality, we feel the immortality of humanity.] The Revolution has given rise to the people, and Hugo will help them retrieve the power lost in 1851.

HUGO'S REVOLT IN *LES MISÉRABLES*

Hugo links ideal and truth, beauty and light, in order to accent the importance of art in the revolutionary struggle. "Cela tient qu'elle est artiste. L'idéal n'est autre chose que le point culminant de la logique, de même que le beau n'est autre chose que la cime du vrai. Les peuples artistes sont aussi les peuples conséquents. Aimer la beauté, c'est voir la lumière" (*LM*, 1264). [Of course she is an artist. The ideal is nothing other than the culminating point of logic, even as the beautiful is nothing other than the summit of the true. Artists are also logical people. To love beauty is to see the light.] If revolutions took place in the relative vacuum of practicality, i.e. politics, the ideal would be absent, and as we have seen, without the ideal, there can be no real revolt. The poet, as the purveyor of truth and beauty, is thus in the forefront of the revolutionary movement. It is up to him to show the way.

Hugo explicitly states his role of explicator of the ideal. "Chose admirable, la poésie d'un peuple est l'élément de son progrès" (*LM*, 1265). [An admirable thing, the poetry of a people is the condition of its progress.] Progress can only come about through the pursuit of the ideal that, in turn, is expressed in poetry. "La quantité de civilisation se mesure à la quantité d'imagination . . . il faut être artiste. En matière de civilisation, il ne faut pas raffiner, mais il faut sublimer. A cette condition, on donne au genre humain le patron de l'idéal" (*LM*, 1265). [The amount of civilization is measured by the amount of imagination . . . we must be artists. In the matter of civilization, we must not refine, but we must purify. On this condi-

tion, we give the human race the model of the ideal.] Imagination
is closely tied to the ideal, because without the imagination to envi-
sion the future, no revolutionary movement will succeed. Just as
Baudelaire sees the poet as the interpreter of beauty, Hugo sees him
as the interpreter of the revolutionary ideal, "cette vision auguste
des poètes: le beau social" (*LM*, 1265) [this august vision of the
poets: social beauty]. If Baudelaire contents himself with beauty,
Hugo goes further, arriving at social beauty, the concept of a world
where the ideal reigns supreme.

Discursive power finds one of its sources in its reliance on a sense
of justice. As long as the written discourse has as its goal the further-
ing of justice, it will dominate images that seek to perpetuate absolute centralized power. Louis Marin presents an ingenious way of
thinking of this question of power and justice:

> 1. Discourse is the mode of existence of an imaginary of force, an
> imaginary whose name is "power."
> 2. Power is the imaginary of force when it is uttered as discourse of
> justice.[9]

Hugo's novel finds its power in its ability to represent characters
and events, in the imaginary world of fiction where the social reigns
over the political, where the discursive wears down the visual over
time. The creator of the "story" has a different power than the recorder of "history," and it is on this power that Hugo relies to rewrite the history of the Second Empire.

Ricœur cites Pascal discussing the relationship between justice
and power: "Not being able to fortify justice we have justified
force. . . . Justice without enforcement is contradictory, because
there are always villains: enforcement without justice is criminal."[10]
We have seen how Hugo and Louis-Napoléon have taken on the
roles of justice and order: political power does not reinforce Hugo's
sense of justice, and Louis' "restoration of order" is a watchword for
the injustice of imposed power. In the struggle for power, however,
brute strength can initially win the day; once someone has achieved
a position of power, imagination comes into play, as the individual
or his group attempt to solidify his position.[11] The way an individual
or party or system represents itself will determine its legitimacy, its
acceptance by the people. Louis attempted to redefine himself in
terms of his uncle and found himself trumped in the end by Hugo's
representation of him as an usurper of power, a fraudulent emperor,

a "Napoléon le petit." Hugo's vision prevails, as we have seen, through a combination of historical events and the strength of Hugo's sense of justice.

Pascal sees man's grandeur in his capacity to see himself as "misérable," an apt word in the context of this analysis of Hugo's novel. It is his consciousness of his miserable state that sets him apart from a tree, for example. This grandeur has a political context as well, for who is more miserable than a king who has been dethroned? Pascal recounts the fable of a people whose king has been lost. A stranger who resembles the lost king arrives and is immediately taken to be the king. He receives all the respect due the king and allows himself to be treated as such. "It is therefore a 'portrait effect,' an 'effect of representation' that makes the king. And it is the image that he, in turn, dedicates to the prince . . . become the 'legitimate usurper,' that gives instructional power to the missive."[12] What better description of how Hugo sees Louis-Napoléon? The people take the nephew, who resembles the great emperor in family name, to be the legitimate heir to the throne. Louis reinforces this misconception through representations of himself in the guise of an emperor and through a discourse emphasizing order and tradition. Hugo's task, as he sees it, is to unmask the imposter.

For Hugo, the best way to escape the abuses of the personalization of power is through a constitutional form of government (*MHF*, 272). As Hegel points out, in this system grandeur lies not with the political power of an individual but with the more general sense of what is just.[13] In place of a discourse of praise (of the king), we find one of blame, which searches out that which is unacceptable to the wellbeing of the community. This constant skepticism regarding the praise of absolutism allows a society to render the most justice to the most people. Hugo becomes the voice of "moral conscience" (*MHF*, 274) as he becomes the voice of blame during the Second Empire. From the night of December 2, 1851 onward, Hugo seeks out injustice wherever he can find it, and that search usually leads him to Louis' door. His competing narrative tarnishes the laudatory images the emperor has established for himself and prepares the collective conscience for a shift of sentiment after 1870.

In *Les Misérables* Hugo presents a group of young idealists, each one calling for justice, each one representing a different aspect of the revolutionary ideal. He contrasts Enjolras, the absolutist, and Combeferre, the moderate. Enjolras represents the revolutionary of 1789 who uses "logique," including the logic of violence, as a means

to an end, while Combeferre's "philosophie" will result in a negoti-
ated peace. "Entre la logique de la révolution et sa philosophie, il y
a cette différence que sa logique peut conclure à la guerre, tandis
que sa philosophie ne peut aboutir qu'à la paix" (*LM*, 664). [Be-
tween the logic of revolution and its philosophy, there is this difference, that its logic can lead to war, while its philosophy can only end
in peace.] These young men allow Hugo to highlight his own conflicting notions about revolution and the Revolution of 1789.[14]
Hugo wanted the ideals of the Revolution to live on without having
to go through another revolutionary upheaval. While presenting the
people as the core of any revolution, he does not envisage a new
society led by Gavroche. Instead, his leaders would resemble Enjolras and Combeferre, educated and idealistic young men. For
Combeferre "mettre peu à peu, par l'enseignement des axiomes et
la promulgation des lois positives, le genre humain d'accord avec
ses destinées, cela lui plaisait mieux. . . . Un incendie peut faire une
aurore sans doute, mais pourquoi ne pas attendre le lever du jour?"
(*LM*, 665). [To put, gradually, by the teaching of axioms and the
promulgation of positive laws, the human race in harmony with its
destinies, pleased him better. . . . A fire can cause a dawn, undoubtedly, but why not wait for sunrise?] Combeferre thus resembles the
side of Hugo's personality that counsels patience: "Combeferre in-
clinait à laisser faire le progrès, le bon progrès; froid peut-être, mais
pur; méthodique, mais irréprochable; flegmatique, mais imperturbable" (*LM*, 666). [Combeferre was inclined to let progress do her
work, the good progress; cold, perhaps, but pure; methodical, but
irreproachable; phlegmatic but imperturbable.] While revolution
may be composed of glorious rushes of action, including violence,
progress must stay pure in order to ensure "L'immense évolution
vertueuse des peuples" (*LM*, 666). [The immense virtuous evolution of peoples.]

Hugo provides us with all the analysis we need of these characters.
Each represents an aspect of his own views toward the Revolution
and revolution in general. "Tous ces jeunes gens, si divers, et dont
. . . il ne faut parler que sérieusement, avaient une même religion:
le Progrès. . . . Tous étaient les fils directs de la révolution française"
(*LM*, 671). [All these young people, so diverse, and of whom . . . we
must only speak seriously, had the same religion: Progress. . . . All of
them were direct descendants of the French Revolution.] Enjolras
gives the republic parental status in much the same way that Hugo
confers it on the Revolution. "Ma mère, c'est la République" (*LM*,

690). [My mother is the republic.] Everything they believe stems from an initiatory experience that is engraved in their and the nation's memories. These are young men who may not be of the people but who are for the people. Prendergast sees this top-down approach of Hugo's as condescendingly bourgeois (92), but Hugo would not see it as anything but idealistic, with the stronger, more educated, more prosperous members of society leading the way for the oppressed. "Affiliés et initiés, ils ébauchaient l'idéal" (*LM*, 671). [Affiliated and initiated, they sketched out their ideal.]

Every group needs its cynic, every thesis its antithesis. Grantaire questions every principle that is close to Hugo's heart, a device that patently allows Hugo to introduce arguments that will show the strength of his ideals. "Tous ces mots: droits du peuple, droits de l'homme, contrat social, révolution française, république, démocratie, humanité, civilisation, religion, progrès, étaient, pour Grantaire, très voisins de ne rien signifier du tout" (*LM*, 672). [All these words: rights of the people, rights of man, social contract, French Revolution, republic, democracy, humanity, civilization, religion, progress, were, for Grantaire, very nearly meaningless.] Grantaire is a pleasant foil who never seriously threatens the hegemony of the true idealists, Enjolras and Combeferre.

After having advocated the kind of revolt that Camus outlines in *L'Homme révolté*, Hugo seems to turn his back on the nobility of revolt and privileges revolution as the natural result of human unhappiness. "Révolution est précisément le contraire de révolte. Toute révolution, étant un accomplissement normal, contient en elle sa légitimité. . . . Les révolutions sortent, non d'un accident, mais de la nécessité" (*LM*, 854). [Revolution is precisely the opposite of revolt. Every revolution, being a normal accomplishment, contains in itself its legitimacy. . . . Revolutions emerge not by accident but of necessity.] Curious language. Hugo would seem to imply that revolt is accidental, thus contradicting the basic tenet of the man who says "no." His argument is more lucid in a later section contrasting "revolt" and "uprising."[15]

Uprisings can sometimes strengthen the government's hold on power by testing the army, solidifying bourgeois public opinion, flexing the muscles of the police, and providing a hard rubdown which makes the government feel better. "Si l'on en croit de certains oracles de la politique sournoise, au point de vue du pouvoir, un peu d'émeute est souhaitable" (*LM*, 1073). [If we believe certain oracles of underhanded politics, from the government's point of view, a bit of uprising is desirable.] While Hugo presents this as coming from a cynic, it is hard to believe that he disagrees. Any uprising that does not overthrow the government renders those in power stronger. He would propose that the people either be sure of success before rising up or take their time and effect change gradually.

Revolt cannot be brutally imposed on a people if the timing is not right. "Chaque époque de l'histoire apporte avec elle la protestation qui lui est possible" (LM, 1077). [Each historical era brings with it the protest it makes possible.] This statement is as close as we will ever get to the core of Hugo's thinking on revolt. In 1789, the time was ripe for revolution; in 1851 it was not. The 1850s and 1860s were a time when only the shifting of public opinion could produce a revolutionary result. Hugo's project was to effect that change, and in order to do so, he claimed the moral high ground by allying himself with the words that represent his ideals: "ces hautes montagnes qui dominent l'horizon moral, la justice, la sagesse, la raison, le droit" (LM, 1079). [these high mountains that dominate the moral horizon, justice, wisdom, reason, right.]

Add to these words la fraternité. "Les grands périls ont cela de beau qu'ils mettent en lumière la fraternité des inconnus" (LM, 1127). [Great perils have this beauty, that they bring to light the fraternity of strangers.] The barricades are the heart of the action in the streets. The coming together of people who have a common goal is a model in miniature of Hugo's conception of la fraternité. Almost ten years later, the Commune will construct barricades of a different nature with different goals in mind . . . but with similar results. Hugo will be there to take up in person the cause of a new republic. The fraternity that he has been preaching in exile will come true in the streets of Paris.

The ideal, while a source of action, is always more than that. "C'est toujours pour l'idéal, et pour l'idéal seul, que se dévouent ceux qui se dévouent. L'enthousiasme peut se mettre en colère; de là la prise d'armes. Mais toute insurrection qui couche en joue un gouvernement ou un régime, vise plus haut" (LM, 1263). [It is always for the ideal, and only for the ideal, that those who devote themselves devote themselves. Enthusiasm can get angry; hence the taking up of arms. But every insurrection that aims at a government or a régime aims higher.] Hugo's position in exile does not allow him to revolt through specific revolutionary channels; his revolution is by necessity one based on an ideal. Beyond the immediate goal of overthrowing the emperor, Hugo's project of the installation of the

ideal republic is vague at best. Here he recognizes the lack of speci-
ficity but calls it inevitable. "Et l'on se sacrifie pour ces visions, qui,
pour les sacrifiés, sont des illusions presque toujours, mais des illusions auxquelles . . . toute la certitude humaine est mêlée" (*LM*,
1264). [And we sacrifice ourselves for these visions, which, for the
sacrificed, are almost always illusions, but illusions with which . . . all
human certainty is involved.] Once the short-term goal is achieved,
the specifics of the ideal may be implemented. Until then, they remain in the realm of the ideal, where the prophet can use them as
a call for change.

"La grandeur de la démocratie, c'est de rien nier et de ne rien
renier de l'humanité" (*LM*, 534). [The grandeur of democracy is
that it denies nothing and renounces nothing of humanity.] At first
glance, this statement would seem to contradict what Hugo has just
said about jettisoning the past, but the key word is *humanity*. The
horrors of the past that Hugo rejects fall outside the sphere of humanity. They are the tools of the wicked used against the ignorant
in an attempt to control the power structure. The totality of humanity that democracy encompasses does not admit anything other than
Hugo's ideals of liberty.

Hugo wants to be the sage who brings fact and right into harmony. In order to do so, he needs history on his side. He needs to
show that his conception of what is right is justified over a length of
time. "Le droit, c'est le juste et le vrai. Le propre du droit, c'est de
rester éternellement beau et pur" (*LM*, 842). [The right is the just
and the true. The quality of the right is that it stays eternally beautiful and pure.] Hugo sets up an opposition between that which is
just, "the right," and the reality of any given political situation, a
reality that, if it does not contain a just core, will lead to something
monstrous.

One of the watchwords of the empire is law, and Hugo shows here
that the law can be manipulated by men in ways that the laws of God
cannot. "Marius, sur les questions pénales, en était encore, quoique
démocrate, au système inexorable, et il avait, sur ceux que la loi
frappe, toutes les idées de la loi. Il n'avait pas encore accompli . . .
tous les progrès. Il n'en était pas encore à distinguer entre ce qui est
écrit par l'homme et ce qui est écrit par Dieu, entre la loi et le droit"
(1434–35). [Marius, on penal questions, although a democrat, was
still stuck on the inexorable system, and he had, on those that the
law strikes, all the ideas of the law. He had not yet reached . . . progress. He could not yet distinguish between what is written by man

and what is written by God, between law and right.] The difference
between law and right is the distinction between empire and republic. The latter is founded on principles of both law and righteousness, of worldly order and spiritual goodness. Marius, the innocent,
has not yet understood this difference; when he and others like him
do so, the empire will fall and be replaced by Hugo's ideal republic.

This struggle between the just ideal and the compromised reality
has been going on for centuries, but Hugo's aim is to reconcile the
two. "Terminer le duel, amalgamer l'idée pure avec la réalité humaine, fait pénétrer pacifiquement le droit dans le fait et le fait dans
le droit, voilà le travail des sages" (*LM*, 842). [To finish the duel, to
combine pure ideal with human reality, to make the right peacefully
penetrate the fact, and the fact the right, this is the work of the
wise.] If "the right" is to remain eternally beautiful and pure, it
must stand the test of time.

Excess idealism can be however just as dangerous as its opposite.

Il y a des êtres . . . qui, ayant l'azur du ciel, disent: c'est assez! . . . L'infini
leur suffit. Ce grand besoin de l'homme, le fini . . . qui admet le progrès,
le travail sublime, ils n'y songent pas. L'indéfini, qui naît de la combinai-
son humaine et divine de l'infini et du fini, leur échappe. (*LM*,
1243–44)

[There are people who . . . having the blue sky, say: "that's enough!" . . .
the infinite is enough for them. They do not think of this great human
need, the finite, which accepts progress, sublime toil. The indefinite,
which is born from the human and divine combination of the infinite
and the finite, escapes them.]

Dreamers can be as oblivious to the ideal in reality as tyrants. It takes
a true thinker such as Hugo to marry idealism and practical solu-
tions to create a better world. Hugo obviously overreaches when he
states that he wants to end the duel between fact and right, but he
at least recognizes its significance in the history of any nation. He is
claiming a role in that duel, one that he intends to win.

What better way for Hugo to sum up his own, sometimes contradictory, feelings than this comment about Jean Prouvaire, another
of the students: "Son esprit avait deux attitudes, l'une du côté de
l'homme, l'autre du côté de Dieu" (*LM*, 666). [His mind had two
attitudes, one toward man, the other toward God.] All day long Prouvaire examines human questions such as money, marriage, religion, freedom of thought, education, and poverty, and in the

evening he studies the stars. The philosopher/poet par excellence wants to improve and save the world at the same time.

Hugo explicitly links the Revolution and God in order to give it the importance and urgency he feels it deserves.

> Même tombés, surtout tombés, ils sont augustes, ces hommes qui, sur tous les points de l'univers, l'œil fixé sur la France, luttent pour la grande œuvre avec la logique inflexible de l'idéal; ils donnent leur vie en pur don pour le progrès; ils accomplissent la volonté de la providence; ils font un acte religieux." (1262–63)

> [Even fallen, especially fallen, they are noble, these men who, from all points of the universe, with eyes fixed on France, struggle to do great work with the inflexible logic of the ideal; they give their lives as a pure gift for progress; they accomplish the will of Providence; they perform a religious act.]

This religious action is done "pour amener à ses splendides et suprêmes conséquences universelles le magnifique mouvement humain irrésistiblement commencé le 14 juillet 1789; ces soldats sont des prêtres. La Révolution est un geste de Dieu" (*LM*, 1263). [to lead to its splendid and supreme universal consequences the magnificent movement of man, irresistibly commenced on the 14 July 1789; these soldiers are priests. The Revolution is a gesture from God.] God will not rest until the next revolution sweeps the illegitimate emperor out of power.

HUGO AND THE PEOPLE

Hugo's view of the power of the people is solidly rooted in the memory of past glory. When they are presented with reminders of their past, they will rise up and strike out at those who are preventing past ideals from becoming present reality. The revolutionary spirit of the French people—and specifically, the Parisians—comes from the depth and strength of their memories of the Revolution.

> Qu'un chat puisse se changer en lion, les préfets de police ne le croient pas possible; cela est pourtant, et c'est là le miracle du peuple de Paris. Le chat d'ailleurs, si méprisé du comte Anglès, avait l'estime des républiques antiques; il incarnait à leurs yeux la liberté. . . . Donnez-lui une pique, il fera le 10 août; donnez-lui un fusil, vous aurez Austerlitz. Il

est le point d'appui de Napoléon et la ressource de Danton. . . . Faites-lui chanter la Marseillaise, il délivrera le monde. (*LM*, 139–40).

[Police prefects do not believe it possible for a cat to change into a lion; nevertheless, it happens, and this is the miracle of the people of Paris. Moreover, the cat, so despised by the Count Anglès, had the esteem of ancient republics; it was in their eyes the incarnation of freedom. . . . Give him a pike and he will produce the tenth of August; give him a rifle, and you will have Austerlitz. He is Napoléon's base, and Danton's resource. . . . Have him sing the Marseillaise, and he will save the world.]

It will take only a catalyst to effect the necessary change from cat to lion. Poverty is always a source and a result of potential unrest. "En temps de révolution la misère est à la fois cause et effet" (*LM*, 869). [In times of revolution, misery is at once cause and effect.] Poverty may indeed be a cause and effect of revolution, but in other times, it does not disappear. The seeds of revolution are sown wherever poverty exists. If hunger and inspirational words were cause enough in 1789, Hugo sees no reason why such anger cannot be resuscitated and channeled by a wordsmith such as himself.

Hugo explicitly states his debt to the French Revolution. "La France est faite pour réveiller l'âme des peuples, non pour l'étouffer. Depuis 1792, toutes les révolutions d'Europe sont la révolution française; la liberté rayonne de France" (*LM*, 383). [France exists to awaken the soul of the people, not to smother it. Since 1792, all the revolutions of Europe have been the French Revolution: liberty radiates out from France.] Throughout his writings from exile, the Revolution, despite the excesses of the Terror, has been associated with all of Hugo's treasured ideals. The Revolution is the example that other European nations follow toward liberty. Hugo sees the principles of the Revolution as a saving grace and condemns monastic conservatism. The nations of Spain and Italy, for example, can only come out of the darkness of their commitment to such a monastic life "grâce à la saine et vigoureuse hygiène de 1789" (*LM*, 527) [thanks to the healthy and vigorous cleansing of 1789].

Hugo never believes that the French people were as docile as they seemed to be under the Second Empire. "La France, ayant rétabli *el rey neto* en Espagne, pouvait bien rétablir le roi absolu chez elle. Ils tombèrent dans cette redoutable erreur de prendre l'obéissance du soldat pour le consentement de la nation" (*LM*, 384). [France, having restored *el rey neto* in Spain, could certainly restore the absolute monarch at home. They fell into that fearful error of mistaking the obedience of the soldier for the consent of a nation.] Louis-Napoléon will make the same error eighteen years later. Only the forces of order were silencing the people's natural desire for freedom.

Hugo's love affair with the French people is based on memory, partly because he is in exile and partly because of their shared experience. "La mémoire du peuple flotte sur ces épaves du passé" (*LM,* 468). [The memory of the people floats over these wrecks of the past.] Here he emphasizes the long-lasting power of the memory of the people. On the other hand, Hugo's view of the people is not always clear. "Pour le peuple ou contre le peuple, c'est la question" (*LM,* 862). [For the people or against the people, that is the question.] As simple as this formulation may seem, there are implications here that Hugo does not fully resolve. As Prendergast points out, Hugo's support of the people is colored by his portrayal of them as inhabitants of the darkness.[16] In Hugo's future utopian republic, it is not always clear what place the people will have. "Or ceux qui ont faim ont droit" (*LM,* 863). [Now those who are hungry have the right.] Yes, but the right to what exactly? Hugo makes a clear distinction between "people" and "populace," the latter being the pejorative version of the former.[17] "Le rire de tous est complice de la dégradation universelle. De certaines fêtes malsaines désagrègent le peuple et le font populace. Et aux populaces comme aux tyrans il faut des bouffons" (*LM,* 1392). [The laughter of all is the accomplice of the universal degradation. Certain unwholesome festivals disintegrate the people and make it a populace. And for populaces as well as for tyrants, buffoons are needed.] For every Jean Valjean, there is a Thénardier. And immorality is not limited to the lower classes: Louis-Napoléon is the Thénardier of the ruling class, seeking profit at every turn, always at the expense of others. Thénardier becomes a slave trader after Jean Valjean assures his exile. Hugo can envisage Louis doing the same, but first the poet must provoke the ouster of the tyrant.

The people can take on multiple roles in Hugo's conception of the future republican ideal. I have often spoken of Hugo as prophet, but here he relinquishes that role to those in the cabarets. "Dans les cabarets du faubourg Antoine . . . une sorte d'esprit prophétique et un effluve d'avenir y circule" (*LM,* 870). [In the cabarets of the *Faubourg Antoine* . . . a sort of prophetic spirit and a whiff of the future circulate.] Even France can take on the same role: "Ce prophète, la France" (*LM,* 1234) [This prophet, France]. By placing the author himself and the French nation in a relationship of equivalence, Hugo elevates himself to a place of supreme power. The people have their ear to the ground; they are sensitive to the past, present, and future. They know how the story will end, and their version is more realistic than Hugo's.

At the same time, Hugo retains his privileged position as a leader of the people through the power of his words. "O pauvre pensée des misérables! Hélas! personne ne viendra-t-il au secours de l'âme humaine dans cette ombre? Sa destinée est-elle d'y attendre à jamais l'esprit, le libérateur . . . le radieux chevalier de l'avenir?" (*LM*, 1017). [Oh, pitiful thought of the miserable! Alas! Will no one come to the aid of the human soul in this darkness? Is it its destiny to wait forever for the spirit, the liberator . . . the radiant knight of the future?] Hugo proposes himself as this chevalier who will lead the people out of ignorance into a better future, a revolutionary who will guide them toward ideals that are etched in the morals of all time. "Le sens révolutionnaire est un sens moral. Le sentiment du droit, dévéloppé, développe le sentiment du devoir. . . . La dignité du citoyen est une armure intérieure; qui est libre est scrupuleux; qui vote règne" (*LM*, 1020–21). [The revolutionary sense is a moral sense. The sentiment of right, when developed, develops the sentiment of duty . . . the dignity of a citizen is his interior armor; he who is free is scrupulous; he who votes reigns.] This is a piece of irony because the votes of 1852 had certainly not fulfilled the role that Hugo envisions for them here. Hugo may have been the genius necessary in the 1850s and 1860s, but his attitude toward revolution was at times ambiguous. Early in *Les Misérables* G., le conventionnel, would seem to be trying to justify the violence of la Terreur of 1793: "Oui, les brutalités du progrès s'appellent révolutions. Quand elles sont finies, on reconnaît ceci: que le genre humain a été rudoyé, mais qu'il a marché" (*LM*, 47). [Yes, the brutalities of progress are called revolutions. When they are finished, we recognize this: that the human race has been mistreated, but that it has advanced.] But in the same sentence we see Hugo's aversion to violence. Even if the human race has the ability to survive violence and even if violence is a necessary condition for revolution, we can see through Hugo's prose a fundamental desire for peaceful transition.

Hugo has repeatedly called for progressive change rather than violence, but at times he seems to be doing the opposite.

> Ce que vous autres appelez le progrès marche par deux moteurs, les hommes et les événements. Mais, la chose triste, de temps en temps l'ex-

ceptionnel est nécessaire. Pour les événements comme pour les hommes, la troupe ordinaire ne suffit pas; il faut parmi les hommes des génies, et parmi les événements des révolutions. (*LM*, 1116)

[What you others call progress works by two driving forces, men and events. But the sad thing is that from time to time the exceptional is necessary. For events as well as for men, the regular company is not enough; geniuses are needed among men, and revolutions among events.]

Even Hugo's beloved notion of progress, always seen as a peaceful concept, is at times represented by violence: "Ce que nous appelons ici combat peut aussi s'appeler progrès" (*LM*, 845). [What we call combat may also be called progress.] Hugo is well aware that his vision of progress will constitute a struggle that is political, social, and psychological.

Just as in 1832 France was not ready for another revolution, thirty years later she is no more inclined in that direction. And yet the principle remains for Hugo: great ideas require great actions. If he could lead the French people into battle against Louis-Napoléon he would, despite his claims of pacifism. But later in the same paragraph, he seems to question the grandeur of the whole concept of revolution:

Une révolution, qu'est-ce que cela prouve? Que Dieu est à court. Il fait un coup d'état, parce qu'il y a solution de continuité entre le présent et l'avenir, et parce que, lui Dieu, il n'a pas pu joindre les deux bouts. (*LM*, 1116–17)

[A revolution, what does that prove? That God is hard up. He makes a *coup d'état*, because there is a solution of continuity between the present and the future, and because he, God, has not been able to join the two ends.]

Revolution comes about solely as a last resort, when even God cannot reconcile present and future. The pendulum soon swings back to pacifism, as Hugo reveals his true aversion to violence. "Le mieux, certes, c'est la solution pacifique" (*LM*, 1262). [The best, certainly, is the peaceable solution.] Rather than revolution, he proposes: "Etudier le mal à l'amiable, le constater, puis le guérir" (*LM*, 1262). [Study evil amicably, state what it is, then cure it.]

While Hugo's imagined revolution is a nonviolent one, his pacifism occasionally gives way to a sense of frustration.

Jusqu'au jour où le grand concordat humain sera conclu, la guerre, celle
du moins qui est l'effort de l'avenir qui se hâte contre le passé qui s'at-
tarde, peut être nécessaire. Qu'a-t-on à reprocher à cette guerre-là? La
guerre ne devient honte que lorsqu'elle assassine le droit, le progrès, la
raison, la civilisation, la vérité. (*LM*, 1150–51)

[Until the day when the great human agreement shall be concluded,
war, that which at least is the struggle of the hurrying future against the
lingering past, may be necessary. How can we reproach that war? War
only becomes shame when it assassinates right, progress, reason, civilization, truth.]

In order to do away with oppression, it may be at times necessary to
resort to force. "Il vient une heure où protester ne suffit plus; après
la philosophie il faut l'action; la vive force achève ce que l'idée a
ébauché" (*LM*, 1151). [There comes an hour when protest no
longer suffices; after philosophy action is necessary; great strength
finishes what the idea has sketched out.] Despite Hugo's prescience,
the French people may be excused for being confused by his mixed
messages throughout the novel. One minute a confirmed pacifist,
the next a banner-waving leader of the insurrection, Hugo presents
a Janus-like figure that grasps at any remedy for the malady of the
status quo.
      Hugo can, however, accomplish something more practical. As a
well-known figure in France, Hugo and great men like him can
bring about change.

Il faut que de grands combattants se lèvent, illuminent les nations par
l'audace, et secouent cette triste humanité que couvrent d'ombre le
droit divin, la gloire césarienne, la force, le fanatisme, le pouvoir irres-
ponsable et les majestés absolues. (*LM*, 1151)

[Great warriors must stand up, illuminate nations by their audacity, and
shake up this sad humanity that is covered with shadow by divine right,
Caesarean glory, force, fanaticism, irresponsible power, and absolute
monarchy]

He is the combattant, the same way we have seen him as the genius.
He will illuminate the French people and take away the shroud of

tyranny that has covered their conscience. He will help them throw off the yoke of absolute power that is based on myths from the past.

Hugo turns his sights from 1832 to 1848 and in so doing brings his own past nearer to the present of 1861. "Juin 1848 fut . . . un fait à part, et presque impossible à classer dans la philosophie de l'histoire." (*LM*, 1194). [June, 1848 was . . . a thing apart, and almost impossible to classify in the philosophy of history.] He sees in the uprising "la sainte anxiété du travail réclamant ses droits" (*LM*, 1194) [the sacred anxiety of labor demanding its rights]. The danger lay in the vulnerability of the new republic, and so the disorder in the streets had to be quelled. These events in turn caused inner turmoil for Hugo, and indeed for the French people. "Mais, au fond, que fut juin 1848? Une révolte du peuple contre lui-même" (*LM*, 1194). [But, at heart, what was June 1848? A revolt of the people against themselves.] While June 1848 may have represented the people fighting themselves, at least legitimate ideals were being espoused on both sides. This unfortunate turn of events would prove to be even more costly than the immediate death toll, since the ultimate price would be the republic itself. Yet Hugo looks back on those fateful days almost nostalgically, since the Second Empire has not given anyone the chance to say what they truly believe or to act on those beliefs.

Hugo continues to develop the idea of the poet as revolutionary, but at the same time he endows ordinary revolutionaries with poetic powers.

> L'insurgé poétise et dore l'insurrection. On se jette dans ces choses tragiques en se grisant de ce qu'on va faire. Qui sait? on réussira peut-être. On est le petit nombre; on a contre soi toute une armée; mais on défend le droit, la loi naturelle, la souveraineté de chacun sur soi-même . . . la justice, la vérité (*LM*, 1264)

> [The insurgent poetizes and gilds the insurrection. He throws himself into these tragic things, intoxicated by what he is going to do. Who knows? They will perhaps succeed. They are just a few; they have against them a whole army; but they defend right, natural law, the sovereignty of each over himself . . . justice, truth.]

The insurgent waxes poetic and the poet revolts. Together they will form the new order, based on basic revolutionary principles. Yet Hugo understands how difficult it is to get the masses to summon the courage to revolt. They have so little that they are afraid of losing even that. "Les lourdes masses . . . craignent les aventures; et il y a de l'aventure dans l'idéal. Quelquefois l'estomac paralyse le cœur" (*LM*, 1264). [The heavy masses . . . fear randomness; and there is randomness in the ideal. Sometimes the stomach paralyzes the heart.]

The French people have however a unique resiliency that will allow them to overcome their fears and rise up against tyranny. "La grandeur et la beauté de la France, c'est qu'elle . . . est la première éveillée, la dernière endormie. Elle va en avant. Elle est chercheuse" (*LM*, 1264). [The grandeur and the beauty of France is that . . . she is the first awake, the last asleep. She goes ahead. She is a seeker.] Herein lies Hugo's hope for victory in the future. The French people, seduced by order and prosperity, will eventually see the truth and awaken to revolt against injustice. The characters that man Hugo's barricades become larger than life through their sense of sacrifice. "Ces hommes . . . devinrent des Titans" (*LM*, 1269). [These men . . . became Titans.] The cause is what counts, not their comfort or even their survival. They are willing to sacrifice for the future of the country. The soldiers and men at the barricades may have differing visions of France, but they are both fighting for her. "Que l'un combatte pour son drapeau et que l'autre combatte pour son idéal, et qu'ils s'imaginent tous les deux combattre pour la patrie" (*LM*, 1271). [Let one fight for his flag, and the other for his ideal, and let them both imagine that they are fighting for the country.] Civil war, as we have seen, may be a necessary evil on the way to the ideal republic, but both sides are fundamentally fighting to save the entity that is France.

THOSE WHO SAY "NO"

In *Napoléon le petit* and *Les Châtiments*, Hugo directly defied the power of the new emperor in his role as the man who dared say "no." In *Les Misérables* such a refusal of blind obedience to a corrupt regime takes several different forms that constantly harken back, through the force of the reader's memory, to Hugo's protest against Louis-Napoléon.

Un général anglais . . . leur cria: Brave français, rendez-vous! Cambronne répondit: "Merde!" . . . Le lecteur français voulant être respecté, le plus beau mot peut-être qu'un français ait jamais dit ne peut lui être répété. Défense de déposer du sublime dans l'histoire. (*LM*, 356)

[An English general . . . cried to them: "Brave Frenchman, surrender!" Cambronne answered, *"Merde!"* . . . Out of respect to the French reader, the most beautiful word, perhaps, that a Frenchman has ever uttered cannot be repeated to him. No including the sublime in history.]

In this famous passage, Hugo is paying homage to a man who dared to say "No," while at the same time criticizing historians for cleansing their accounts of all that might be unseemly. Hugo's Romantic project of the inclusion of opposites here acts as a counterpoint to the dominant discourse as it is enunciated in the writings of historians.[18]

Hugo succinctly describes the man whose "no" unleashes the forces of history: "Il fallait donc à la bourgeoisie comme aux hommes d'État, un homme qui exprimait ce mot: Halte. Un Quoique Parce que. Une individualité composite, signifiant révolution et signifiant stabilité, en d'autres termes affermissant le présent par la comptabilité évidente du passé avec l'avenir" (*LM*, 845). [The bourgeoisie, then, as well as statesmen, needed a man who would say this word: Halt! An Although Because. A composite individuality, signifying revolution and signifying stability; in other words, assuring the present through the obvious compatibility of the past with the future.] If Hugo had been a statesman, he would have been the man he describes. In the absence of this perfect man who says, "Stop," Hugo's voice will have to substitute for true leadership. He will have to remind the people at every turn of what they need in the future and of how the past and future are inextricably intertwined. He will be the writer who supplies the ideas that finally lead to action.

The notion of the superiority of ideas over action is prevalent in *Les Misérables:* "Cette époque passera, elle passe déjà . . . il ne peut y avoir de puissance que dans un cerveau. . . . Ce qui mène et entraîne le monde, ce ne sont pas les locomotives, ce sont les idées" (*LM*, 975). [This time will pass, it is already passing by. . . . There can only be power in a brain . . . that which leads and sweeps the world along is not locomotives but ideas.] It is not the Platonic idea or even the Flaubertian one where idea becomes synonymous with style; it is simply what it says: without a thinking people, all action will be destined to lead to tyranny. Without an enlightened population, those in power will take advantage of their ignorance.

Hugo takes a major step in *Les Misérables* toward advocating universal public education as an incubator of enlightened revolutionary activity. "Revenons à ce cri: Lumière! . . . les révolutions ne sont-elles pas des transfigurations? Allez, philosophes, enseignez, éclairez, allumez" (*LM*, 608). [Let us return to that cry: Light! Are not revolutions transfigurations? Come on, philosophers, teach, enlighten, spark.] The poor, with their bare feet and their ignorance, can become weapons in the conquest of the ideal. "Regardez à travers le peuple et vous apercevrez la vérité" (*LM*, 608). [Look through the people, and you will see the truth.] In his earlier works, he addressed his reader and more or less accepted the fact that the uneducated portion of the population would not be enlightened enough to help in the struggle against the empire. Here, on the other hand, the people become an effective arm against tyranny because they possess the ideal of truth and the thirst for deliverance from ignorance and poverty. Hugo proposes to educate the people first, to use the "idea" as a weapon against the darkness. Only then will true revolution be possible.

As we have seen however, the poet must speak when the time is right. Hugo puts this concept in judicial terms: "C'est à l'heure de l'évidence que le démonstrateur paraît" (*LM*, 1079). [It is at the hour of evidence that the demonstrator appears.] When armed insurrection will not be enough, the poet must take up his pen in place of the sword. His is a project whose goal is the overthrow, preferably by peaceful means, of an elected government.

Le livre que le lecteur a sous les yeux en ce moment, c'est . . . la marche du mal au bien, de l'injuste au juste, du faux au vrai, de la nuit au jour, de l'appétit à la conscience, de la pourriture à la vie, de la bestialité au devoir, de l'enfer au ciel, du néant à Dieu. Point de départ: la matière; point d'arrivée: l'âme. L'hydre au commencement, l'ange à la fin. (*LM*, 1267)

[The book which the reader has now before his eyes is . . . the march from evil to goodness, from injustice to justice, from lies to truth, from night to day, from appetite to conscience, from rottenness to life, from bestiality to duty, from hell to heaven, from nothingness to God. Starting point: matter; goal: the soul. Hydra at the beginning, angel at the end.]

Ambitious words, but they are backed up by Hugo's commitment, his proximity to the events of 1851, and finally by his distance during his years in exile. He must convince the French people that he is right and the government is wrong.

A genius or a great warrior trying to lead his people to freedom is often poorly received by the society that he is trying to change. "Les génies attirent l'injure, les grands hommes sont toujours plus ou moins aboyés" (*LM*, 1204). [Geniuses attract insult, great men are always more or less hounded.] Exile and renunciation are in store for those who dare speak out against the powers that be, those who control public opinion. Hugo was not of course the only genius to be exiled: Napoléon Bonaparte remained a powerful weapon in Hugo's arsenal. In a single passage, Hugo outlines the origins of his admiration of Napoléon and the beginnings of a comparison between the emperor and himself. Both have been defeated, Hugo by Napoléon's nephew; both have been exiled; yet both have such a "quantity of revolution" inside them that their enemies tremble lest they return.

> Chose singulière, on s'éprit en même temps de cet avenir, Liberté, et . . . de ce passé, Napoléon. La défaite avait grandi le vaincu. . . . Ce fantôme donnait le tremblement au vieux monde. Les rois régnèrent mal à leur aise, avec le rocher de Sainte-Hélène à l'horizon (*LM*, 366–367)

> [Curious thing, we fall in love with this future, Liberty, and at the same time with this past, Napoléon. Defeat increased the stature of the vanquished. . . . This phantom made the old world tremble. Kings reigned ill at ease with the rock of Saint Helena on the horizon.]

This admiration of the true emperor by the novelist comes ironically more from defeat than from triumph. The emperor in exile finds his power in memory, the same way the novelist in exile does.

Not everyone longs for a return to Napoleonic glory, however, and Hugo presents this opposing view. We see here again a generational conflict, this time between royalists and liberals.

> La révolution, dont nous sommes les héritiers, doit avoir l'intelligence de tout. Attaquer le royalisme, c'est le contre-sens du libéralisme. Quelle faute! et quel aveuglement! La France révolutionnaire manque de respect à la France historique. . . . Pourquoi ne pas vouloir toute l'histoire? Pourquoi ne pas aimer toute la France? (*LM*, 638–39)

> [The revolution, whose heirs we are, must understand everything. To attack royalism is a misinterpretation of liberalism. What a mistake! and

what blindness! Revolutionary France lacks respect for historic
France. . . . Why not want all of history? Why not love all of France?]

From the royalist point of view, French heritage includes more than
just the revolutionary period. If we include all of French history, we
must accept the role of the monarchy in France's destiny. From
Hugo's point of view, such a conclusion is nonsense. It is impossible
to include all of French history in one's view of the future of the
country. One must choose between the ideals one believes in and
the alternatives. If everyone were able to accept all of French history
as a legitimate model for the future, then Hugo and Louis-Napoléon
would have had nothing to disagree about. Napoléon I would have
been the same model for both of them instead of the ideological
sword that inexorably and definitively placed them on opposing
sides. History is thus as subjective as life itself. No single view dominates until its legitimacy is proven through time.

Hugo recognizes the importance of temporal distance in the judgment of historical figures. He establishes a comparison between
Louis-Napoléon and Louis-Philippe who was king during the climac-
tic events of *Les Misérables*, ironically preferring the monarch to the
"elected" head of state. "Louis-Philippe, comme tous les hommes
historiques sortis de la scène, est aujourd'hui mis en jugement par
la conscience humaine. Son procès n'est encore qu'en première instance" (*LM*, 851). [Louis-Philippe, like all historic men who have
left the scene, is to be put on trial today by human conscience. His
trial is still in the preliminary stages.] Time and the development of
the collective memory over that time will determine the final public
opinion of any historical figure.

Earlier Hugo had accused Louis-Philippe of putting the "useful"
before the "grand" (*LM*, 848). Here he goes one step farther by
privileging the "good." "Or pour nous, dans l'histoire où la bonté
est la perle rare, qui a été bon passe presque avant qui a été grand"
(*LM*, 852). [Now, for us, in history where goodness is a rare pearl,
he who has been good comes almost before he who has been great.]
Louis-Philippe, portrayed sympathetically by Hugo, stands in contrast to Louis-Napoléon, who had, according to Hugo, no concept
of goodness. "Entre l'attaque du passé et l'attaque de l'avenir, l'ét-
ablissement de juillet se débattait. Il représentait la minute, aux
prises d'une part avec les siècles monarchiques, d'autre part avec le
droit éternel" (*LM*, 855). [Between the attack of the past and the
attack of the future, the establishment of July was struggling. It rep-

resented the present, in conflict on the one hand with the monar-
chical centuries, on the other hand with the eternal right.] Twenty
years later, France would find itself in a similar situation, as the Second Empire struggled to find its place in history, caught between
memories of empire, republic, and monarchy. Where was right and
legitimacy? Whose version of the past would serve as the model for
all time and not just for the present?

Hugo's own maturation of political thought paralleled Marius's,
and both had close ties to their opinion of Napoléon Bonaparte.
"Comme ceci est l'histoire de beaucoup d'esprits de notre temps,
nous croyons utile de suivre ces phases pas à pas et de les indiquer
tous" (*LM*, 645–46). [As this is the history of many minds of our
time, we believe it to be useful to follow these phases step by step,
and to indicate them all.] Both Hugo and Marius saw events and
men embodied in two enormous constructions: the republic and the
empire. They saw emerge from the Revolution the spirit of the people and from the empire the spirit of France. Before becoming ad-
herents of the revolutionary ideal, they had been devoted royalists.
Only the unfolding of events over a number of years convinced
them that they had been wrong. For Marius, it was the sudden realization that his father had been a heroic soldier under Napoléon I;
for Hugo the process was gradual, just as progress itself takes time:
"Les progrès ne se font pas tous en une étape" (*LM*, 646). [Progress
is not accomplished in one go.]

Marius, like Hugo, came to an understanding of Napoléon I and
the Revolution through study, specifically the study of history
through its documentation. "En lisant l'histoire, en l'étudiant sur-
tout dans les documents et dans les matériaux, le voile qui couvrait
Napoléon aux yeux de Marius se déchira peu à peu" (*LM*, 647). [On
reading this history, especially in studying it in documents and materials, the veil that hid Napoléon from Marius's eyes was gradually
ripped away.] This is precisely the sort of enlightenment that Hugo
would like to bring to all the French people.

Marius goes too far in his admiration of Napoléon I and becomes
an example of what can happen when belief becomes fanaticism.

Napoléon fut [pour Marius] le constructeur prédestiné du groupe français succédant au groupe romain dans la domination de l'univers. . . .
Despote, mais dictateur; despote résultant d'une république et résumant
une révolution. Napoléon devint pour lui l'homme-peuple comme Jésus
est l'homme-Dieu. (*LM*, 648)

[Napoléon was (for Marius) the predestined builder of the French group, succeeding the Roman group in the domination of the universe. . . . Despot, but dictator; despot emerging from a republic and summing up a revolution. Napoléon became to him the people-man just as Jesus is the God-man.]

Rational thinking gives way to blind adulation. Rational action cannot result from such blind faith. Hugo hopes to convey the idea that the revolutionary ideal is one that in practice must be moderate in order to succeed. Extremism will only lead to more tyranny.

In describing the mood in France in 1832, Hugo points out how history works. "On se transformait presque sans s'en douter, par le mouvement même du temps. L'aiguille qui marche sur le cadran marche aussi dans les âmes" (*LM*, 661). [People were transformed almost without suspecting, by the very movement of time. The hand which moves around the dial moves also among souls.] The gradual changes in attitude that take place over time are the ones that will have a lasting impact on the collective memory of the time. These transformations can be influenced—by people such as Hugo for example—but they must develop deep inside each individual in order for them to be effective over time. The juxtaposition of history and opinions can be found throughout Hugo's works written in exile. History is made as the result of public opinion, which itself is created by an agglomeration of individual beliefs.[19]

The days of Napoléon Bonaparte are just a memory, and the men who rule the present political situation are traitors to his legacy. "Les hommes d'État, cela équivaut quelquefois à dire: les traîtres" (*LM*, 843). ["Statesmen" is sometimes equivalent to saying "traitors."] Hugo does not condemn, however, politicians out of hand. The word "sometimes" is significant because it allows Hugo to soften his stand. If men of state are not always traitors, then some of them must be loyal to the ideals of the nation. Such benevolence is a weakness in Hugo's argument, for no matter how idealistic men of state have been since the Revolution, none could be said to be the kind of pure leader that Hugo desires. His examples must thus come from further back in history, often from ancient Rome.

Two questions persist throughout Hugo's writings from exile: What is power and where does it come from? The legitimacy of those in power must always be questioned, and in order to answer that question, the source of power must be known. For Hugo, the greatest travesty of Louis-Napoléon's reign is the way in which he took power. The illegitimacy of the coup d'état strikes deeper at the heart of French history than even the usurpation of the uncle's mantle. For Hugo, power must emanate from the nation, made up of a free and educated population. Until the people are free and educated, the "wise men" must oversee any transfer of power in order to ensure its legitimacy. They do so by comparing it with what has happened through history. While some of these wise men may disagree, certain concepts such as the rule of law remain eternal.

Hugo remains acutely aware of class differences, and the bourgeoisie are certainly not the wise men to whom he refers.

> On a voulu, à tort, faire de la bourgeoisie une classe. La bourgeoisie est tout simplement la portion contentée du peuple. Le bourgeois, c'est l'homme qui a maintenant le temps de s'asseoir. Une chaise n'est pas une caste. Mais, pour vouloir s'asseoir trop tôt, on peut arrêter la marche même du genre humain. Cela a été souvent la faute de la bourgeoisie. (*LM*, 844–45)

> [We have tried, wrongly, to make a social class of the bourgeoisie. The bourgeoisie is simply the contented portion of the people. The bourgeois is the man who now has time to sit down. A chair is not a caste. But, by wishing to sit down too early, we may even stop the progress of the human race. That has often been the mistake of the bourgeoisie.]

As ironically bourgeois as Hugo's project often sounds, the bourgeoisie is an easy target. They have neither the lost grandeur of the monarchy nor the romantic suffering of the people. They stand in the way of both new and old ideals by putting their own, usually economic, interests first. For Hugo, Louis-Napoléon is the typical bourgeois, a man who will do anything to conserve the comforts and powers that he has gained, whether legally or illegally. Once he has attained power, he will suppress all opposition in order to maintain the perquisites that go with that power.

The empire has become in Hugo's imagination a continuing masquerade ball where pleasure and celebration carry on at the expense of the poor, where everyone is masked to hide their evil doings. "On ne voit plus de ces mardi gras-là aujourd'hui. Tout ce qui existe étant un carnaval répandu, il n'y a plus de carnaval" (1390).[20] [We no longer see such Mardi Gras nowadays. Everything being an expanded carnival, there is no longer any carnival.] There is no need for a real carnival because real life provides the necessary masquerade.

If Rome can love Nero, Paris can love Louis-Napoléon.

Paris est la grande ville folle toutes les fois qu'il n'est pas la grande cité sublime. Le carnaval y fait partie de la politique. Paris se laisse volontiers donner la comédie par l'infamie. Il ne demande à ses maîtres—quand il a des maîtres—qu'une chose: fardez-moi la boue. Rome était de la même humeur. Elle aimait Néron. Néron était un débardeur titan (*LM*, 1392–93)

[Paris is the great crazy city whenever she is not the great sublime city. The carnival is a part of her politics. Paris willingly supplies herself with comedy through infamy. She demands only of her masters—when she has masters—one thing: "Cover the mud for me!" Rome was in the same mood. She loved Nero. Nero was a titanic dock worker.]

As long as crime and tyranny are cloaked in riches and celebration, no one will notice the stench under the surface. "Tout peut être parodié, même la parodie" (*LM*, 391). [Everything can be parodied, even parody.] If the Second Empire is a parody of the first, Hugo is adept at parodying the parody.

EXILE AND THE SECOND EMPIRE/LE GAMIN IN PARIS

Hugo never wavers in his belief that the Second Empire will not last, either in fact or in history.

Dans cette minute que nous traversons, minute qui heureusement ne laissera point au dix-neuvième siècle sa figure, à cette heure où tant d'hommes ont le front bas et l'âme peu haute, parmi tant de vivants ayant pour morale de jouir, et occupés des choses courtes et difformes de la matière, quiconque s'exile nous semble vénérable. (*LM*, 538)

[In this moment through which we are passing, a moment which fortunately will not leave its stamp on the nineteenth century, in this hour when many have their brows lowered and their souls downtrodden, among so many of the living whose watchword is pleasure, and who are occupied with the brief, misshapen things of matter, whoever is self-exiled seems venerable to us.]

One way to combat the evil of the times is to go into exile, to lift one's head and look at the empire from the outside in order to gain a new perspective. Exile is not the easy road taken by those who choose to stay and profit from the new regime; it is the way of deprivation and hardship, but it leads to revelation and commitment to a better future.

The personification of the exile in *Les Misérables* is the figure of the gamin, Gavroche. Hugo's admiration for the gamin comes from his persistence and his joie de vivre. "Il y a deux choses dont [le gamin] est le Tantale et qu'il désire toujours sans y atteindre jamais: renverser le gouvernement et faire recoudre son pantalon" (*LM*, 601–2). [There are two things of which (the gamin) is the Tantalus, which he is always wishing for, but never attains—to overthrow the government, and to have his pants mended.] Always on the edge of starvation, he uses his wits to survive. Exiled within the confines of the city, he manages to make himself a part of the fabric of the town, darting in and out, stealing where necessary, but most often finding ways to satisfy his material needs in ways that are harmless and creative. Hugo sees himself in the gamin; he is the outsider who knows he will not single-handedly bring down the Second Empire but who will use his wits to outsmart the powers that be. "Cet enfant du bourbier est aussi l'enfant de l'idéal. Mesurez cette envergure qui va de Molière à Bara" (*LM*, 603). [This child of the mire is also the child of the ideal. Measure this breadth which spreads from Molière to Bara.] While the gamin has his antecedents in literature, he has his ideal as a guide. Hugo sums up his description of the gamin: "Le gamin est un être qui s'amuse, parce qu'il est malheureux" (*LM*, 603). [The *gamin* is a being who has fun because he is unfortunate.] This sentence describes Hugo's plight in exile; the man who unhappily resides away from home and rails at the government from a distance is at the same time a man who is having a good time doing so. The humor in Hugo's works is a counterweight to the potentially lugubrious nature of the writing.

The outsider as hero is reflected in Hugo's view of himself as exile, as hero-in-waiting. "Je ne suis d'aucune famille, moi . . . Je ne suis pas de celles des hommes . . . j'y suis de trop. . . . Je suis le malheureux, je suis dehors" (*LM*, 1418). [I am of no family . . . I am not of the family of men . . . I am an encumbrance. . . . I am the unfortunate; I am outside.] Jean Valjean spoke these lines, but Hugo certainly felt similar emotions. The exile is someone who, not necessarily through any fault of his own, is no longer a part of society. "Je suis hors de la vie, monsieur" (*LM*, 1420). [I am outside of life, sir.] His experience is so different that he has no place in the ongoing world around him. His past negates his future and renders his present problematic, to say the least. Only a sea change in that society will permit him to find his way. For Jean Valjean, that change, in the guise of the revelation of his true identity to Marius and Cosette, comes too late. Hugo hopes that such will not be his lot in the future. He wants the empire to fall and to permit him to retake his rightful place in French society.

The exile is not someone who will compromise to be taken back into society. "Pour qu'on me respecte, il faut qu'on me méprise" (*LM*, 1421). [For someone to respect me, he must despise me.] On the contrary, he has no desire to be part of a world of injustice. Neither Jean Valjean nor Hugo is willing to relinquish his principles for the minimal reward of personal happiness. Only when the full truth is known and only when the reign of injustice is lifted from the chests of the oppressed will the exile be able to return. Hugo's description of Gavroche's place of lodging, the Napoleonic-era elephant standing at the Place de la Bastille, endows it with symbolic power. "Etant du passé, il était de la nuit; et cette obscurité allait à sa grandeur" (*LM*, 975). [Being of the past, he was of the night; and this obscurity went well with his greatness.] Erected as a tribute to the Egyptian campaign, the elephant is neglected under subsequent regimes. Its only standing is as a reminder of the past. Yet Hugo gives it a new signification by making it the home of Gavroche, who symbolizes not only *les misérables* but also a certain joy found in the freedom of the streets. The statue of the past becomes a home for the future of the revolution, as Gavroche joins the barricade and gives his life for the cause of greater freedom. The geographical significance of the elephant, coupled with Gavroche's representation of revolutionary potential, enhances Hugo's portrayal of Paris as the home of French revolutionary movement, and it is on the Parisian stage that the novel's climax takes place.

Hugo's vision of Paris, especially as outlined in *Les Misérables*, acts as a problematization of the history of the city in the present, even though he writes of Paris in 1832 and not his present, 1862. "[Paris] construit dans tous les esprits l'idée du progrès" (*LM*, 607). [[Paris] builds in everyone's mind the idea of progress.] The city comes to represent for Hugo not only all of France, but all of Europe. The city is alive with all that is good and evil, and, it is especially the center of progress. "L'histoire passe par l'égout. . . . Elle retrouve dans ce qui reste ce qui a été . . . la trace" (*LM*, 1287).[21] [(History) passes through the sewer. . . . It finds in what remains what has been . . .

the trace.] At the same time, Paris is a repository of French history, and those who control the city can manipulate its historical meaning to the French people. During the Second Empire Louis-Napoléon tried to re-create many of the institutions his uncle had put in place. "L'entêtement des institutions vieillies à se perpétuer ressemble à l'obstination" (*LM*, 530). [The stubbornness of bygone institutions in perpetuating themselves resembles obstinacy.] Louis used the memory of such institutions to create his own version of his uncle's history.

Hugo finds such slavery to the past a dangerous way to proceed: "Rêver la prolongation indéfinie des choses défuntes et le gouvernement des hommes par l'embaumement, restaurer les dogmes en mauvais état . . . imposer le passé au présent, cela semble étrange" (*LM*, 530). [To dream of the indefinite prolongation of things that are dead and the government of mankind by embalming; to restore dilapidated dogmas . . . to impose the past on the present, all this seems strange.] Those who perpetuate the past do so through the use of slogans and catchwords that trigger sympathetic reactions in the people: social order, divine right, morality, family, respect for one's ancestors, tradition, legitimacy and religion. Hugo is not fooled by the slogans and he asks his reader to reflect on them with caution. We can certainly learn from the past, but we must not become slaves to outmoded ways of living and thinking. One could argue that Hugo's own calls for the people to follow Revolutionary ideals is the same sort of slavery to the past, but he clearly delineates his ideals, principles that are eternal, from the superficial tools of totalitarian structures: "Superstitions, bigotismes, cagotismes, préjugés, ces larves, toutes larves qu'elles sont, sont tenaces à la vie" (*LM*, 530). [Superstition, bigotry, hypocrisy, prejudice, these larvae, larvae though they may be, cling to life.]

Paradoxically, Paris often forgets its recent history so fast that necessary lessons are not learned. "Paris s'accoutume très vite à tout—ce n'est qu'une émeute—et Paris a tant d'affaires qu'il ne se dérange pas pour si peu. Ces enceintes immenses peuvent seules contenir en même temps la guerre civile et on ne sait quelle bizarre tranquillité" (*LM*, 1092). [Paris accustoms itself very quickly to everything—it is only an uprising—and Paris is so busy that it does not trouble itself for so little. These colossal walls alone can contain both a civil war, and an indescribably strange tranquility.] Hugo has lived through such scenarios. Here he is talking about 1832, but he could just as easily have been referring to 1851. Paris's ability to shrug off the violence going on within her is an obstacle to Hugo in exile, as he tries to make the French people remember the outrage and the violence of the coup d'état. If the people's revolt did not succeed at that time in overcoming a more general apathy, what chance does he have to make the people revolt years later against an illegitimate emperor?

If Paris were just Napoléon's city, Hugo would have a much easier time convincing the people of Paris to rise up against the emperor's ineffective nephew. "Rien n'est plus étrange; et c'est là le caractère propre des émeutes de Paris qui ne se retrouve dans aucune autre capitale. Il faut pour cela deux choses, la grandeur de Paris, et sa gaieté. Il faut la ville de Voltaire et de Napoléon" (*LM*, 1093). [Nothing is more strange; and this is the particular characteristic of Parisian uprisings, which is not found in any other capital. Two things are needed, the greatness of Paris and its gaiety. It requires the city of Voltaire and Napoléon.] But the gaiety of Paris, which in normal times Hugo would embrace, here acts as a hindrance to his project by providing an affective distance that dulls the senses of the people to revolt and makes them susceptible to a political apathy that allows for the installation of an illegally elected government.

Paris is the temptress, the holder of all that is beautiful and true, yet she can turn on you and sting you with the power of a million bees if you try to control her. "Paris, cette cité modèle . . . cette métropole de l'idéal . . . cette ruche de l'avenir. . . . Imitez Paris, vous vous ruinerez" (*LM*, 1283–84). [Paris, this model city . . . this metropolis of the ideal . . . this hive of the future. . . . Imitate Paris and you will be ruined.] The only way to govern her is with ideas that play to people's self-interest and dampen their revolutionary spirit. In a linguistic tour de force, using only verbs ending in "-ue," Hugo despairs that revolution can be understood and therefore effective. "Oui, me revoilà triste! Ce que c'est que d'avaler un huître et une révolution de travers! Je redeviens lugubre. Oh! L'affreux vieux monde! On s'y évertue, on s'y destitue, on s'y prostitue, on s'y tue, on s'y habitue" (*LM*, 1118). [Yes, here I am, sad again. What a thing it is to swallow an oyster or a revolution the wrong way! I am becoming gloomy. Oh! The frightful old world. They strive, they dismiss, they prostitute themselves, they kill one another, they get used to it!] Instead of using revolution to create a better world in the future, the people fall into the old traps of self-interest and apathy, creating new tyrannies that lead to new revolutions. The past is full of such examples and the poet despairs at being able to break the cycle. He also recognizes that power is based on self-interest: "La civilisation, malheureusement représentée à cette époque plutôt par une agrégation d'intérêts que par un groupe de principes, était ou se croyait en péril" (*LM*, 1232). [Civilization, unfortunately represented at that time by an aggregation of interests rather than by a group of principles, was, or thought itself to be in danger.] The words "at that time" are important for they imply that it has not always been this way and does not have to remain so. The future can actually be better if everyone applies a set of principles that benefits the population as a whole.

Hugo has just lived through ten years of viewing this materialistic France from afar. He is in a better position than most to observe its characteristics without being caught up in the wheels of materialism. He is confident that it is just a phase and that the true France will rise again.

> La France est de la même qualité de peuple que la Grèce et l'Italie. Elle est athénienne par le beau et romaine par le grand. En outre elle est bonne. . . . La France a ses rechutes de matérialisme. . . . La géante joue la naine; l'immense France a ses fantaisies de petitesse. Voilà tout. (*LM*, 1265–66)

> [France is of the same quality of people as Greece and Italy. She is Athenian by beauty, and Roman by greatness. In addition she is good. . . . France has her relapses of materialism. . . . The giant plays the dwarf; immense France has her petty whims. That sums it all up.]

Hugo never underestimates, however, the self-interested power of his principal adversaries, politicians, whose power to seduce the people into apathy is immense. Hugo would agree with Péguy that the philosopher is preferable to the politician.[22] "Une nation est illustre; elle goûte à l'idéal, puis elle mord dans la fange, et elle trouve cela bon; et si on lui demande d'où vient qu'elle abandonne Socrate pour Falstaff, elle répond: 'C'est que j'aime les hommes d'État'" (*LM*, 1266). [A nation is illustrious; it tastes the ideal; then it bites the filth, and finds it good; and if we ask why it abandons Socrates for Falstaff, it answers: "Because I love statesmen."] The philosopher never loses sight of the ideal, while the politician is mired in expediency. Moreover, when the politician does not have the advantage of having been elected, his legitimacy is even more questionable. Yet a head of state who convinces the people that his vision is the right one is the most dangerous creature of them all, because once he accomplishes that goal, there is nothing to stop him from achieving any personal ends he desires. It is often difficult for the people to resist his seduction because he holds the key to the money and the information systems of the country. The people are attracted by what he can give them and kept in ignorance of any alternative methods of government. For any other voice to be heard, it must not only be right but powerful.

ORDER AS A THREAT TO PROGRESS

For Hugo, the government's reactions to events will always be negative in comparison with those of the people, whose values are fundamental to the preservation of liberty.

> Les opinions avancées avaient des doubles fonds. Un commencement de mystère menaçait 'l'ordre établi,' lequel était suspect et sournois. Signe au plus haut point révolutionnaire. L'arrière-pensée du pouvoir rencontre dans la sape l'arrière-pensée du peuple. L'incubation des insurrections donne la réplique à la préméditation des coups d'État (*LM*, 661)

> [Advanced opinions had false bottoms. A hint of mystery threatened "the established order," which was untrustworthy and sullen, a sign that was revolutionary to the highest degree. The ulterior motives of those in power meet the reservations of the people. The incubation of insurrections corresponds to the premeditation of coups d'état.]

Both the people and the government are working from the same belief system at the outset, yet their reflexes develop differently according to their own interests. The regime in power wants to stay there; the people want to be treated fairly and with dignity.

While the government may, in the short run, consolidate its power by putting down an insurrection, the fabric of the nation is weakened by such repression. "Massacres qui déshonoraient trop souvent la victoire de l'ordre devenu féroce sur la liberté devenue folle" (*LM*, 1075). [Massacres which too often dishonored the victory of order grown ferocious over liberty gone mad.] Here the poet can shore up his own power base by both educating the public and by calling for change. The people, less inclined to support the government blindly, will be more receptive to such subversive language after the suppression of a revolt.

Hugo's conception of what order represents could not be more

different from the emperor's. "Qui désespère a tort. Le progrès se
réveille infailliblement. . . . Jusqu'à ce que l'ordre, qui n'est autre
chose que la paix universelle, soit établi, jusqu'à ce que l'harmonie
et l'unité règnent, le progrès aura pour étapes les révolutions" (*LM*,
1260–61). [He who despairs is wrong. Progress inevitably wakes
up. . . . Until order, which is nothing more than universal peace, is
established, until harmony and unity reign, progress will have revolutions as its stages.] Hugo's use of the word "order" is a conscious
reference to Louis-Napoléon's dependence on the same word to
maintain power. Order as the representative of universal peace is a
notion only an idealist could espouse. For the emperor, it is a means
of controlling the population. For Hugo, the new order will come
out of revolution; for Louis, order will prevent such revolutions
from toppling his regime.

Inspector Javert is the character that most closely responds to
Hugo's critique of Louis-Napoléon and the Second Empire. Javert
represents the concept of social order, and no slippage in his belief
could be permitted or the whole social edifice might crumble. His
appetite for power renders him a representative of the evil inherent
in the misuse of power.[23] "L'idéal pour Javert . . . c'était d'être irréprochable. [L'ordre] était son dogme et lui suffisait" (*LM*, 1348). [Jav-
ert's ideal . . . was to be irreproachable. . . . Order was his dogma
and was enough for him.] Unlike the order espoused by Louis-
Napoléon's propaganda machine, however, Javert's devotion to
order was sincere. In this context he can be seen as Hugo's vision of
the Second Empire, whose very existence came about through a call
for order. At the same time, Louis shows himself to be more dangerous than Javert because he subverts the very concept of order for
which he supposedly stands.

When Jean Valjean saves his life at the barricade, Javert's world,
unbeknownst to him, is about to be shaken at its foundation. When
he recaptures Valjean coming out of the sewer, he must decide between order and humanity, between sending Valjean back to the gallows and freeing the man who saved his life. Unable to decide, he
throws himself into the Seine and drowns. "L'autorité était morte
en lui" (*LM*, 1349). [Authority had died in him.] Javert, unlike
Hugo's vision of the empire, is not all bad. It is the society he represents that is the perpetrator of the injustice to Valjean and *les misérables*. Javert, "le guetteur de l'ordre, l'incorruptibilité au service de la
police" (*LM*, 1351) [the spy of order, incorruptibility in the service
of the police], finally realizes that the society he considered infalli-

ble has proven to be corrupt, and he cannot accept it. Hugo hopes that all of French society will come to the same conclusion.

Hugo presents a fascinating contrast between revolutionaries ("les barbares de la civilisation") [the barbarians of civilization] and the representatives of "order" ("les civilisés de la barbarie") [the civilized of barbarism]. "Quant à nous, si nous étions forcés à l'option, entre les barbares de la civilisation et les civilisés de la barbarie, nous choisirions les barbares. . . . Ni despotisme, ni terrorisme. Nous voulons le progrès en pente douce. L'adoucissement des pentes, c'est là toute la politique de Dieu" (*LM*, 871). [As for us, if we were forced to choose between the barbarians of civilization and the civilized of barbarism, we would choose the barbarians. . . . Neither despotism, nor terrorism. We want progress on a gentle slope. . . . The smoothing of the way is God's whole agenda.] The "barbarians of civilization" want to end oppression and abolish tyranny. They want all the things Hugo does: "le travail pour l'homme, l'instruction pour l'enfant, la douceur sociale pour la femme, la liberté, l'égalité, la fraternité, le pain pour tous, l'idée pour tous, l'Edenisation du monde, le Progrès" (*LM*, 870) [employment for men, instruction for children, social gentleness for women, liberty, equality, fraternity, bread for everyone, ideas for all. The Edenization of the world, Progress.] Their methods may not always be pretty, but their ideals are a beacon of light for the whole nation.

The "civilized of barbarism" are "souriants, brodés, dorés, enrubannés, constellés, en bas de soie, en plumes blanches," etc. (*LM*, 871) [smiling, embroidered, gilded, covered with ribbons and stars, in silk stockings, in white feathers] and insist on maintaining divine right, fanaticism, ignorance, slavery, the death penalty and war. Hugo's conflicts are seen here in terms of class: the aristocracy and bourgeoisie clinging to injustices of the past, the people loudly proclaiming that the day of reckoning is nigh. Hugo himself proposes something in between. He wants revolutionary change but without revolution. He calls for nonviolent action based on clear religious principles of love and respect for the rights of others. While Prendergast may see this as a fundamentally bourgeois proposal, the ideal is as pure as ever.[24]

Hugo recognizes that the struggle is a social one, and not just a philosophical construct. "C'étaient les éléments sociaux qui entraient en lutte, en attendant le jour où ils entreront en équilibre" (*LM*, 1232). [It was the social elements entering into conflict while awaiting the day when they will enter into equilibrium.] France is a society that retains its strict divisions between social classes, and Hugo, despite some theoretical bluster, does not dispute the status quo in this context. On the other hand, he will combat the power of one class to oppress another, so that one day power will be more harmoniously distributed.

No matter how evil and corrupt politicians may be, Hugo never gives in to a cry for vengeance. We saw in *Les Châtiments* that he did not believe that Louis-Napoléon should be executed upon his inevitable demise, and he repeats this call for amnesty in *Les Misérables.* "Les émeutes, dans l'état où est la société, sont tellement la faute de tout le monde qu'elles sont suivies d'un certain besoin de fermer les yeux" (*LM*, 1359). [Uprisings, in the present state of society, are so much the fault of everyone that they are followed by a certain need to close your eyes.] This spirit of forgiveness comes not just from Hugo's opposition to the death penalty, but from a longstanding French governmental tradition of forgiveness after times of difficulty. The amnesties after World War II averted the spectacle of putting thousands of collaborators on trial and the risk of undermining national healing. On the other hand, such amnesties lead to a general tendency to sweep ugly matters aside and pretend they never existed. This can result in the return to power of those who should rightfully have been separated from public life. Louis-Napoléon is one example. In this episode, the person who is spared execution is Marius, the innocent who fights at the barricade to save the honor of the country his father had defended. Yet even Marius is not blameless, as Hugo points out. Everyone must share the responsibility of blood in the streets, even if the government does the bulk of the killing. We are left then with an ambiguous message from Hugo. Everyone is to blame, yet no one is permanently removed from public life. The government is repressive, yet no one should be guillotined for his actions. In Hugo's ideal republic, justice will be merciful.

Les Misérables gives Hugo a chance to develop these ideas about the future, based on memories of past ideals. Progress, as we have seen, is the key to any future world seen by Hugo. The notion of progress is forever present in the novel. G., le conventionnel says: "Le droit a sa colère, monsieur l'évêque; et la colère du droit est un élément du progrès" (*LM*, 43). [Justice has its anger, Bishop, and the wrath of justice is an element of progress.] Here progress is propped up by that which is right, even if rightness must rise up in anger against the forces of oppression. Enjolras echoes Hugo's vision of the ideal future.

> Or, la loi du progrès, c'est que les monstres disparaissent devant les anges, et que la Fatalité s'évanouisse devant la Fraternité. . . . Amour, tu es l'avenir. . . . Dans l'avenir personne ne tuera personne, la terre rayonnera, le genre humain aimera. Il viendra, citoyens, ce jour où tout sera concorde, harmonie, lumière, joie et vie, il viendra, et c'est pour qu'il vienne que nous allons mourir. (*LM*, 1141)

> [Now, the law of progress is that monsters disappear before angels, and that Fatality disappears before Fraternity. . . . Love, you are the future. . . . In the future no one will commit murder, the earth will be radiant, the human race will love. It will come, citizens, that day when all will be in agreement, harmony, light, joy, and life; it will come, and it is in order to make it come that we are going to die.]

Hugo's idealism is never in short supply, and this fundamental optimism is necessary to provide a contrast to the bitter reality of the present.

Hugo's ideal always includes faith as a central pillar. Monseigneur Bienvenu says: "Le progrès doit croire en Dieu" (*LM*, 47) [Progress must believe in God], and Hugo's appeal from exile to the French people always contains the wish that they look to their faith to find the reasons to follow him into a better future. Monseigneur Bienvenu continues: "Oh, je ne voudrais pas avoir tout ce superflu-là à me crier sans cesse aux oreilles: il y a des gens qui ont faim! il y a des gens qui ont froid! il y a des pauvres! il y a des pauvres!" (50). [Oh! I wouldn't want to have all these unnecessary possessions yelling forever in my ears: "There are people who are hungry! There are people who are cold! There are poor people! There are poor people!"] Jean Valjean inherits his generous spirit from the bishop and adopts an attitude of forgiveness and giving that coincides with Hugo's ideals.

The Second Empire championed the accumulation of wealth, but the poor continued to struggle. For Hugo, only through a return to the revolutionary spirit of sharing and progress could France return to glory. "Qu'on ne se méprenne pas sur notre pensée, nous ne confondons point ce qu'on appelle 'opinions politiques' avec la grande aspiration du progrès, avec la sublime foi patriotique, démocratique et humaine, qui, de nos jours, doit être le fond même de toute intelligence généreuse" (*LM*, 51–52). [Let no one misunderstand our

idea; we do not confuse what are called "political opinions" with
that grand hope of progress, with that sublime patriotic, democratic,
and human faith, which, in this time, should be the very foundation
of all generous intelligence.] These last two words are the key to
Hugo's view of progress in the future.

Belief and love are consciously religious words that symbolize the
Hugolian ideal. "Nous ne comprenons ni l'homme, comme point
de départ, ni le progrès comme but, sans ces deux forces qui sont
les deux moteurs: croire et aimer" (*LM*, 536). [We understand neither man as a starting-point, nor progress as the goal, without these
two forces that are the two great driving forces, faith and love.] Believe in God, certainly, but believe the poet as well when he shows
you the way toward the future through a restructuring of the past.
Love God, but love your fellow man as well in order to avoid the
mistakes of the past.

> "Le progrès est le but, l'idéal est le type.
> Qu'est-ce que l'idéal? C'est Dieu.
> Idéal, absolu, perfection, infini; mots identiques." (*LM*, 536)

> [Progress is the goal, the ideal is the model.
> What is the ideal? It is God.
> Ideal, absolute, perfection, the infinite; these words are synonymous.]

Hugo succinctly sums up his project of showing the people the way
to a perfect future through belief in progress and in the eternal ideals of freedom and love. Progress comes only from daring. Paris
dares and Hugo dares to write about it. Reminiscent of his call for
someone to say "no," he outlines how he sees daring as a way to
lead: "Le cri: *Audace!* est un Fiat Lux. Il faut, pour la marche en
avant du genre humain, qu'il y ait sur les sommets en permanence
de fières leçons de courage. Les témérités éblouissent l'histoire et
sont une des grandes clartés de l'homme" (*LM*, 607). [The cry, "Audacity," is a *Fiat Lux.* The onward march of the human race requires
that there be on the heights noble lessons of courage. Deeds of daring dazzle history, and form one of the guiding lights of man.]
Hugo's vision of the future is fundamentally utopian, and he sees
the realization of his dreams as being impossible without the willingness of the people to dream as he does. "Rien n'est tel que le rêve
pour engendrer l'avenir. Utopie aujourd'hui, chair et os demain"
(*LM*, 661). [There is nothing like a dream to create the future. Uto-

pia today, flesh and blood tomorrow.] If we remain always in the realm of the practical and the possible, we will never be able to reach beyond the banal.

Progress is always linked in Hugo's mind with honesty. "Le progrès est honnête homme; l'idéal et l'absolu ne font pas le mouchoir" (*LM*, 1021). [Progress is an honest man; the ideal and the absolute pick no pockets.] The fundamental difference between himself and Louis-Napoléon, as he sees it, is one of honesty versus dissimulation, of integrity versus expediency, of right versus hypocrisy. Honest progress will come about gradually. "Le progrès tout entier tend du côté de la solution. . . . L'effacement de la misère se fera par une simple évolution de niveau" (*LM*, 1023). [All progress tends toward a solution. . . . The abolition of misery will be brought about by a simple evolution of level.] No talk of revolution here, only evolution. Hugo had been in exile for almost ten years as he completed *Les Misérables*, and he knew that Louis-Napoléon would not be easily unseated. This distance made his role as the conscience of the nation that much more important. His is the constant drumbeat of progress toward a future peace. "L'évanouissement des guerres, de la guerre des rues comme de la guerre des frontières, tel est l'inévitable progrès. Quel que soit aujourd'hui, la paix, c'est Demain" (*LM*, 1080). [The vanishing of war, of war in the streets as well as border wars, such is inevitable progress. Whatever may be today, peace is Tomorrow.] By capitalizing "Tomorrow," Hugo personifies and deifies the future, the time of peace, in order to contrast it with the present, the time of unrest and despotism. While Louis-Napoléon had used universal suffrage to his own advantage, Hugo still remains faithful to this fundamental part of representative democracy.

Up to this point, we have seen Hugo limit his vision to the boundaries of France. Every call for a new republic has been for a French version of Hugo's ideal. Now he goes further and includes the entire world.

> Combeferre sortait peu à peu de la forme étroite du dogme et se laissait aller aux élargissements du progrès, et il en était venu à accepter, comme évolution définitive et magnifique, la transformation de la grande république française en immense république humaine. (*LM*, 1213)

> [Combeferre had been leaving little by little the narrow form of dogma, and allowing himself to tread the broad paths of progress and he had

come to accept, as its definitive and magnificent evolution, the transformation of the great French Republic into the immense human republic.]

This is not merely hyperbole; Hugo is truly an idealist and as such he includes everyone in his vision of a better world. This global view is no more unrealistic than the French version. Reach for the moon and you may get the stars.

Enjolras's long discourse on the future represents the climax of the novel of ideas.

> Enjolras s'écria: 'Citoyens, vous représentez-vous l'avenir? . . . plus de haine . . . à tous le travail, pour tous le droit. . . . Dompter la matière, c'est le premier pas; réaliser l'idéal, c'est le second. Réfléchissez à ce qu'a déjà fait le progrès. . . . Et quelle révolution ferons-nous? Je viens de le dire, la révolution du Vrai. (*LM,* 1213)

> [Enjolras exclaimed: "Citizens, can you imagine the future? . . . no more hatred . . . to all, employment, for all, law. . . . To subdue matter is the first step; to realize the ideal is the second. Reflect upon what progress has already done. . . . And what revolution shall we effect? I have just said, the revolution of Truth.]

From a political point of view, there is one guiding principle: the sovereignty of the individual, otherwise known as *Liberté.* The protection of the individual by the whole is called *Fraternité.* If liberty is the summit, equality is the foundation. Here is the juncture of those who think and those who suffer. "La misère rencontre l'idéal" (*LM,* 1213–16). [Misery encounters the ideal.] Hugo puts into his character's mouth his own ideas about the future and about the sacrifice necessary to achieve his idealistic ends. *Les misérables* have found their ideal in the future proposed by the poet.

Progress is not something that is chosen; it is inherent in every society. "Le progrès est le mode de l'homme. La vie générale du genre humain s'appelle le Progrès; le pas collectif du genre humain s'appelle le Progrès. Le progrès marche; il fait le grand voyage humain et terrestre vers le céleste et le divin" (*LM,* 1260). [Progress is man's way. The general life of the human race is called Progress; the collective advance of the human race is called Progress. Progress advances; it makes the great human and terrestrial journey towards the celestial and the divine.] Since 1851 Hugo has been the thinker unable to awaken the march of progress. Yet his optimism, based on faith and history, has never wavered. "Qu'est-ce donc le progrès? Nous venons de le dire. La vie permanente des peuples" (*LM*, 1261). [What, then, is progress? We have just said. The permanent life of societies.] Progress is an inevitable part of social life, and until the perfect society is established, revolution will be necessary to restore progress after the tyrants have taken it away temporarily. Past and future resemble each other in the way they influence the actions of today. Only the result is different, as the lies of the past give way to the truth of the future. "L'utopie . . . sort de sa sphère radieuse en faisant la guerre. Elle, la vérité de demain, elle emprunte son procédé, la bataille, au mensonge d'hier. Elle, l'avenir, elle agit comme le passé" (*LM*, 1261). [Utopia . . . leaves its radiant sphere by making war. The truth of tomorrow borrows her process, battle, from the lie of yesterday. She, the future, acts like the past.]

In the years following the publication of *Les Misérables*, Louis-Napoléon's status in French history, although far from universally agreed upon, was clearly diminished by Victor Hugo. While the nation prospered and saw great technological, financial, and architectural changes under the Second Empire, Louis has not been remembered as a strong leader whose vision led to a better France. His obsession with wealth, both personal and national, has overshadowed his contribution to social progress, such as improved conditions for workers. Because of texts like *Les Misérables*, history has stripped Louis of his privileged position and given the principal roles to men such as Haussmann, leaving the moral high ground to the people.

The power of narrative lies in its hold on the collective imagination, which is always based on the group's collective memory of historical events. By influencing the way people see history, literary texts can actually affect the course of history, whether it be in the way historical events are portrayed in the classroom, in history books, in the development of a new constitution, or even in immediate political action. As a competitive reaction to the *Les Misérables'* popularity, for example, Louis-Napoléon put in place new measures to help the poor. Victor Hugo, a master chronicler of his time, not only influenced the emperor's policies but also played a significant role in how the Second Empire and Louis have been remembered over time.

CONCLUSION

Les Misérables was Hugo's last and greatest effort to expose the empire for what it was. By putting into novel form what he had begun in an exposé (*Napoléon le petit*) and poetry (*Les Châtiments*), Hugo not only continued to bludgeon the emperor, but he also brought the power of fiction to bear in his struggle. Hugo was France's preeminent poet and had already charmed his readers with *Notre-Dame de Paris*, so the success of *Les Misérables* was predictable. The novel represents a problematization on a number of different levels. In each case, Hugo delves deeply into the psyche of the group being studied in order to understand what makes them tick. By understanding that, he will have a better chance of changing people's thinking about a wide range of topics that the empire has prevented from being shown the light of day. By explaining his own understanding of the memories, problems and hopes of his readers, Hugo will have a better chance of having his dreams come true.

Hugo shows to full advantage the powers of historical fiction that traditional history does not have. While documented history is read by and affects mainly those of a scholarly bent, fiction is accessible to all, through the potent combination of memory and imagination. *Les Misérables* represents the culmination of Hugo's thinking in exile. While it is certainly a work of great idealism, it is also one of significant realism. Hugo's goals are clear from the outset of *Napoléon le petit*, but it is not until he puts his feelings into novel form that Hugo's majestic imagination takes hold and delivers a crushing blow to Louis-Napoléon. While it is not enough to dethrone the emperor, Hugo stakes a claim to be heard that cannot be denied. The novel's success will redound through the years until his triumphant return to Paris in 1870. While his ideal republic has not yet come to pass, a republic emerges from the ruins of the empire and the Commune. In *Les Misérables*, Hugo made an indelible place for himself in the collective memory that he had tried so hard to influence.

It remains to look, in the conclusion to this study, at how Hugo's version of history in the three works we have examined, coupled with his utopian vision of the future, helped the French people recuperate their revolutionary ideals, put the recent past behind them and move into the next phase of their history, the Third Republic. Through Ricœur's articulation of forgetting and pardoning, we can more easily explain the great success of *Les Misérables* and, more generally, of Hugo's historical and political vision. While we have dealt here with interpretations of the past, Hugo's favorite realm was the future, and his utopian vision of that future has come to pass in many ways. No society arrives at its present without remembering and then forgetting its past; Hugo's works helped France accomplish that goal.

Conclusion: Visions of the Future

Victor Hugo's place in history is secure; he remains one of the most beloved and widely read authors in the world. (He is even a considered a saint in Viet Nam's Cao Dai religion.) In the preceding pages, I have undertaken to reposition him as a historian of his time, as well as a writer of poetry and fiction. This allows us to reconsider a text that was less well known (*Napoléon le petit*) and classics (*Les Châtiments* and *Les Misérables*) as historical documents. At the same time, Hugo's imagined twentieth century adds another dimension to the historical perspective by showing the prescience of his vision of the future. He was convinced that the upheaval and dishonesty he saw around him would give way to a new age of freedom and equality. In order to reach such a place, however, Hugo and his society would have to pass through a period of healing, forgiving, and forgetting. In this conclusion, I will examine briefly the significance of these processes in the historiographical process in order to better position Hugo as a historian and a prophet.

The Historical Condition

The relationship between past and present has been at the heart of this study, and it is fitting to conclude with a final look at it in order to clarify Hugo's position as historian of the present. Hugo had an ambivalent posture concerning the rapport between past and present because he revered them both and because he understood the power that each held over the society. The past was a source of tradition and strength, the present the agent of change, foreshadowing a new world. He also understood that in order for a community to move into the future, it had to relinquish parts of its past, the elements of stagnation that were dragging it back toward the reliance on tradition for meaning. In this context, history plays a nonhistorical role in society by reinforcing the importance of the present and future. The ability and the right to judge the past rely

204

on an individual's desire to build a future. The "constructive urge" comes at the price of rejecting the past (*MHF*, 291). A forward-looking historian and critic turns toward the nonhistorical, such as art and religion, in order to cure himself of "historical sickness" the impulse to rely on the past to find meaning in the present (*MHF*, 292).

Every society finds its present day different from, and ultimately preferable to, eras that have come before it. The three arbiters of such a judgment are the judge, the historian, and the individual citizen. But it is ultimately history itself that decides the matter, as long duration corrects the short-term memory of events. As time passes, the present evolves, as does our view of both the past and the future. Hugo situates himself in time through his view of progress, an ideal that drives him to judge both his past and his present in order to construct the best world for the future. Progress is not always easy and success is mixed, but "a global newness widens the distance between the space of experience and the horizon of expectation" (*MHF*, 297).[1] Hugo sees himself in all three arbiters' roles—judge, historian, and citizen—as he seeks to help the French people find an equilibrium between past and present that will lead to a better future.

Hugo's constant point of reference is the French Revolution, a moment of crucial significance in the development of history as a modern genre. History in the nineteenth century takes up one role of religion in society by providing the means of understanding the past. This displacement of traditional forms of understanding allowed the rise of new ways of thinking such as idealistic philosophy.[2] Hugo does not, of course, replace religion; he modifies its role in the historical process by assigning it a place of honor, by designating it the keeper of the ideal, while allowing history to take over as both a preserver of tradition and an agent of change.

Hugo's idealistic vision of the United States of Europe reflects a recognition of the need to unify different modes of thinking, aiming, both on the practical and political fronts, at the establishment of peace between nations and the worldwide diffusion of democratic ideals (MHF, 302). Implicit in this unifying view is the need to find a new way of thinking about the future, which in turn leads to a new conception of the past. In order to attain the goal of European democracy, the different societies will have to reject their reliance on tradition and, by inference, religion, in order to understand one another. Within each state, people of differing views will have to find common ground, and the best hope for doing so lies in the ideals of the French Revolution.[3]

Historical relativism touches every domain of human experience; for each observer there is a different point of view (*MHF*, 304). The double meaning of the word *histoire* (history and story) comes into play again, as the accumulation of past events and the reporting of those events. Critical philosophy has as its goal to reflect on the limits of an understanding that history would like to see as universal (*MHF*, 305). Each era sees its "modernity" as new and different, and therefore superior. The urge is to analyze the new era and compare it to ones that have come before, while all the time remembering that any attempt to assign "truth" to the analysis will lead to controversy (*MHF*, 305). This possessive stance leads to a new view of the future because the future that was our parents' is no longer ours.[4] Hugo wants to take possession of the vision of the future for all the French people by painting Louis-Napoléon as an agent of the past, desperately hanging onto outdated traditions in order to stay in power.

Ricœur reaches back to Aristotle to argue for the superiority of fiction (epic and tragic) over historical narrative when it comes to expressing the truth. The French Revolution changed, however, the way we look at truth by emphasizing our (modern) dissatisfaction with the present. This "rupture on the level of mores and taste" gave rise to Romanticism (*MHF*, 308). Baudelaire, for example, defined modernity as "historical self-consciousness" (*MHF*, 310), this belief that "our" modernity is different from and superior to previous ones. Hugo is convinced that his era's modernity can flourish only when the yoke of the past, represented by Louis-Napoléon and the forces of repression, is thrown off. His works, and in this instance his novel, are an attempt to re-create the epic on a Greek scale in order to provoke his audience to see the truth of the historical situation. Hugo thus takes on the double role of historian and judge.

While the historian searches for the truth and the judge for justice, both are supposed to be impartial. Each represents a third party in relation to the public space occupied by the protagonists of social action (*MHF*, 314). In the dispute pitting Hugo against Louis-Napoléon, there are no impartial judges. Hugo and Louis become adversarial lawyers in a long running trial. No attempt is made to pretend that impartiality exists. Meanwhile the French people, the ultimate arbiters of the case, may not be perfect judges but at least their impartiality is based on a theory of justice supported by the idea of equality. Such judges would neither curry favor nor show anger.[5] The French people will render a judgment after the fact, after the historians, including Hugo, have spoken.

Both the historian and the judge rely on eyewitness testimony in order to arrive at the truth. In both cases, the testimony given is submitted to rigorous criticism: cross-examination in a trial, corroborating or conflicting evidence in the documentation stage of the writing of history. The judge and the historian must be experts in recognizing falsehood. In this sense, the historian often acts as a judge as he sifts through the documentary evidence available to him (*MHF*, 317). In both a trial and a historical narrative, there is a representation of the facts of the case, written in the present tense, as a reconstruction, a mise en scène. Since witnesses often disagree, the representation of "facts" is also a representation between adversarial parties. In a trial, the opposing sides are present, but in a historical document, they exist only in writing (*MHF*, 319). A trial depends on language, as each side argues his case: "This organized debate is intended to be a model of discussion in which the passions that fed the conflict are transferred into the arena of language" (*MHF*, 319). Such is the case for Hugo and Louis, since their dispute takes place in the court of public opinion, although their "trial" lasts eighteen years.

The greatest difference between a sentence and a historical judgment is that the former cannot be changed after the normal appeals process has run its course. Public opinion concerning the case will continue to evolve (*MHF*, 319). A historical narrative represents just one piece of an ever-evolving puzzle, constructed by various voices representing a multitude of points of view during different eras. History becomes "an unending process of revision, which makes the writing of history a perpetual rewriting" (*MHF*, 320). Historical judgment is always provisionary while a sentence at the end of a trial is definitive. The historian reopens the circle of potentially limitless explanation that the judge eventually closes (*MHF*, 321). Hugo, as prosecutor and historian, has the luxury of keeping the circle open at all times since he has no pretense of impartiality. Louis, in his eyes, is guilty from the beginning. His job, as chief prosecutor, is to convince the people that his case is the strongest.

The historian is a judge of not one case, but of a collection of cases, and as such, his ear is attuned to testimony in a different manner than the judge's. A judge listens to a small number of actors, and if it is a historical trial, these are usually people at the highest level of the societal structure. The historian casts a much wider net, as he hears from not only those at the top of the hierarchy, but those at the bottom as well, even from "bystanders, those more or less passive witnesses that are the silent populations in their complicity" (*MHF*, 324). This is Hugo's project in *Les Misérables*. After having heard from eyewitnesses in *Napoléon le petit*, and after analyzing the testimony in *Les Châtiments*, Hugo descends to the bottom of the social scale in *Les Misérables* in order to paint a comprehensive picture of the effects of injustice and inequality. Only by allowing his readers to hear the voices of the "bystanders" will Hugo be able to win his case in the court of collective memory. These "crowds . . . currents and . . . anonymous forces" (*MHF*, 324) are what allow the historian to at least approach the kind of definitive judgment that a trial produces.

While every trial begins with the pretense that each piece of testimony will be equal in strength and believability to any other, the fact remains that some witnesses tell more convincing tales than others and that some testimonies are based on truth and others are not (*MHF*, 325). A judge and jury must decide whose version of events is most plausible and must do so within the limits of their competence. The historian, on the other hand, can at least pretend to be impartial and attempt to come to some sort of consensus concerning what happened. He has the "possibility and the duty to transgress over and over again" (*MHF*, 326). Hugo finds himself in between these two poles: on the one hand, he has a certain number of years in which to obtain historical perspective on the events of December, 1851; on the other hand, his field of vision is limited because he has the short-term goal of helping to drive Louis from the throne. The French people, through their collective memory of the era, and professional historians of the Second Empire will be the ones who finish the history that Hugo began.

How will Louis-Napoléon be judged after the fall of the empire in 1870? The role of historian as judge is as problematic as that of the historian as witness.[6] Ricœur asks in what measure historiography can contribute to establishing the right sentence for the greatest criminals of the twentieth century and the inverse question of how a sentence already handed down can influence historical debate (*MHF*, 326). While Ricœur is referring specifically to judgments concerning the Holocaust, we can extrapolate these same notions to the conflict between Hugo and Louis-Napoléon. Hugo was testifying against Louis while the latter was still in power and, therefore, sus-

ceptible to judgment by his people. Historians later debated Louis'
status when he had already thrown away the empire through a des-
perate desire to emulate his uncle's conquests. The defeat at Sedan
sealed Louis' fate in the eyes of public opinion, although historians
have not always been as harsh on him.

Ricœur sees the inability to condemn someone completely as a
modern counterpart of the elimination of absolute praise of the
monarch (*MHF*, 326). Such an inability can lead to the construction
of new myths, such as the revisionist theories about the Holocaust.
Such revisionism leads to a crisis between historical judgments and
judgments that are more moral, judicial, or political (*MHF*, 328). All
of these kinds of judgment are present in the dispute between Hugo
and Louis-Napoléon, and the boundaries between prosecutor,
judge, and historian become blurred. The fact remains, however,
that Hugo's version of events will be the one that constitutes both
the judgment and the history of Louis' reign. And it will be the people, through their collective memory, who confirm such a judgment.

Ricœur is at his most eloquent when describing the role of ordinary citizens in the formation of "historical knowledge." This idea
is fundamental to the project of the historian of the present. "The
intervention of citizens is never completed, placing them more on
the side of the historian. But the citizen is in search of an assured
judgment, intended to be as definitive as that of the judge. In every
respect, the citizen remains the ultimate arbiter. It is the citizen who
militantly carries the 'liberal' values of constitutional democracy. In
the final analysis, the conviction of the citizen alone justifies the fairness of the penal procedure in the courts and the intellectual honesty of the historian in the archives" (*MHF*, 333). The fact that the
citizen plays this important role in a democracy is key to Hugo's
whole project. During the Second Empire, the citizens of France
could not sit in judgment on their emperor because they had not
been afforded the power to do so. Hugo's call for a return to representative democracy is based in part on his desire to restore the
power of citizens as judges and ultimately historians. As long as the
empire was in place, stifling all voices of opposition, Hugo had to
play the role of citizen-judge-historian. Only when the empire was
replaced could the process of healing begin.

Even before the fall of the empire, Hugo worked toward forgetting disagreeable past events, such as the coup d'état. We have seen
that forgetting is not always a negative thing, as it allows a person
or a society to evolve. Memory may be defined as the fight against

forgetting, but paradoxically, forgetting sets us free to move into the future. An appeased memory equals a happy forgetting (*MHF*, 412). If memory can be defined as the enemy of forgetting, then a constant negotiation must go on between the two to find the equilibrium necessary for us to function (*MHF*, 413). Forgetting defies memory's attempt to be absolutely reliable and sets the terms for the necessary negotiation (*MHF*, 414).

Forgetting exists to different degrees: total oblivion, partial memory, or a sort of reserve from which memories can be plucked at any time. Ricœur calls the former "forgetting through effacement of traces" (*MHF*, 414) and the latter "the reserve of forgetting" (*MHF*, 417). It is from this last group that the historian, through perseverance, builds his story (*MHF*, 417). Memories reappear in various forms: written, oral, sensual, and so on, and the historian weaves his story from them. In many cases, the writing of this history allows the events to become a definitive part of the past, which in turn permits the reader to come to terms with the memories and move forward into the future. The reserve of forgetting thus becomes forgetting through effacement of traces through the writing of history.

Forgetting can be abused in much the same way as memory: through forbidding, manipulating, or ordering. This often takes the form of an amnesty. When a society is forbidden to forget, unpleasant memories become part of its existence, creating a state of discouragement and fear. When the natural process of forgetting is manipulated, people can be forced to remember that which they would have chosen to forget. When a society grants amnesty to criminals, history is distorted, and the forgetting process is aborted before it can run its course. Hugo saw all of these things happening under Louis-Napoléon, and he decried the manipulation of forgetting as much as the distortion of memory.

Throughout his writing from exile, Hugo constantly said that Louis, once dethroned, should not be put to death. Obviously, Hugo's sentiment against capital punishment is the driving force behind these statements, but can we go so far as to infer a sense of pardon? Perhaps not, but by taking the high road on execution, Hugo puts the possibility of pardon on the table.

Ricœur ends *Memory, History, Forgetting* with a chapter examining the relationship between pardon, memory, forgetting and history. "Forgiveness—if it has a sense, and if it exists—constitutes the horizon common to memory, history and forgetting" (*MHF*, 457). Pardoning is never easy, and the lack of fixed limits in history at times makes it seem impossible, but there is a certain "consideration due to every human being" (*MHF*, 458) that calls for a contemplation of pardoning at every turn. Because the relationship between memory and forgetting is so fluid, any chance to establish what Ricœur calls a "peaceful memory' (*mémoire heureuse*) (*MHF*, 459) relies on our examining the possibility of a pardon before executing the sentence handed down.[7]

Ricœur's section on political culpability provides us with some clues as to Hugo's thinking about Louis-Napoléon and the French people who "collaborated" with the emperor. Ricœur makes a distinction between the criminal culpability of those who actually committed crimes and the collective guilt of the people, which can never be criminalized (*MHF*, 474). In between these two groups lies the political establishment, which may not have actively participated in criminal activity but which, to one degree or another, acquiesced to the behavior of those committing the crimes. From the very beginning, Hugo designates the coup d'état a criminal act, and even entitles his story about the events of December 2 to 4, 1851 *Histoire d'un crime*. And even as he railed against the emperor, he included Louis' associates and those who accepted positions in the new government as part of the guilty group.

Once the culpability of the perpetrators has been established, the way they are dealt with becomes critical to the collective memory of the times. For Ricœur, the representation of responsibility is more important than what form punishment takes.[8] In an extraordinary twist on historical precedent, Hugo tries, convicts and sentences Louis-Napoléon and his closest supporters before they have spent a year in power. He finds them guilty of crimes—political, social, moral, and physical—against the French people and condemns them all to prison, yet, as we saw in *Napoléon le petit*, he sentences none of them, not even Louis, to death.

Hugo understood that punishment has limits. While Louis may have been indisputably guilty in Hugo's eyes, the fact remains that a defense lawyer could have made a case for the emperor. History has shown that Louis had his supporters. In a democratic society, every citizen has a voice, and the death penalty would effectively snuff out the voices of those who support the condemned. Ricœur cites Karl Jaspers: "The ethos of politics . . . is the principle of a state in which all participate with their consciousness, their knowledge, their opinions, and their wills"[9] (Cited in *MHF*, 475). And for Hugo, stopping short of execution represents the moderation necessary for a just society to function.[10] Vengeance was never Hugo's motivation in his writing from exile; his focus was on the political more than the personal, despite the strident tone of a text such as *Napoléon le petit.*

While communities may not be criminally liable for complicity with evil regimes, they are of course morally responsible for their lack of action. By refusing to see or simply by remaining passive, people become individually responsible for collaboration, and when a political change comes and it is time to suffer the consequences of one's actions or inaction, the focus should remain on the individual's responsibility. Such individual accounting does not always happen, however, because the victors who were once victims have their own collective memory of the wrongs done to them as a group. "The collectivity has no moral conscience," writes Ricœur and we end up with reprisals such as those seen at the end of the German occupation of France (*MHF,* 477). Old hatreds resurface; humiliations are not forgotten. Political proposals are generally ineffective in the face of fundamental friend-foe relationships, and even areas of common experience such as the national memory, cannot overcome them. "Love and hate operate differently, it seems, on the collective scale of memory" (*MHF,* 477). Vengeance no doubt also played a role in the violent nature of the Commune, but that was a much more confused situation, politically, militarily, and morally.

For Hugo, what mattered was that the emperor was gone, and a return to normalcy was greatly anticipated. In view of this, Hugo was more inclined to moderation and clemency toward the emperor, but not toward his memory. While Hugo may have recommended sparing the emperor the death penalty, he would never forgive him for his misdeeds. In contrast to so many postwar reprisals around the world, however, Hugo would be more receptive of an attitude of "understanding, not revenge" (*MHF,* 483), and his works were part of the means of helping the French people understand the implications of Louis' policies throughout his reign.

The events of the Commune prevented the French people from having a period during which they could calmly reflect on the Second Empire. It was only in the years after the establishment of the Third Republic that stock could be taken of what they had lived through. During that time, Hugo did not relent, publishing *Histoire d'un crime* in 1877, thus supporting Ricœur's assertion that "an enterprise of reconciliation . . . requires a great deal of time" (*MHF,* 485). With the coup d'état and its aftermath continually before their

eyes, the French people could not help but reevaluate their historical view of the emperor.

Hugo's greatest wish was that the memory of the Second Empire
be the right one, echoing Ricœur 's "peaceful memory" (*la mémoire
heureuse*). Without a past that is true, a nation is deceiving itself and
cannot fully realize its potential as a democratic state in which transparency is a necessity. But peaceful memory can be elusive, and so
Hugo continued his refrain against the emperor. "Faithfulness to
the past is not a given, but a wish" (*MHF*, 494). The winds of collective memory are constantly shifting, and history is constantly being
rewritten. Hugo's texts took their place in the history of the Second
Empire and continue to affect our view of this crucial period, even
today. As each generation acts as a "transmitter of meaning,"[11]
Hugo's words have been passed down from one era to the next.
Louis-Napoléon is not, in the French imagination, anywhere near
the figure that his uncle was, partly because of the writings of Hugo.
Any accomplishments of the Second Empire are generally credited
to the times, the industrial revolution or an increasingly enlightened
population. Hugo indeed helped ensure Louis' place in history as
Napoléon le petit.

Hugo's Ideology of the Future

Hugo's fascination with progress remains one of his most lasting
and appealing obsessions, and it is echoed in the writings of count-
less modern philosophers and historians. Ricœur devotes an entire
chapter to Heidegger's *Being and Time,* with its orientation toward
the future rather than the past. I will not repeat his summary except
to highlight ideas that touch upon Hugo's vision of the future, always closely linked to his notion of "progress." For Heidegger,
"there are three times, past, present, and future. . . . The present of
past things is memory; the present of present things is direct perception . . . and the present of future things is expectation" (Cited in
MHF, 352). The word expectation (*attente*) is crucial to Hugo's
thinking about the future. He expects the Second Empire to fall and
to be replaced by a democratic republic. He expects capital punishment to be outlawed. He expects to see the founding of a new political structure, under the general rubric of the United States of
Europe. While not all of these predictions come true in his lifetime,
the desire for them in Hugo's mind spurs him to continue his fight

against Louis during the long years in exile. The only limit to his struggle would be his own death, but he is confident that others will join him and continue on if he were to die. This potentiality of the "possible being" (*pouvoir-être*) and the open-endedness of the unknown future are cornerstones of Heidegger's thinking on time.

The past plays the role for Heidegger of reminding us of our debt to our heritage.[12] This idea is the counterpart to Ricœur's conception of mourning, the forgetting of parts of the past in order to move forward. The historian is, in many ways, he who makes the dead speak, and Hugo certainly fills this role. His constant comparisons of Louis to his uncle create a dialogue between past and present figures. In this way, history becomes for Heidegger as well as for Hugo "still acting; history as the sum of things transmitted; the authority of tradition" (*MHF*, 377). Hugo chooses the tradition represented by the principles of the French Revolution (his debt to the past) over the stagnation of the past represented by Louis. By recognizing his debt to one aspect of history, he is able to "mourn" the rest through forgetting.

Kierkegaard had a slightly different take on the relationship between the past and the future. His emphasis on repetition allows him to see the past as an opening on what is to come. "The creative power of repetition is contained entirely in this power of opening up the past again to the future" (*MHF*, 380). The historian plays a critical role as the catalyst for the transfer of vision from the past to the future. "The historian, providing a place for the dead, makes a place for the living" (*MHF*, 380). Those from another era who have died were, at their time, living, and history confers upon them the status of a living "having been." They are as alive in history as we are in the present.

Jules Michelet became the first French practitioner of this bringing to life of the past through its "living unity."[13] Through this theme of "resurrection," Michelet hoped to study life "not in its surfaces but in its internal and profound organisms" (*MHF*, 380). By linking the past so closely with the present, Michelet decreased the historian's distance between himself and his subject, and became a precursor of twentieth-century New Historians who find their subject matter in every facet of human experience. In this regard, history can never be considered final; a new interpretation can be made at any time, depending on the historian's point of view.

One of the aspects of human experience that has become critical in the modern conception of the writing of history is of course memory. It is often listed as one of the "new" objects of history, along with the body, cooking, death, sex, carnival, and so on (*MHF*, 385). Jacques Le Goff's *Mémoire et Histoire* outlines clearly the rise of memory as an object of study for the New Historian. Memory is part of a "history of history" and is recognized as the "raw material of history."[14] History enriches memory and enters "the great dialectical process of memory and forgetting lived by individuals and societies" (Le Goff, *Mémoire et Histoire*, 10–11). Memory must not be overemphasized but must take its place as part of the pairing memory/history, parallel to other pairings such as antiquity/modernity and progress/reaction (*MHF*, 386). Memory's crucial role in the writing of history is found in the modes of transmission of that history (*MHF*, 386). The dialectic set up between history and collective memory, creating a constant reappraisal of those links, keeps alive the close relationship between past and present, and ultimately the future as well.

Victor Hugo's vision of the future evolves from memory and is, as we have seen, idealistic in the extreme. When he speaks of "progress," he envisions a world in which the ideal will transcend the historical, in which we can find again our humanity. This vision, while rooted in history, seeks to eliminate history as a determining factor in our behavior. In order to achieve the ideal, a cleansing of the past must take place, and his works from exile attempt to serve such a purpose. Claude Dijon analyses this process: "Victor Hugo loved to praise the future, and we know also that his marvelous predictions played a double role. One that denounces, accusing the present, the bloody ignominy of the coup d'état and the execrable empire; the other announces the future, and Victor Hugo sets in opposition to all human history the century of peace, of universal brotherhood and of happiness: the 20th century."[15] The future, to be lived in the United States of Europe, will be the opposite of what has come before, at least of what has come to pass since 1851.

Digeon points out that Hugo's idealistic project requires going beyond history, a prospect that makes his ideology unworkable and leads us to an impasse "in which man succeeds, in and by history, in surpassing history, attaining the ideal transparency of the 'real governed by the true': where man, liberated from his inhuman history, will become human again" (*LM*, 17). Hugo thus paradoxically calls for the French people to remember the first emperor in order to forget the second, and in so doing, they will be able to get beyond the evils of their recent historical past and attain a new and purer world.

Such a view of the future supposes a formidable attachment to history, even as it calls for us to imagine a world beyond history (Digeon, "Victor Hugo," 17). This process parallels the workings of memory in that one must both remember and forget in order to move forward. The past holds the key to the ideal of the future, but one must not become a slave to memories of past glories. Hugo can be accused of being a slave to the memory of Napoléon I, but he would argue that he simply uses the first emperor as a comparison to the second. Until Louis-Napoléon is ousted, the country will be looking backward, not forward to Hugo's ideal future. His job is to make them forget the present so they can move into a new world.

And what a new world it has become. Many of Hugo's dreams have become reality in societies around the world. Many states, based on the rule of law, now abide by principles of equality and freedom for all, including women, children, minorities, and the poor. Organized religion no longer holds sway, particularly in the West, in affairs of state or education, which is most often free and accessible to all. A redistribution of wealth has been brought about by raising the standard of living through education. And penal systems have been humanized, including the abolition of the death penalty in all but a few countries.[16] Much remains to be done, of course, and no one could argue that the modern world is a utopia, but Hugo's crusade to see a United States of Europe has come to pass in much the way he envisioned it.

CONCLUSION

This is the story of a "historian" who dared to tell a different story. His counter-discourse left him open to charges of sedition and the possibility of exile, both physical and communal. His voice was at first unwanted at the time of expression because his community was not ready to reevaluate its common past. He was an uncommon crusader because he was a teller of tales, a writer of autobiography, fiction and poetry, who dared to enter the realm of politics and historical struggle, who dared to say "no" in order to right a wrong ingrained in the collective conscience.

In this study, we have seen the power of literature as a historical document. As we move into a new century and the study of history takes on an increasingly personal tone, one based more on collective memory than archival interpretation, literature has become an increasingly potent historiographical tool. The historical novel remains one of the world's most popular genres and is the way much of humanity learns its history. At the same time, history written by professionals has become more "novelistic." The blurring of these genres reveals a desire on the part of the reading public to absorb history through metaphor, the same kinds of texts Hugo, Walter Scott, and others provided in the past. Hugo's continuing popularity can be traced to this desire for the blending of fiction and history, of history and memory. The best storytellers adapt to the exigencies of their age and find ways to touch the most readers in the most profound ways. Hugo remains a bestseller today for precisely those reasons. He taught his contemporaries to remember, to forget and to move forward, never losing sight of the utopian ideals shared by all.

Notes

INTRODUCTION

1. Paul Ricœur: *Time and Narrative*, trans. Kathleen McLaughlin and David Pellauer (Chicago: University of Chicago Press, 1984); *Memory, History, Forgetting* (Chicago: University of Chicago Press, 2004).

Time and Narrative, vol. 3 will hereafter be abbreviated *T&N*. *Memory, History and
Forgetting* will be abbreviated *MHF*. In *Memory, History, Forgetting* Ricœur puts it in
terms of "relations." He sees "external relations between memory and history and
internal relations between individual memory and collective memory" (*MHF*, 96).

CHAPTER 1. MEMORY AS HISTORIOGRAPHICAL PROCESS

1. "Memory and history, far from being synonymous, appear now to be in fundamental opposition. Memory is life, borne by living societies founded in its name.
It remains in permanent evolution, open to the dialectic of remembering and forgetting, unconscious of its successive deformations, vulnerable to manipulation and
appropriation, susceptible to being long dormant and periodically revived. History,
on the other hand, is the reconstruction, always problematic and incomplete, of
what is no longer. Memory is a perpetually actual phenomenon, a bond tying us to
the eternal present; history is a representation of the past. Memory, in so far as it is
affective and magical, only accommodates those facts that suit it. . . . History, because it is an intellectual and secular production, calls for analysis and criticism.
Memory installs remembrance within the sacred; history, always prosaic, releases it
again. Memory is blind to all but the group it binds, which is to say, as Maurice
Halbwachs has said, that there are as many memories as there are groups, that
memory is by nature multiple." Pierre Nora, "Between Memory and History: *Les
lieux de mémoire*," trans. Marc Roudebush, *Représentations* 26 (Spring 1989): 7–25.
(Cited in *R&H*, 633).

2. For a definition and discussion of the theory of counter-discourse, see Richard Terdiman, *Discourse/ Counter-Discourse: The Theory and Practice of Symbolic Resistance in Nineteenth-Century France* (Ithaca, NY: Cornell University Press, 1985).

3. See Michel Foucault, *Language and Counter-Memory, Practice* (Ithaca, NY: Cornell University Press, 1977).

4. "It is in relation to individual consciousness and its memory, that collective
memory is held to be a collection of traces left by the events that have affected the
course of history of the groups concerned, and that it is accorded the power to

place on stage these common memories, on the occasion of holidays, rites, and public celebrations" (*MHF*, 119).

5. Maurice Halbwachs's major works are *Les Cadres sociaux de la mémoire* (Paris: Albin Michel, 1994), hereafter abbreviated as *CS*, and *La Mémoire collective* (Paris: Albin Michel, 1997).

6. Halbwachs writes: "One judges a functionary based on the duties he currently performs, and one wishes him to be well-adapted to the present conditions and his immediate task: one takes note, no doubt, of his previous duties, but only in as much as they attest to his current competence and ability. The rank of a nobleman, on the other hand, is determined by the extreme age of his title. In order to appreciate it, perspective is necessary" (*CS*, 231).

7. Cited in Maurice Crubellier, *La Mémoire des Français* (Paris: H. Veyrier, 1991), 7.

8. See Michel Foucault, *Surveiller et punir* (Paris: Gallimard, 1975), 30.

9. Marc Ferro, *L'Histoire sous surveillance. Science et conscience de l'histoire* (Paris: Calmann-Levy, 1985, 196). (Cited in *CMF*, 9–10).

10. "A culture, because it is made up of representations, only coincides in part with the world it is supposed to represent. It is no different for memory, which is the temporal aspect. Its apparent coherence matters more than an impossible adequacy to the transformation of the group. It is the framework that holds the elements of the picture together, that consecrates its existence by giving it a direction. There lies, no doubt, the power of memory: in its capacity for organization" (Crubellier, *Mémoire*, 10).

11. Marc Bloch, *Apologie pour l'histoire ou Métier d'historien* 1974; repr., (Paris: Masson, Armand Colin, 1993–97). (Cited in *MHF*, 13.)

12. Bergson, Henri, "Matière et Mémoire: Essai sur la relation du corps à l'esprit," 1896, in *Œuvres* (Paris: PUF, 1963), 225–35. (Cited in *MHF*, 24.)

13. Cited in *MHF*, 25.

14. Charles Taylor calls this "inwardness," in *Sources of the Self*, (Cambridge, MA: Harvard University Press, 1989), 109.

15. Pierre Nora, "L'ère des commémorations," in *Les Lieux de mémoire*, 3:977. (Cited in *MHF*, 91).

CHAPTER 2. MEMORY AS NARRATIVE

1. In *Memory, History, Forgetting*, Ricœur puts it in terms of "relations." He sees "external relations between memory and history and the internal relations between individual memory and collective memory" (*MHF*, 96).

2. "The role of fiction in this memory of the horrible is a corollary to the capacity of horror and also of admiration, to address itself to events whose explicit uniqueness is of importance" (*T&N*, 187).

3. "Over the past few years, another new theme has claimed a growing, at times rather obsessive place in French historical production, namely, the theme of historical memory. To understand this, one must no doubt allow for changes in a society's relation to time and to its own past. . . . Memory became a focal point for considerable investment because it offered a kind of alternative to history (that is, to actual history, not the history one finds in books). Yet that alone probably cannot account

for a complex phenomenon that reflects a variety of interests and concerns. Memory can reveal hidden or repressed historical processes, particularly when misfortune or shame is involved. It can also be an instrument for exploring collective identity (or identities)" (Jacques Revel and Lynn Hunt, eds. *Histories: French Constructions of the Past* [New York: The New Press, 1995]) 1:50.

4. "Historians must stop regarding time in the constraining sense of linear chronology and, instead, look upon it as a laboratory in which it should be possible to demonstrate and study the existence of variations and recurrences," ibid.

5. Albert Camus, *L'Homme révolté* (Paris: Gallimard [Folio], 1951).

6. Edmund Husserl, *ZurPhänomenolgie des innern Zeitbewusstseins* (The Hague: Nijhoff, 1966), 24. (Cited in *T&N*, 27.)

7. See also Jacques Derrida, *La Voix et le phénomène* (Paris: PUF, 1967), 67–77.

8. "Each new now, by pushing the preceding past into the recent past, makes it a retention that has its own retentions. This second-order intentionality expresses the unceasing recasting of earlier retentions by more recent ones, which makes up temporal fading away" (*T&N*, 30).

9. "This intentional reduplication of the intentionality characteristic of retention ensures the integration of recollection into the constitution of internal time-consciousness" (*T&N*, 35).

10. "The realization, or lack of realization, of an expectation related to a remembered event acts upon the memory itself and retroactively gives a particular coloring to the reproduction" (*T&N*, 36).

11. "In addition to this, the representation of time, on the level of schemata and principles, is always accompanied by a determination of time, that is, by a particular lapse of time, a determination that adds nothing to the presupposition of an infinite time of which all times are the successive parts. It is in the determination of particular successions that this indirect character of the representation of time becomes clearer" (*T&N*, 49).

12. "In conclusion, the three dynamic relations of inherence, consequence, and composition, by organizing appearances in time, determine, by implication, the three relations of temporal order that define duration as a quantity of existence, regularity in succession, and simultaneity in existence" (*T&N*, 52).

13. Michel Foucault, *Surveiller et punir* (Paris: Gallimard, 1975) 30.

14. Robert Castel, "'Problematization' as a Mode of Reading History," in *Foucault and the Writing of History*, ed. Jan Goldstein, 237–52 (Cambridge: Blackwell, 1994). Castel's chapter was translated by Paula Wissing.

15. "Le Souci de la vérité," *Magazine Littéraire* 207 (1984), 18. Cited in Castel, "Problematization," 237–38.

16. *L'Impossible Prison: Recherches sur le système pénitentiaire au XIXe siècle*, ed. Michelle Perrot (Paris: Seuil, 1980), 47. (Cited in Castel, "Problematization," 238).

17. Ibid., (Cited in "P," 242).

18. *Les Ecrits de Fernand Braudel* (Paris: Fallois, 1997), 156.

19. *New York Tribune*, April 27, 1858. Cited in *R*, 20–21.

20. Karl Marx, *The 18th Brumaire*. (Cited in *R*, 33).

CHAPTER 3. *NAPOLÉON LE PETIT*

1. Hugo wrote *Napoléon le petit* between June 12 and July 14, 1852. It was published in August of that year. Edmond Biré, *Victor Hugo après 1852* (Paris: Perrin, 1894).

2. The *Constitutionnel* did not share, of course, Hugo's view: "Pour nous, nous ne redoutons pas que le prince Louis-Napoléon vienne parodier en 1852 l'Empire du commencement du siècle. . . . Il mettra sa gloire à faire un empire" (September 20, 1852). [For our part, we do not fear that the prince Louis-Napoléon will create a parody in 1852 of the empire of the early part of the century. . . . He will use his glory to create an empire] Hugo will later say exactly the opposite: that Louis's reign is a parody of his uncle's.

3. *Oeuvres complètes de Victor Hugo.* Présentées par Jeanlouis Cornuz, no. 30, 4 (Paris: Editions Rencontre, 1968). All subsequent references will be to this edition. Translations in text by Natalie Handel, Alexandra Harris, and William VanderWolk with consultation of Victor Hugo, *Napoleon the Little* (Boston: Estes and Lauriat).

4. "I shall call the documentary phase the one that runs from the declarations of eyewitnesses to the constituting of archives, which takes as its epistemological program the establishing of documentary proof" (*MHF*, 136).

5. E. Benveniste, *Problèmes de linguistique générale* (Paris: Gallimard, 1966). (Cited in *MHF*, 153).

6. Censorship had been abolished in France between 1848 and 1850 but was reinstated even before Louis took absolute power in 1851. "Victor Hugo played an important part in defending the abolition of censorship. But the SACD (Society of Authors and Dramatic Composers) was itself divided, between Victor Hugo and Langlé on one hand, Scribe and Baron Taylor on the other. After two years of freedom, censorship was reinstituted in 1850, and for a long time to come." Alain Vaillant "Les Sociétés d'auteurs et la censure au XIXe siècle" (in Ory, *La Censure*, 107–8).

7. " More and more, this bond of trustworthiness extends to include every exchange, contract, and agreement, and constitutes assent to others' word, the principle of the social bond, to the point that it becomes a *habitus* of any community considered, even a prudential rule. First, trust the word of others, then doubt if there is good reason for doing so" (*MHF*, 165).

8. Marc Bloch, *Apologie pour l'histoire ou Métier d'historien* (Paris: Armand Colin, 1993–97). (Cited in *MHF*, 169–70).

9. "If we can speak of observation in history, it is because the trace is to historical knowledge what direct or instrumental observation is to the natural sciences," *MHF*, 170. "The notion of the trace can be taken to be the common root of testimony and clue" (*MHF*, 175).

10. "On the 2nd of December 1852, the Faider Law, passed in Brussels after pressure from the French government had been applied, decided to punish 'whoever is guilty of any offense toward foreign sovereign monarchs or anyone attacking their authority.'" Gabrielle Chamarat, Preface to *Les Châtiments* (Paris: Pocket, 1998), 6–7.

11. Karl Marx, Article in the *New York Tribune*, April 27, 1858. (Pierre Albouy, "Hugo fantôme," *Littérature* 13 (1974): 115. (Cited in *R*, 60.)

Chapter 4. *Les Châtiments*

1. "*Napoléon le petit* was an appeal to French society to react against the imposter; *Châtiments* addresses the people and history from the point of view of the

prophet." Chamarat, Gabrielle, ed., *Nommer l'innommable* (Orléans: Paradigme, 1994), 8.

2. "What is at stake from now on is less a possible uprising than a text which is so connected to reality that it will inevitably act, in the long run, on one's thoughts" (ibid., 10).

3. "Political discourse was already, since the beginning, considered by Hugo to emanate from a moral, political and social conscience; but it remained subjected to a philosophy of retreat in the artist: the enunciation kept its distance from that which was being enunciated. . . . With *Châtiments*, things begin to move, one could almost say that they are inverted. That which is spoken, its precise pertinence to reality, finds its strength and its validity in the enunciation. The word 'kills' and, in so doing, awakens consciences because it speaks of a place that is different from the current indignity" (ibid., 19).

4. "What the long time span structures on the temporal plane is the priority of series of repeatable facts, rather than singular events likely to be remembered in a distinctive way. In this sense, these facts are open to quantification and to being dealt with mathematically" (*MHF*, 184).

5. "The writing of history becomes literary writing. An embarrassing question then invades the intellectual space thereby opened: how does the historical operation preserve, even crown at this stage, the ambition for truth by which history distinguishes itself from memory and eventually confronts the latter's avowal of trustworthiness. More precisely: how does history, in its literary writing, succeed in distinguishing itself from fiction? (*MHF*, 190).

6. Robert Mandrou, *Introduction à la France moderne: Essai de psychologie historique* (Paris: Albin Michel, 1998). (Cited in *MHF*, 195).

7. The goal of "the history of mentalities" (*l'histoire des mentalités*) is "the reconstitution of behaviors, expressions, and silences that express conceptions of the world and collective sensibilities . . ." ibid. (Cited in *MHF*, 195).

8. Mandrou calls these operating concepts "worldviews, structures, conjunctures" (*MHF*, 195).

9. "But one is not great or small at no price. One becomes great when, in a context of discord, one feels justified in acting in the way that one does" (*MHF*, 221).

10. "Luc Boltanki and Laurent Thévenot have added a complementary component of intelligibility to that of status by taking into account the plurality of regimes of justification resulting from the plurality of types of conflict. Someone who has high status in the commercial order may not be so in the political order or in the order of public reputation or in that of aesthetic creation." Laurent Thévenot, "L'action qui convient," Patrick Pharo and Louis Quéré, eds., *Les Formes d'action* (Paris: EHESS, 1990), 39–69. (Cited in *MHF*, 221).

11. Yves Gohin. "Le Patriotisme de Victor Hugo," (in *Victor Hugo et l'Europe de la pensée*, 115).

12. "But this democratic ideal does not justify the fate of the country being subject without reservation to the opinion of the majority of the citizens. A citizenry is necessary to make a republic; a republic is necessary to make a citizenry: this is the hard logic of history, which is only circular logic for some pure reason" (ibid).

13. "Hugo knows that he is, in a way, the victor . . . purified, freed from the society whose hostage he almost was and from which he was able, just in time, to

disengage himself. He is the victor because he represents the citizenry in exile."
Jean Gaudon, *Le Temps et la contemplation* (Paris: Flammarion, 1969), 157.

14. "Hugo has the power and the grace, thanks to poetry, to put himself above those whose target he has been for so long and who have just compromised themselves in the coup of December 2. Hugo sees a sort of coronation in the fact that the judicial branch, the army, the church, the businessmen and the merchants have thrown themselves joyously into the imperial adventure. He, the banished one, who incarnates . . . justice, honor and patriotism, and who claims to be the century's conscience, will become the magus" (ibid.).

15. "Seizing criminals, calling for an immediate result, making poetry into a whip or a red-hot iron, these are not ends in themselves, and we must remember, when we read *Les Châtiments*, the successive layers of this 'going beyond' (*dépassement*) of the every day, in the cosmic. We must remember also the presence, in the poetic voice of a prophetic voice that seems to come from the belly of reality" (ibid., 159).

16. Gaudon sums up how Hugo manipulated the style of *Napoléon le petit* to suit his particular project: "The writer has not lost in advance, and *Naploéon le petit*, despite the exigencies of its discourse, shows brilliantly that a caricaturist's technique can give rise to a literary technique. He need only abandon the worn out idea of continuous metaphor—a source of artificial coherence—and add in some violent images that find their source in skillfully constructed allegory. Thus he will be able to strike hard without interference from reason" (ibid., 165).

17. "The operation consists of plunging Louis Bonaparte and his crowd in what *Les Misérables* will later call 'the dregs' (*les bas fonds*) by reconstituting around them its vocabulary. The language of prisoners, gamblers, prostitutes and underworld characters is appropriated by the poet to create a hell to fit the condemned" (ibid., 167).

18. "*Les Châtiments* remains exposed to all criticism: monotony, abuse of force or of virtuosity, disproportion between the presumptuous lover of justice and the criminal, who didn't deserve quite so much." Guy Rosa, *Hugo, Les Misérables* (Paris: Klincksieck, 1995), 8.

19. "[His philosophy] gives him authority in that it requires this superhuman leap that opposes the text to the world, as a reality to an illusion. It also requires that he produce a text that is more real than the world, to which the world will end up succumbing, and in which history recovers its course, words their meaning, the distinction between good and evil its pertinence, and art itself its beauty, the shape of the absolute" (ibid., 11).

20. "The teaching of the prophets is neither science nor pedagogy, and the oracle is not prediction. God is the source and protector of the inspired prophetic pronouncement. It participates in the divinity whose intervention it effects in history. . . . Its effectiveness does not depend on its audience—on the contrary, it depends on its nature. The disdain that greets it is the best proof of its transcendence. It need only be pronounced to be true and to fulfill itself" (ibid.).

21. Pelletan gives Dante as an example of this phenomenon. Camille Pelletan, *Victor Hugo, homme politique* (Paris: Offendorff, 1907). (Cited in Rosa, *Hugo*, 72).

22. "The relative popular failure of *Les Châtiments*, in its historical context, in no way affects its current effectiveness. It simply makes us wonder. We generally believe that a literature 'of circumstance' loses its impact almost immediately. This could

very well show the opposite. Perhaps we could say that the fate of great satiric poetry is not to have an immediate affect, the example of Dante coming immediately to mind. *Les Châtiments* spoke very loudly, but that was in 1870. They are still speaking today" (Rosa, *Hugo*, 72).

CHAPTER 5. *LES MISÉRABLES*

1. Victor Hugo, *Les Misérables* (Paris: Gallimard (Pléïade), 1951), 134. All further references will be to this edition and will be abbreviated as LM. All translations are by Natalie Handel, Alexandra Harris, and the author, with consultation of Victor Hugo, *Les Misérables* (New York: The Modern Library, 1992).

2. See Kathryn Grossman, *Figuring Transcendence in* Les Misérables: *Hugo's Romantic Sublime* (Carbondale: University of Southern Illinois Press, 1994), 104. (Hereafter abbreviated as *FT.*)

3. Ricœur defines this term in his chapter entitled "The Critical Philosophy of History," *MHF*, 293.

4. "Nevertheless, despite the distinction in principle between 'real' past and 'unreal' fiction, a dialectical treatment of this elementary dichotomy imposes itself through the fact of the interweaving of the effects exercised by fictions and true narratives at the level of what we can call the 'the world of the text,' the keystone to a theory of reading," *MHF*, 262.

5. Hayden White's *Metahistory* (Baltimore: Johns Hopkins University Press, 1973) and his notion of the "linguistic turn" is an important source for Ricœur.

6. See Bernard Le Petit, *Les Formes de l'expérience: Une autre histoire sociale* (Paris: Albin Michel, 1995). (Cited in *MHF*, 251).

7. "The king is not really a king, that is, monarch, except through the images that confer upon him a reputedly real presence," *MHF*, 264.

8. "Cette clarté, l'histoire, est impitoyable; elle a cela d'étrange et de divin que, toute lumière qu'elle est, et précisément parce qu'elle est lumière, elle met souvent de l'ombre là où l'on voyait des rayons; du même homme elle fait deux fantômes différents, et l'un attaque l'autre, et en fait justice, et les ténèbres du despote luttent avec l'éblouissement du capitaine. De là une mesure plus vraie dans l'appréciation définitive des peuples. Babylone violée diminue Alexandre; Rome enchaînée diminue César; Jérusalem tuée diminue Titus. La tyrannie suit le tyran. C'est un malheur pour un homme de laisser derrière lui de la nuit qui a sa forme" (*LM*, 327). [This light of history is pitiless; it has this strange and divine quality that, all luminous as it is, and precisely because it is luminous, it often casts a shadow just where we saw a radiance; of the same man it makes two different phantoms, and one attacks and punishes the other, and the darkness of the despot struggles with the splendor of the captain. Hence results a truer measure in the final judgment of nations. Babylon violated lessens Alexander; Rome enslaved lessens Caesar; massacred Jerusalem lessens Titus. Tyranny follows the tyrant. It is woe to a man to leave behind him a shadow that has his form.]

9. Louis Marin, *Le Portrait du roi* (Paris: Seuil, 1981), 23. Ricœur's explanation of Marin's formulation is just as revealing: "On the one side, therefore, force becomes power by taking hold of the discourse of justice; on the other, the discourse of justice becomes power in standing for the effects of force. Everything takes place

within the circular relation between standing for and being taken for. This is the circle of coming to believe. Here the imaginary does not designate merely the visibility of the icon that sets before the eyes the events and characters of a narrative, but a discursive power" (*MHF*, 268).

10. *Pensées*, fragment 81. (Cited in *MHF*, 269.)

11. "So these bonds securing respect for a particular person are bonds of imagination," Pascal, fragment 828. (Cited in *MHF*, 270.)

12. Louis Marin, *Le Portrait du roi* [Portrait of the King], 265. (Cited in *MHF*, 353.)

13. Hegel, *Principes de la philosophie du droit* [Philosophy of Right] (Paris: Gallimard, 1963), 275. (Cited in *MHF*, 272).

14. See Christopher Prendergast, *Paris and the Nineteenth Century* (Oxford: Blackwell, 1992), 97.

15. See *LM*, 1194.

16. See Prendergast, *Paris*, 90.

17. Ibid., 92.

18. See in particular Richard Terdiman, *Discourse/Counter-Discourse* (Ithaca: Cornell University Press, 1985).

19. "Nous faisons ici de l'histoire. . . . Les opinions traversent des phases" (*LM*, 661). [We are now writing history. . . . Opinions go through phases.]

20. See especially Matthew Truesdell, *Spectacular Politics: Louis-Napoléon Bonaparte and the Fête Impériale, 1849–1870* (New York: Oxford University Press, 1997).

21. The whole notion of trace is one that Paul Ricœur has treated with great care. See especially *MHF*, 415–43.

22. See particularly Péguy's *Clio* (Paris: Gallimard, 1932).

23. Louis-Napoléon "fulfills not his Javert-like duty to uphold the law but the appetite for power that, in Hugo, typifies malefactors and legalists alike," (*FT*, 5).

24. "Of course, to say that *Les Misérables* is saturated through and through with the more sentimental and evasive forms of bourgeois ideology is to say something truly important about it" (Prendergast, *Paris*, 97).

CONCLUSION

1. "The opening of a horizon of expectation designated by the word 'progress' is the prior condition for the conception of modern times as new. . . . In this regard, one can speak of the 'temporalization of the experience of history'" (*MHF*, 297).

2. "It is by virtue of this kinship, and this substitution, that the idealist philosophy of history was able to rise above simple causal analyses, integrate multiple temporalities, open itself to the future, or better, open a new future, and in this way reinterpret the ancient *topos* of history, teacher of life, following the promises of redemption spilling out upon humanity to come by the French Revolution, the mother of all ruptures" (*MHF*, 300–301).

3. "We have already mentioned the rupture effect ascribed to the French Revolution by the European intelligentsia of the nineteenth century. Even then, the lights of reason made Medieval times appear shadowy, dark; following them, the revolutionary impulse made past times appear dead" (*MHF*, 302).

4. "What matters is that the projection of the future is, henceforth, of a piece

with the retrospection on past times. From then on, the century can be seen with the eyes of the future" (*MHF*, 307).

5. "Neither complaisance, nor spirit of vengeance" (*MHF*, 315).

6. "to what extent . . . can historiographical argumentation legitimately contribute to formulating a penal sentence for the great criminals of the twentieth century and thus to nourishing a *dissensus* with an educational purpose? The inverse question is the following: to what extent can a debate be conducted among professional historians under the surveillance of a previously decided guilty verdict, not only on the plane of national and international public opinion, but on the judicial and penal plane?" (*MHF*, 326).

7. "Formulated in the optative mood, this eschatology is structured starting from and built on the wish for a happy and peaceful memory, something of which would be communicated in the practice of history and even in the heart of the insurmountable uncertainties that preside over our relations to forgetting" (*MHF*, 459).

8. "But more important than punishment . . . remains the word of justice that establishes the public responsibilities of each of the protagonists and designates the respective places of aggressor and victim in a relation of appropriate distance" (*MHF*, 475).

9. Karl Jaspers, *La Culpabilité allemande* (Paris: Editions de Minuit, 1990), 49. (Cited in *MHF*, 475).

10. "the consideration due to the accused, on the political level, takes the form of moderation in the exercise of power, of self-limitation in the use of violence, even of clemency with respect to the vanquished . . . clemency, magnanimity, the shadow of forgiveness" (*MHF*, 475–76).

11. Henri-Pierre Judy, "Entretiens sur le Patrimoine" (lecture, Paris, Nov. 26, 2001).

12. "Anticipatory resoluteness can only be the assumption of the debt that marks our dependence on the past in terms of heritage" (*MHF*, 363).

13. Jules Michelet, Preface to *Histoire de France* (1869). (Cited in *MHF*, 380).

14. Jacques Le Goff, *Mémoire et Histoire*, 10. (Cited in *MHF*, 385).

15. Claude Digeon, "Victor Hugo et l'idée d'avenir," in *Victor Hugo: Les Idéologies*, 11 (Nice: Serre, 1985).

16. See Henri Pena-Ruiz and Jean-Paul Scot, *Un Poète en politique: Les Combats de Victor Hugo* (Paris: Flammarion, 2002).

Select Bibliography

Works by Victor Hugo

Les Châtiments. Paris: Pocket, 1997.

Les Misérables. Paris: NRF (Bibliothèque de la Pléiade), 1951.

Les Misérables. New York: The Modern Library, 1992. [English version]

Napoléon le petit. Paris: Laffont, 1987.

Napoleon the Little. Boston: Estes and Lauriat.

Œuvres complètes. Paris: Laffont, 1987.

Œuvres complètes de Victor Hugo. Présentees par Jean Louis Cornuz. Paris: Editions Rencontre, 1968.

Œuvres poétiques. Paris: Gallimard, 1967. *Paris*. Paris: Bartillat, 2001.

Victor Hugo, Politique. Paris: Laffont, 1985.

Secondary Works

Adereth, M. *Commitment in Modern French Literature*. New York: Schocken, 1968.

Albouy, Pierre. *La Création mythologique chez Victor Hugo*. Paris: Corti, 1985.

———. *Mythographies*. Paris: Corti, 1976.

Angrand, Pierre. *Victor Hugo raconté par les papiers d'État*. Paris: Gallimard, 1961.

Aref, Mahmoud. *La Pensée sociale et humaine de Victor Hugo dans son œuvre romanesque*. Geneva: Slatkine, 1979.

Arsac, Louis, ed. *Analyses et réflexions sur Victor Hugo, "Les Châtiments."* Paris: Ellipses, 1998.

Baczko, Bronislaw. *Les Imaginaires sociaux Mémoire et espoir collectifs*. Paris: Payot, 1984.

Baguely, David. *Napoléon III and his Régime: An Extravaganza*. Baton Rouge: Louisiana State University Press, 2000.

Bellet, Roger. *Presse et journalisme sous le Second Empire*. Paris: Colin, 1967.

Bierman, John. *Napoléon III and his Carnival Empire*. New York: St. Martin's Press, 1988.

Biré, Edmond. *Victor Hugo après 1852*. Paris: Perrin, 1894.

Borrut, Edith. *Etude sur souvenirs et mémoire*. Paris: Ellipses, 1995.

Brombert, Victor. *Victor Hugo and the Visionary Novel*. Cambridge, MA: Harvard University Press, 1984.

Butler, Thomas, ed. *Memory: History, Culture and the Mind.* New York: Blackwell, 1989.

Camus, Albert. *L'Homme révolté.* Paris: Gallimard, Folio, 1951.

Carrard, Philippe. *Poetics of the New History.* Baltimore: Johns Hopkins University Press, 1992.

Chamarat, Gabrielle, ed. *Nommer l'innommable.* Orléans: Paradigme, 1994.

Combes, Claudette. *Paris dans "Les Misérables'".* Nantes: Editions CID, 1981.

Connerton, Paul. *How Societies Remember.* Cambridge: Cambridge University Press, 1989.

Crubellier, Maurice. *La Mémoire des Français.* Paris: H. Veyrier, 1991.

De Certeau, Michel. *L'Ecriture de l'histoire.* Paris: Gallimard, 1975.

Ducatel, Paul. *La Vie tumultueuse et échevelée de Louis-Napoléon Bonaparte.* Paris: Grassin, 2000.

Foucault, Michel. *Language, Counter-Memory, Practice.* Ithaca: Cornell University Press, 1977.

Gaudon, Jean. *Le Temps et la contemplation.* Paris: Flammarion, 1969.

Gaudon, Sheila, ed. *Correspondance entre Victor Hugo et Pierre-Jules Hetzel.* Paris: Klincksieck, 1979.

Gildea, Robert. *The Past in French History.* New Haven, CT: Yale University Press, 1994.

Goldstein, Jan, ed. *Foucault and the Writing of History.* Oxford: Blackwell, 1994.

Grant, Richard B. *The Perilous Quest: Image, Myth, and Prophecy in the Narratives of Victor Hugo.* Durham, NC: Duke University Press, 1968.

Grossman, Kathryn. *Figuring Transcendence in "Les Misérables": Hugo's Romantic Sublime.* Carbondale: Southern Illinois University Press, 1994.

Guillemin, Henri. *Hugo.* Paris: Seuil, 1984.

Halbwachs, Maurice. *Les Cadres sociaux de la mémoire.* Paris: Albin Michel, 1994.

———. *La Mémoire collective.* Paris: Albin Michel, 1997.

———. *On Collective Memory.* Translated by Lewis Coser. Chicago: University of Chicago Press, 1992.

Hutton, Patrick. *History as an Art of Memory.* Hanover, NH: University of Vermont Press, 1993.

Idéologies hugoliennes. Actes de colloque. Nice: Serre, 1985.

Isser, Natalie. *The Second Empire and the Press.* The Hague: Nijhoff, 1974.

Journet, René, and Robert Guy. *Le Manuscrit des "Misérables."* Paris: Les Belles Lettres, 1963.

———. *Le Mythe du peuple dans "Les Misérables."* Paris: Editions Sociales, 1964.

Kahn, Jean-François. *L'extraordinaire métamorphose, ou cinq ans dans la vie de Victor Hugo, 1847–51.* Paris: Seuil, 1984.

Kozicki, Henry. *Developments in Modern Historiography.* New York: St. Martin's Press, 1993.

Kulstein, David. *Napoléon III and the Working Class: A Study of Government Propaganda under the Second Empire.* Los Angeles: Ward Ritchie Press, 1969.

Le Goff, Jacques. *Histoire et mémoire.* Paris: Gallimard, 1988.

———, ed. *La Nouvelle Histoire.* Paris: Editions Complexes, Historiques, 1978.

Le Goff, Jacques, and Pierre Nora, eds. *Faire de l'histoire II: Nouvelles Approches.* Paris: Gallimard, 1974.

Manuel, Jean. *Victor Hugo philosophe.* Paris: PUF, 1985.

Marx, Karl. *The 18th Brumaire of Louis Bonaparte.* New York: International Publishers, 1963.

Maurois, André. *Olympia: The Life of Victor Hugo.* New York: Carroll and Graf, 1956.

Mehlman, Jeffrey. *Revolution and Repetition.* Berkeley and Los Angeles: University of California Press, 1977.

Meschonnic, Henri. *Ecrire Hugo. Pour une poétique IV. Poétique politique dans "Les Châtiments."* Paris: Gallimard, 1977.

———. *Victor Hugo, la poésie contre le maintien de l'ordre.* Paris: Maisonneuve et Larose, 2002.

Nash, Suzanne. *"Les Contemplations" of Victor Hugo: An Allegory of the Creative Process.* Princeton, NJ: Princeton University Press, 1976.

Noiriel, Gérard. *Qu'est-ce que l'histoire contemporaine?* Paris: Hachette, 1998.

Nora, Pierre, ed. *Lieux de mémoire.* Paris: Gallimard, 1984–92.

Ory, Pascal, ed. *La Censure en France à l'ère démocratique.* Paris: Editions Complexe, 1997.

Pelletan, Camille. *Victor Hugo, homme politique.* Paris: Ollendorff, 1907.

Pena-Ruiz, Henri, and Jean-Paul Scot. *Un Poète en politique: Les Combats de Victor Hugo.* Paris: Flammarion, 2002.

Petit, Philippe, and Henry Rousso. *La Hantise du passé.* Paris: Textuel, 1998.

Pirouet, Georges. *Victor Hugo romancier ou le dessus de l'inconnu.* Paris: Denoël, 1985.

Price, Roger. *The French Second Empire: An Anatomy of Political Power.* Cambridge: Cambridge University Press, 2001.

———. *Napoléon III and the Second Empire.* London: Routledge, 1997.

Renouvin, P. *L'Idée de la Fédération européenne dans la pensée politique du dix-neuvième siècle.* Oxford: Clarendon Press, 1949.

Revel, Jacques, and Lynn Hunt, eds. *Histories: French Constructions of the Past.* New York: The New Press, 1995.

Ricœur, Paul. *La Mémoire, l'histoire, l'oubli.* Paris: Seuil, 2000.

———. *Memory, History, Forgetting.* Translated by Kathleen Blamey and David Pellauer. Chicago: University of Chicago Press, 2004.

———. *Temps et récit.* Paris: Seuil, 1985.

———. *Time and Narrative.* Translated by Kathleen McLaughlin and David Pellauer. Chicago: University of Chicago Press, 1984.

Rosa, Guy. *Hugo,* Les Misérables. Paris: Klincksieck, 1995.

Rousso, Henry. *La Hantise du passé.* Paris: Textuel, 1998.

Roy, Claude. *Victor Hugo, témoin de son siècle.* Paris: J'ai lu, 1962.

Seebacher, Jacques. *Victor Hugo ou le calcul des profondeurs.* Paris: P.U.F., 1993.

Seebacher, Jacques, and Ubersfeld, Anne, eds. *Actes du Colloque de Cérisy.* Paris: Seghers, 1985.

Spitzer, Alan. *Historical Truth and Lies about the Past.* Chapel Hill: University of North Carolina Press, 1996.

Strenski, Ivan. *Four Theories of Myth in Twentieth-Century History.* London: MacMillan Press, 1987.

Terdiman, Richard. *Discourse/Counter-Discourse.* Ithaca, NY: Cornell University Press, 1985.

Thinès, Georges. *Victor Hugo et la vision du futur.* Tournai, Belgium: La Renaissance du Livre, 2001.

Truesdell, Matthew. *Spectacular Politics: Louis-Napoléon Bonaparte and the Fête Impériale, 1849–1870.* New York: Oxford, University Press, 1997.

Ubersfeld, Anne, and Guy Rosa, eds. *Lire "Les Misérables."* Paris: José Corti, 1985.

Vesser, H. Aram, ed. *The New Historicism.* New York: Routledge, 1989.

Victor Hugo et l'Europe de la pensée. Actes de colloque. Paris: Nizet, 1995.

Victor Hugo, l'écriture et l'histoire. Actes de colloque. Tunis: Publications de la Faculté des Lettres de la Manouba, 1991.

Victor Hugo: Les Idéologies. Actes de Colloque Interdisciplinaire. Nice: Serre, 1985.

Voyenne, Bernard. *Histoire de l'idée europénne.* Paris: Payot, 1964.

Ward, Patricia, and Bernadette L. Murphy. *Victor Hugo, œuvres et critiques, 1981–3.* Paris: Lettres Modernes, 1992.

White, Hayden. *Metahistory: The Historical Imagination in Nineteenth-Century Europe.* Baltimore: Johns Hopkins University Press, 1973.

ARTICLES

Albouy, Pierre. "Des hommes, des bêtes, et des anges." *Europe* 40.394–95 (February–March 1962): 46–54.

———. "Hugo fantôme." *Littérature* 13 (1974): 115–31. Reprinted in *Mythographies,* 248–64.

———. "Hugo, ou le Je éclaté." *Romantisme* 1–2 (1971): 53–64.

Armstrong, M. S. "Hugo, Egouts and *Le Ventre de Paris.*" *FR* 69, 3 (Feb. 1996): 394–408.

Bell, W. M. L. "Victor Hugo and the Republican Tradition." *Quinquereme* 10.1 (1987): 2–25.

Bergson, Henri. "Matière et mémoire: Essai sur la relation du corps l'esprit" (1896). In *Œuvres,* 225–35. Paris: PUF, 1963. (Cited in MHP, 24)

Bigeard, Guy. "L'Ecrivain témoin de son temps." Besançon: Imprimerie Jacques et Demontrond (1980): 163–70.

Braudel, Fernand. "La Longue Durée." *Annales* (October–December 1958): 725–53.

Castel, Robert. " 'Problematization' as a Mode of Reading History." In *Foucault and the Writing of History,* 237–52. Edited by Jan Goldstein (Cambridge: Blackwell, 1994).

Comeau, P. "The Rise of the Social Conscience of Victor Hugo . . . [?]" *NCFS* 16, nos. 1–2 (1987): 47–58.

Coombes, John E. "State, Self and History in Victor Hugo's *L'Année terrible.*" *Studies in Romanticism.* 32, no. 3 (Fall 1993): 367–78.

Delabroy, Jean. "L'Accent de l'histoire." *Lendemains* 7, no. 28 (1982): 15–24.

De la Carrera, Rosalina. "History's Unconscious in Victor Hugo, *Les Misérables*." *MLN* 96, no. 4 (1981): 839–55.

Digeon, Claude. "Victor Hugo et l'idée d'avenir." In *Victor Hugo: Les Idéologies*, 11–18.

Fizaine, Jean-Claude. "Aspects d'un centenaire." *Romantisme* 60 (1988): 5–36.

———. "Hugo et le désœuvrement: l'Histoire, l'exil, le fragment." *Romantisme* 19, no. 67 (1990): 87–99.

Gaudon, Jean. "Writing on the 19th Century—The Unfinished Epic. *RHLF* 86, no. 6 (1986): 1101–08.

Gemie, S. "The Republic, the People and the Writer: Victor Hugo's Political and Social Writing." *French History* 14 (2000): 272–94.

Gohin, Yves. "The Concept of the People, the Individual and Humanity in the Works of Victor Hugo." *La Pensée* 245 (May–June 1985).

———. "Le Patriotisme de Victor Hugo." In *Victor Hugo et l'Europe de la pensée*, 115–26.

Goldstein, Robert Justin. "Fighting French Censorship, 1815–1881." *The French Review* 71, no. 5 (1998): 785–96.

Grossman, Kathryn. "Louis-Napoléon and the Second Empire: Political Occultations in *Les Misérables*." In *Correspondances: Studies in Literature, History and the Arts in Nineteenth-Century France*, edited by Keith Busby, 103–11. Amsterdam: Rodopi, 1992.

———. "Narrative Space and Androgyny in *Les Misérables*." *NCFS* 20, nos. 1–2 (Fall–Winter 1992): 97–106.

Guillemin, Henri. "Un itinéraire politique exemplaire." *Les Nouvelles Littéraires* 2771 (January 22, 1981): 22.

Journet, René. "Victor Hugo et la métamorphose du roman." *Romantisme* 18, no. 60 (1988): 110–14.

Laforgue, P. "Mythe, révolution et histoire. La reprise des *Misérables* en 1860." *La Pensée* 245 (May–June) 1985.

Laurent, Franck. "The Question of the 'grand homme' in the works of Victor Hugo." *Romantisme* 28, no. 100 (1998): 63–89.

Leuilliot, Bernard. "*Quatrevingt-treize dans Les Misérables*." *Romantisme* 18, no. 60 (1988): 99–107.

Leys, Simon. "Victor Hugo." In *Protée et autres essais*, 45–67. Paris: Gallimard, 2001.

Malandain, Pierre. "La Réception des *Misérables* ou 'Un lieu où des convictions sont en train de se former.'" *RHLF* 86, no. 6 (November–December 1986): 1065–79.

Meschonnic, Henri. "Portrait de Victor Hugo en homme siècle." *Romantisme* 18, no. 60 (1988): 57–70.

Messières, René de. "Victor Hugo et les Etats-Unis d'Europe." *FR* 25 (1952): 413–29.

Metridakis, Angelo. "Victor Hugo and the Idea of the United States of Europe." *NCFS* 23, nos. 1–2 (Fall-Winter 1994): 72–84.

Neefs, Jacques. "Accomplir l'œuvre du XIXᵉ siècle." *Romantisme* 18, no. 60 (1988): 71–76.

Raser, Timothy. "Victor Hugo et l'oubli de l'histoire." *Romantisme* 18, no. 60 (1988): 91–97.

Richard, Jean-Pierre. "Hugo." In *Etudes sur le Romantisme*, 177–99. Paris: Seuil, 1970.

Roman. M. "'Ceci que nous jetons souvent.' Progress according to Victor Hugo." *Romantisme* 30, no. 108 (2000): 75–90.

Rosa, Guy. "Victor Hugo poète romantique ou le droit à la parole." *Romantisme* 18, no. 60 (1988): 37–56.

Savey-Casard, Paul. "Le Pacifisme de Victor Hugo." *Revue de Littérature Comparée* 35 (1961), 421–32.

Schumann, Maurice. "Victor Hugo, Social Visionary." *Historia* 468 (1985): 22–27.

Seebacher, Jacques. "La Prise à partie de Louis-Napoléon." *Romantisme* 18, no. 60 (1988): 77–82.

Vade, Yves. "The Myth of France, the Chosen Nation in the Works of Victor Hugo." *History of European Ideas* 16, nos. 4–6 (January 1993): 447–56.

Vaillant, Alain. "Les Sociétés d'auteurs et la censure au XIXᵉ siècle." In *La Censure*, edited by Pasal Ory, 103–18.

Vernier, France. "*Le Dernier Jour d'un condamné*: une intervention de l'écriture dans l'histoire." In *Victor Hugo: l'écriture et l'histoire*, 132–49.

Winegarten, Renée. "Victor Hugo, On the Legacy of Myth." *Encounter* 69, no. 3 (1987): 25–35.

Wilson, Nelly. "Plebs and Peuple in the *Châtiments*." *Quinquereme* 10, no. 1 (January 1987): 26–36.

PUBLIC LECTURES

Foucault, Michel. "Discourse and Truth: the Problematization of Parrhesia." 6 lectures delivered at University of California, Berkeley (October–November 1983.)

Judy, Henri-Pierre. "Entretiens sur le Patrimoine." Lecture, Paris, Nov. 26, 2001.

Laurent, Franck. "'Car nous t'avons pour Dieu sans t'avoir eu pour maître.' Le Napoléon de Victor Hugo dans l'œuvre d'avant l'exil." Communication au Groupe Hugo (équipe de recherche "Littérature et civilisation du XIXᵉ siècle, Université de Paris 7), Sept. 16, 2000.

EXHIBITS

"Victor Hugo, l'homme océan." Site François-Mitterrand (Bibliothèque Nationale de France), Paris, March–May 2002.

Index

Major discussions of topics can be found on bolded pages.